THE NEW NATURALIST LIBRARY

GARDEN
NATURAL
HISTORY

STEFAN BUCZACKI

Collins

This edition published in 2007 by Collins,
an imprint of HarperCollins Publishers

HarperCollins Publishers
77–85 Fulham Palace Road
London W6 8JB
www.collins.co.uk

First published 2007

A CIP catalogue record for this book is available
from the British Library.

Set in FF Nexus by
Rowland Phototypesetting Ltd
Bury St Edmunds, Suffolk

Printed in China by Imago
Reprographics by Saxon Photolitho, Norwich

Hardback
ISBN-13 978-0-00-713993-4
ISBN-10 0-00-713993-4

Paperback
ISBN-13 978-0-00-713994-1
ISBN-10 0-00-713994-2

Contents

Editors' Preface

F OR MANY PEOPLE, a garden is the only easily accessible place to see
plants and animals, and gardening provides the readiest opportunity
for interacting with the natural world. The natural history on the
doorstep deserves wider recognition. Although gardening is an exercise in
applied natural history, there are few publications that introduce the cast and
encourage observers to follow the ecological dramas unfolding under the leaves
or in the compost heap. In this book, Stefan Buczacki reviews the diversity of
organisms and processes waiting to be explored. Integrating gardening lore with
horticultural and ecological science, he interprets familiar observations. He also
offers gardeners recommendations for management to enhance wildlife, together
with ideas that will enrich their appreciation of horticultural natural history.
It is hoped that this much-anticipated addition to the New Naturalist series will
stimulate further work on this relatively unexplored, yet accessible, world, and
encourage gardeners to notice, perhaps even welcome, the unplanned diversity
of organisms, often uninvited, that shares the garden.

Well known as an author and broadcaster on various aspects of gardens and
gardening, and a connoisseur of New Naturalists, owning a complete collection
of titles, Stefan Buczacki is the ideal author for a New Naturalist on *Garden
Natural History*. We are delighted that he accepted the invitation to write this
book for the series.

Author's Foreword and Acknowledgements

APART FROM Max Walters' *Wild and Garden Plants*, no previous New Naturalist volume has considered gardens in any other than a fleeting and superficial manner, let alone had the word 'garden' in its title. To a naturalist like myself who is also a gardener, this seems an astonishing omission. It is nonetheless an understandable one, as the garden has for long been considered something wholly artificial that has little in common with or relevance to 'natural' habitats, somewhere that has no part to play in 'A Survey of British Natural History'. I am privileged to be able to rectify the omission and correct the record, although for someone who thought the task would be straightforward, the exercise has proved a daunting journey of discovery. At the outset, I believed I had simply to tell a story based on my own lifetime's experience and observations in natural history and horticulture, and substantiate it with data from the scientific literature. But there was the rub. I had not reckoned on how tiny, disparate and perfunctory was the scientific literature, how sparse the studies of garden wildlife. Apart from birds, almost no group of organisms that live in gardens have been studied in relation to this particular habitat in any depth. Even the scientific literature of commercial horticulture was of little help, because arable cropping is so different in approach, practice and scope from domestic gardening.

The realisation that I had rather few facts to support my beliefs and ideas has resulted in a book that may be perceived as judgemental, dogmatic and opinionated. I make no apology for that, and whether readers agree or disagree with the views I have expressed and the conclusions I have drawn, I can only articulate the fervent wish that those in a position to do so will now take matters into their own hands. I hope my fellow scientists will at last view the garden seriously, recognise its huge importance in the overall context of a threatened environment, and embark on the studies that are so urgently needed to show how it can most effectively be used and managed for the complementary purposes of enjoyment and conservation.

It is my pleasure to acknowledge with real gratitude the patience, understanding and forbearance of Myles Archibald and the Natural History staff at HarperCollins and the support and confidence expressed in me by the New Naturalist Editorial Board.

CHAPTER 1

British Gardens – the Background

A GARDEN IS 'An enclosed piece of ground devoted to the cultivation of flowers, fruit or vegetables, often with defining word, as flower-, fruit-, kitchen- etc.'; alternatively, it means 'Ornamental grounds, used as a place of public resort' (OED). Today, without adjectival qualification, it carries two connotations: first, that it is essentially a non-commercial undertaking; and second, that it is attached to or associated with a dwelling place. These meanings are what I intend here, a consideration of what is sometimes called, certainly in North America, the 'home garden'. Add an adjective ('market', 'botanic') and it can have other meanings, and although I shall have a few things to say about the botanic garden, the market garden is in effect a small arable farm and falls largely outside my scope.

Historically, it is impossible to see where farms end and gardens begin, but what can loosely be called the artificial management of plants has been a feature of human society for at least 10,000 years. It is known to have developed first in the area we now call the Middle East, especially the region presently occupied by Israel, Iran, Syria and Iraq, and it later spread from there to other parts of the eastern Mediterranean. Recent studies by a British and American research team at a site called Abu Hureyra have not only narrowed the likely geography to Syria, but also extended the timescale to a date around 13,000 BP (Moore *et al.*, 2000). The Abu Hureyra village discoveries neatly linked the first farmers to a hunter-gatherer culture that existed in the same locality for around 400 years before the growing of cereals, including rye, first began. These studies therefore place the origins of plant cultivation in the Late Upper Palaeolithic period, when the glaciers of the last ice age were still retreating from northern Europe. Later still, the organised growing of crops began in India, China and South America, so

that by around 4,000 BP it was an established feature of societies in many
parts of the world.

EARLY CULTIVATION OF PLANTS IN BRITAIN

In Britain, plants were being cultivated at an early date at the village site of
Skara Brae on Orkney which, following its discovery in the mid-nineteenth
century and preliminary study in the early twentieth, was at first believed to
be an Iron Age 'Pictish' settlement. Following radiocarbon dating in the 1970s,
however, Skara Brae was reinterpreted as Neolithic and is now known to have
been inhabited between 5,200 and 4,200 BP (Fig. 1). Recent studies elsewhere
on Orkney suggest that plants may have been grown at an even older locality
which would push the origins of British crop cultivation back to around
6,000 BP. But the growing of crops does not make a garden. For me, a garden
is an area that gives at least a modicum of pleasure as well as practicality to
its owners. Here, however, the archaeological record can do little more than
provide pointers, and precisely when the use of gardens for any sort of
decoration first began is obscure. Quite possibly it arose through the careful
choice of some of the more attractive among edible crops, herbs for instance,
or, even earlier, I have often thought, through the deliberate growing close to

FIG 1. Skara Brae on Orkney was inhabited between 5,200 and 4,200 BP and is probably
one of the first sites in the British Isles at which plants were cultivated.

the home of appealing wild species that arose as weeds among the cereals. I admit it takes a leap of horticultural faith to interpret the presence in an ancient village of the seeds or pollen of field poppy *Papaver rhoeas* or corncockle *Agrostemma githago* as evidence that someone was either specifically tolerating or deliberately growing them; but it must have happened at some time. I have been interested to see the rather more precise expression of the same notion by Harlan & de Wet (1965), who believed prehistoric plants were divided into 'domesticated crops', 'encouraged weeds', 'tolerated weeds', 'discouraged weeds' and 'noxious weeds'. I am not sure how they managed so carefully to analyse the prehistoric mind to discover this, but it seems pragmatic enough, and it would not have taken many seasons to realise which weed was which. My putative ancient ornamental garden would, I suppose, have contained 'encouraged weeds' only.

THE FIRST 'GARDENS'

There is an intriguing claim by Groenman-van-Waateringe (1978) for palynological evidence of the earliest known garden in the Neolithic of the Netherlands. He postulates the existence of blackthorn *Prunus spinosa* as evidence for hedges being used to enclose small settlements, but whether these were real gardens is more a matter of semantics than palaeohorticulture. Conventional wisdom understandably places the origin of 'proper' gardening in Britain with the Romans and the Romano-British. There are indications of the existence of gardens at many villa sites in Britain, but the most extensive evidence of an ancient garden is at the late first century AD Romano-British palace of Fishbourne in Sussex. There the main body of the palace comprised four ranges enclosing a rectangular garden of around 100 by 75 metres with a further similarly sized garden to the south, closer to the sea (Fig. 2). There is evidence of a small kitchen garden and other more modest plots. The main garden was strictly formal, divided into two halves by a central path and created by terracing into a slope of clay and gravel and replacing the spoil with topsoil. There is a clear indication of trenches, amended with loam, being cut into the subsoil and indicating where deep-rooted plants, probably shrubs, were planted. The perimeter paths were hedge-lined, perhaps with box *Buxus sempervirens*, and further formality was achieved by an upright structure along the eastern side, presumably some sort of timber pergola. Fishbourne was clearly similar in overall concept to the contemporary gardens of Italy itself, of which much more is known from paintings and archaeological evidence. It is a mistake, however,

FIG 2. The earliest proper gardens in Britain were at Roman and Romano-British sites such as Fishbourne in Sussex.

to consider these Roman (and Romano-British) gardens as entirely formal. On the Roman site at Latimer in Buckinghamshire (around AD 300), for example, Branigan (1973) found small areas close to the house that seemed to have been kept free of sheep and pigs, and he interpreted these as possibly informal kitchen plots or orchards. But more importantly, it is clear that the Roman garden, in concept and reality, made significant, even if coincidental, concessions to wildlife.

The Roman garden was, according to Jellicoe *et al.* (1986):

> ... *at the centre of a network of feelings and inclinations, inherent in the Roman sensibility: the sense of universal life, expressed by the presence of divinities; a taste for luxuriant vegetation, picturesque topiary remaining exceptional, answering the desire to unite art and Nature; and flowing water.*

But the best evidence of the importance of naturalism comes from no less a source than Pliny (V. Letter 6): 'Beyond the wall lies a meadow which owes as many beauties to Nature as all I have been describing within does to art'

(Bosanquet, 1907). The south garden at Fishbourne may perhaps have been just such a wild garden, one that easily led the eye from the south wing to the natural landscape beyond the tidal inlet (Cunliffe, 1971).

Knowledge of the types of plants that grew in Romano-British gardens is tantalising in what it does and does not reveal. There is ample evidence for the deliberate growing of native shrubs, including box, hawthorn *Crataegus* sp. and juniper *Juniperus communis* because their use as hedges can be inferred from their planting positions. There is ample evidence too for the growing of vegetables (Table 1) and it is commonly believed that vegetable cultivation was introduced to Britain by the Romans (Zeepvat, 1991). Practically all Roman vegetables in Britain, including cabbage *Brassica oleracea*, carrot *Daucus carota*, parsnip *Pastinaca sativa*, celery *Apium graveolens* and turnip *Brassica rapa* subsp. *campestris*, were derived from species that were probably native, although it seems likely that the Romans brought at least some selected forms with them. Many culinary and medicinal herbs were grown too, including coriander *Coriandrum sativum*, dill *Anethum graveolens* and fennel *Foeniculum vulgare*. These were almost certainly introduced, although they have close relatives among the native flora. Some other garden crops have been claimed as Roman introductions to Britain, but macrofossil records substantiating these claims cannot be found.

TABLE 1. Garden and orchard crops identified from macrofossils at Roman sites in Britain (after Murphy & Scaife, 1991).

Anethum graveolens	dill	*Mespilus germanica*	medlar
Apium graveolens	celery	*Morus nigra*	black mulberry
Asparagus officinalis	asparagus	*Papaver somniferum*	opium poppy
Beta vulgaris	beet	*Pimpinella anisum*	anise
Brassica spp.	cabbages	*Pinus pinea*	stone pine
Castanea sativa	sweet chestnut	*Pisum sativum*	pea
Corylus avellana	hazel	*Prunus avium*	cherry
Coriandrum sativum	coriander	*Prunus* cf. *cerasifera*	cherry plum
Cucumis sativus	cucumber	*Prunus* cf. *cerasus*	dwarf cherry
Daucus carota	carrot	*Prunus domestica* s.l.	bullace/damson/plum
Ficus carica	fig	*Prunus persica*	peach
Foeniculum vulgare	fennel	*Pyrus communis*	pear
Fragaria vesca	strawberry	*Rubus fruticosus* agg.	blackberry
Juglans regia	walnut	*Rubus idaeus*	raspberry
Linum usitatissimum	flax	*Vicia faba* var. *minor*	horse bean
Malus sp.	apple	*Vitis vinifera*	grape-vine

Evidence for the ornamental elements in the Roman garden presents more of a problem, although perhaps not as great as some archaeologists have thought. Zeepvat (1991) said:

As regards the 'pleasure' gardens, the available evidence is slight. With respect to flowers, many would be domestic versions of native plants, and as such would not be distinguishable in environmental analysis.

That would be true if the only flowers being grown in Roman-British gardens had been collected from nearby, which would imply that the gardeners were little more advanced in their ambitions than the prehistoric weed cultivators. That seems highly improbable, and I would have expected that even if he was restricted to native species, the Roman or Romano-British garden owner might have wanted to plant forms that he could not see in the neighbouring countryside, and that would therefore show up in seed or pollen analyses as alien to the locality.

Whilst there were a number of what I call 'near-exotics' – plants such as peaches *Prunus persica* that certainly do not grow here wild but originate from not far away – and a few truly exotic plants (cucumbers *Cucumis sativus* among them), the Romano-British garden was largely a garden of native plants or their close relatives. As such it could easily have been a wildlife haven and this was a pattern that was to continue in British gardens in one manifestation or another until the nineteenth century.

After the departure of the Romans in the fifth century, life in Britain changed dramatically, although it is now clear that the Anglo-Saxon period was far from the Dark Ages of traditional textbook teaching. Just over a century ago an authoritative writer on garden history could say with little fear of contradiction:

The fall of the Roman Empire, and the subsequent invasions of barbarians, struck a death-blow to gardening as well as to all other peaceful arts. During the stormy years which succeeded the Roman rule in Britain, nearly all knowledge of horticulture must have died out. (Amherst, 1896)

It is now recognised, however, that it is essentially the absence of almost any documentary record, and an awareness that it was a period of constant internecine warfare, which cloud our view of what was in some respects a time of great artistic creativity. A culture that could produce the Alfred Jewel, the artefacts of the Sutton Hoo ship burial and the Lindisfarne Gospels, and that was settled rather than nomadic, might be expected to have appreciated the pleasure, beauty and solace of the garden almost as much as the Romans before them or the medieval nobility and clergy later. It is our loss that we know almost nothing of it and are limited to what can be gleaned from archaeology and from the Old English plant names that have survived in recognisable form. The fact that essentially ornamental plants such as *lilie* (lily), *mealuwe* (mallow), *popæg* (poppy) and especially *róse* (rose) existed in Old English alongside the more utilitarian *béte* (beet), *rædic* (radish) and *hænep* (hemp) indicate that at least they were noticed, although it is of course arguable that this was for their medicinal rather than aesthetic appeal. Harvey (1979) considered that 'the basis of English gardening, a thousand years ago, consisted ... of fewer than one hundred different plants'. The archaeological evidence, however, is scant (Murphy & Scaife, 1991).

Not until after the Norman Conquest were there written references to English gardens and gardening. One of the first and most celebrated indications that eleventh-century gardens could be pleasing to the eye as well as functional comes in the writings of the Benedictine monk, Eadmer of Canterbury (c.1060–c.1126) (Rubinstein, 2004; Southern, 1963). Eadmer wrote of King William Rufus visiting Romsey Abbey around 1092 to see the young Scottish Princess Matilda (also known as Edith) (1080–1118), who was later to marry King Henry I. She was being educated there by the nuns but, suspicious of the King's motives, the Abbess distracted William and his entourage by inviting them to see the garden wherein grew 'roses and other flowering herbs' while Matilda slipped out under a veil. It seems evident, therefore, that the garden must have been well worth a visit – after all, the King and his chums would be unlikely to have been distracted by something that was little more than a vegetable plot. Interestingly, Romsey Abbey still proudly displays a relic of its early horticultural history in the shape of the 'Romsey Rose', a rather pathetic-looking object found in the 1970s in an ancient scaffolding hole behind a twelfth-century wall painting. Any notion that it was one of the flowers that entranced its ancient residents and visitors can, however, be dispelled. It was more likely to have been flavouring for their broth, as it is apparently some form of shrivelled *Allium* bulb; possibly garlic.

It was not until the following century that the first illustrations of English gardens appeared, among the earliest a beautiful plan in the Eadwine Psalter (Cambridge, Trinity College MS R.17.1), created around 1165 and showing the features associated with the monastic buildings at Canterbury (Fig. 3). It depicts the cathedral water supply, orchard, vineyard and 'herbarium' with its trellises. Over the following three centuries, gardening spread through England, pre-eminently among the monastic houses, but also among the homes and palaces of the grander secular clergy and of the nobility. As people travelled more and further into the European continent and were influenced by what they saw, so

FIG 3. The twelfth-century Eadwine Psalter includes the first illustrations of English gardens, those associated with monastic buildings in Canterbury.

an increasing number of alien plants were seen here too, although most were still essentially European and most not far removed from the wild plants of the English countryside. Arguably, one of the most significant trends for the wildlife of these medieval gardens was that they became increasingly isolated from the neighbouring area by the erection of walls.

The practice of enclosing an area of land within a palisade or even a wall had a multiplicity of benefits. Around the wide expanse of the park, it served to confine deer and boar for hunting, and kept out potential predators such as wolves and the local peasantry. But on a smaller scale, it could also be applied to the garden where, just as in the enclosed housing estate garden of today with its 2-metre panels of softwood fence, potential pest species such as foxes, badgers, cats and dogs might be kept at bay. For the medieval garden, this enclosure might be a palisade or stockade, but might as easily have been an enclosed courtyard surrounded by buildings. One of the earliest recorded examples of an enclosed garden was that of King Henry I at Havering-atte-Bower in Essex, while King Edward I's garden at the Tower of London in 1274 was said to be surrounded by an earthen wall (Harvey, 1979). Later, King Henry III commanded works to be undertaken at Woodstock:

> To make round about the garden of our Queen two walls, good and high, so that
> no-one may be able to enter, with a becoming and honourable herbary near our fish
> pond ... (Liberate Roll, 34 Hen. III., m. 6)

Such enclosure would also assist in the development of a microclimate within the garden and thus in the elevation of temperature, lengthening of the growing season, enhancement of humidity, minimising of wind and the many other environmental features that affect plant growth and maturity. It was soon appreciated that the enhanced warmth and shelter lent themselves to the growing of fruit such as peaches, cherries and vines, but also encouraged aphids, snails and other pests and must incidentally have increased the garden bird population no end.

The ever-increasing use of hedges and of clipped shrubs – which by the early Tudor period were taking the form of topiary – valuably increased bird nesting sites. The arbour too brought more bird life to the garden. There is some uncertainty about what was meant by 'arbour' in early writings, but in the modern sense of a small, enclosed and partly covered area with a turf seat surrounded by climber-clad trellis or trained trees they seem to have been here at an early date. Evidence for a fourteenth-century origin is often deduced from the fact that they were described in *The Flower and the Leaf*, a piece long attributed to Chaucer, though now thought to be a pseudo-Chaucerian creation from the sixteenth century. Nonetheless, by 1523 the poet John Skelton (1460–1529) was noticing the phenomenon:

The clowdis gan to clere, the myst was rarified
In an herber I saw, brought where I was,
There birdis on the brere sange on euery syde …

John Skelton, *The Garlande of Laurell* (Scattergood, 1983)

Pleached alleys too, with a disproportionately large number of twiggy branches, attracted both birds and insect pests, although they were spared that scourge of modern fruit tunnels and espaliers, the woolly aphid *Eriosoma lanigerum*, which did not appear here until Sir Joseph Banks found it in London in 1787. Another of the characteristic features of the Tudor garden, which became especially popular after the early sixteenth century, was the knot, a planting of low hedges, often of box, intricately clipped to give the impression of knotted ropes. The contemporary resurgence of interest in knot gardens has also been blighted, in a literal sense, by a recent arrival in the shape of the fungal pathogen *Cylindrocladium buxicola*, which causes a serious leaf and shoot blight of box, and this is probably yet another instance of historic gardens being considerably healthier than their modern counterparts – the absence of pesticides and labour-saving aids notwithstanding.

Although the lawn as we understand it today was not possible before Budding's invention of the lawnmower in the nineteenth century (p. 35), closely cut areas of grass date back much further. Before Budding's lawnmower, the

FIG 4. The geometric formality of the Tudor garden is well seen in the reconstruction at Tudor House in Southampton.

scythe was the means of cutting grass, and in skilled hands it does seem to have been possible to cut grass both short and even. Well-kept turf was being bought, sold and admired as early as the thirteenth century: Colvin (cited in Landsberg, 1995) reported that in July 1272, Eleanor of Castile (1246–90) was paying one of her squires 3d. for night-time watering of two cartloads of turves that had been laid in the previous month. Undoubtedly, then as now, the all-grass lawn was an ideal rarely achieved, and it seems to have merged imperceptibly into flowering turf (often incorrectly referred to today as a 'flowery mead', which was strictly 'a carpet bejewelled with flowers as depicted in medieval paintings') rather as some modern gardeners excuse their weed-strewn lawns as wild-flower gardens.

THE INTRODUCTION OF EXOTIC PLANTS

As the sailors of Tudor England crossed the world and returned with their treasures, so the numbers of exotic or 'outlandish' plants, especially but not exclusively from the Americas, increased in British gardens: crown imperial *Fritillaria imperialis* (Fig. 5; pre-1590), black hellebore *Helleborus niger* (sometime in the sixteenth century), balsam *Impatiens balsamea* (1596), jasmine *Jasminum officinale* (1548), snowflake *Leucojum autumnale* (1629), mock orange *Philadelphus coronarius* (1596) and tagetes *Tagetes patula* (1573), among many. The steady trickle became a constant flow, and although it was not to rival the nineteenth-century flood, these new introductions played an increasingly important part in our gardens. Some brought their own livestock in the form of specific pests and diseases with them, while all presented challenges to the native wildlife to which they adapted with varying success. A late sixteenth-century garden arrival that is often cited as an example of how valueless introduced trees are in enhancing our biodiversity is the sycamore *Acer pseudoplatanus*, and certainly this has fewer other organisms associated with it, much less dependent on it, than almost any other British tree. Apart from the fungi *Rhytisma acerinum*, the cause of tar spot disease, and *Cryptostroma corticale*, the cause of sooty bark, several ubiquitous species of aphid and sooty mould and another introduction, the grey squirrel *Sciurus carolinensis*, it is hard to think of anything that would suffer significantly by sycamore's absence. By contrast, one of the plants that arrived at this time and that has arguably changed garden wildlife more than any other was *Solanum tuberosum*, the Andean potato, introduced from Colombia and Peru around 1570 (Fig. 6). Admittedly, a number of the organisms affecting it are viruses, and therefore hardly to be noticed by the casual observer, but the list of pests and pathogens that are now associated with potatoes in Europe (and most in Britain)

FIG 5. *Fritillaria imperialis*, one of the many exotic species introduced to British gardens before the end of the sixteenth century.

FIG 6. The potato, introduced from the Andes around 1570, brought with it numerous pests and diseases – including blight caused by *Phytophthora infestans*.

is still remarkably long for a non-native half-hardy plant (Table 2). Although some are exclusive to potatoes, a considerable number, especially among the insect pests, have a wide range of other host plants too.

TABLE 2. The most common pests and diseases of potatoes in Europe/Britain.

INSECTS AND MITES

Agriotes spp.
Aphis fabae
A. gossypii
A. nasturtii
Aulacorthum solani
Conodorus spp.
Ctenicera spp.
Empoasca devastans
Helicoverpa armigera
Leptinotarsa decemlineata
Limonius spp.
Macrosiphum euphorbiae
Myzus persicae
Phthorimaea operculella
Spodoptera exigua

NEMATODES

Ditylenchus destructor
D. dipsaci
Globodera pallida
G. rostochiensis
Meloidogyne chitwoodi
M. hapla
Paratrichodorus spp.
Pratylenchus penetrans
Trichodorus spp.

VIRUSES

Leaf roll virus
Mop top virus
Tobacco rattle virus
Virus A (mild mosaic)

VIRUSES – *cont.*

Virus M
Virus S
Virus X (mild mosaic)
Virus Y (severe mosaic)

BACTERIA

Clavibacter michiganensis var. *sepedonicus* (ring rot)
Erwinia carotovora ssp. *atroseptica* and subsp. *carotovora* (blackleg, soft rot)
Streptomyces scabies (common scab)

FUNGI AND OOMYCETES

Alternaria solani (early blight)
Botrytis cinerea (grey mould)
Colletotrichum coccodes (black dot)
Fusarium solani var. *coeruleum* (dry rot)
Helicobasidium purpureum (violet root rot)
Helminthosporium solani (silver scurf)
Phoma exigua var. *exigua* (gangrene)
P. foveata (gangrene)
Phytophthora erythroseptica (pink rot)
P. infestans (late blight)
Polyscytalum pustulans (skin rot)
Pythium ultimum (watery wound rot)
Rhizoctonia solani (black scurf)
Sclerotinia sclerotiorum (stalk break)
Spongospora subterranea (powdery scab)
Synchytrium endobioticum (wart)
Verticillium alboatrum (wilt)
V. dahliae (wilt)

Data taken from Hide & Lapwood, 1992; Evans & Trudgill, 1992; Raman & Radcliffe, 1992; Hooker, 1986; Valkonen, 1994.

The demise of monastery gardening came, unsurprisingly, with the demise of the monasteries themselves at the hands of Henry VIII and the Reformation. Commonly the only significant feature to remain was the fishpond, which may thus have played a part in one of the more improbable aspects of garden natural history in helping to establish the most important edible pond fish such as common carp *Cyprinus carpio* as naturalised British species, and to spread more widely formerly localised natives such as the pike *Esox lucius*, perch *Perca fluviatilis* and tench *Tinca tinca*.

As kitchen gardening prospered and expanded through the sixteenth and seventeenth centuries, and as ever more lush and luscious exotic crops were grown, so garden wildlife prospered at its expense. The bloated and distorted reproductive and vegetative parts that are the very essence of vegetable and fruit crops attracted molluscs and diplopods, insects and rodents in ever increasing numbers, and the garden was now starting to become the preferred habitat for a considerable number of them. There was little that could be done: pick them off by hand 'and tread them under foot' was William Lawson's contribution to snail control (Lawson, 1618). Moles *Talpa europaea* also caused much anxiety because they disfigured the formality and neatness of the ornamental garden. The gardeners of the time had little more idea or success than their counterparts today in controlling them:

> Take red herrings and cutting them in pieces burn the pieces on the molehills, or you may put garlicke or leeks in the mouths of their Hills, and the moles will leave the ground. I have not tried these ways, and therefore refer the reader to his own tryal, belief or doubt. (Sharrock, 1694)

A garden, often a good garden, was becoming the *sine qua non* for every house of note. Celia Fiennes (1662–1741), who travelled extensively throughout England and made her 'great journey' on horseback in 1698 (Morris, 1947), found and described gardens everywhere she stopped and made especial mention of the 'waterworks' then becoming so fashionable under the Dutch influence of William and Mary. But indoor gardening too, in glasshouses provided with stove heat, was on the increase for those who could afford it. By the early eighteenth century, the garden at Fulham first made famous in Queen Elizabeth I's time by Archbishop Edmund Grindal had so prospered under Bishop Henry Compton that:

> He had a thousand species of exotick plants in his stoves and gardens, in which place he had endenizoned [there's a word due for a comeback] a great many that have been formerly thought too tender for this cold climate. (Switzer, 1718)

No doubt Bishop Compton endenizoned (naturalised) a considerable number of exotick pests too. It is not recorded when such everyday garden animals as the glasshouse whitefly *Trialeurodes vaporariorum* (Fig. 7) or mealybug *Pseudococcus*

FIG 7. The glasshouse whitefly *Trialeurodes vaporariorum* came to Britain from somewhere in 'the tropical and subtropical Western Hemisphere' at an unknown date.

obscurus first arrived here, but how Bishop Compton and his contemporaries managed to keep glasshouse pests of any sort under even a modicum of control is anyone's guess. Subsequently, the unregulated flow of subtropical plants into Britain to satisfy gardeners' demands meant that whiteflies and mealybugs among others were probably well established by the time the repeal of the Glass Tax in 1845 led to a vast increase in glasshouse gardening in the nineteenth century; although it is worth bearing in mind that before 1833, almost all plant imports from far-flung places were in the form of seeds on which relatively few pests (although a fair number of diseases) are transmitted. The significance of the year 1833 was that it heralded the first practical demonstration of the value of the Wardian case, an enclosed glass plant container invented by the botanist Nathaniel Bagshaw Ward (1791–1868). Ward sent plants in such a travelling case to Australia and:

> ... when opened three months later, the plants inside were found to be still growing sturdily; the cases were then refilled and on the return journey their contents again passed unharmed through snow and equatorial heat alike. (Allen, 1994)

By the time the glasshouse gardeners were grappling with their sap-sucking pests, the gardening English were beginning to tire of formality, of neat clipped lines and of topiary around their houses (Fig. 8). Joseph Addison expressed it most succinctly:

> *Our British gardeners, instead of humoring Nature, love to deviate from it as much as possible. Our Trees rise in Cones, Globes and Pyramids. We see the marks of scissors upon every Plant and Bush. I do not know whether I am singular in my Opinion, but for my own part, I would rather look upon a tree in all its Luxuriancy and Diffusion of Boughs and Branches than when it is cut into a Mathematical Figure ...*
> (Addison, 1712)

Addison certainly was not singular in his opinion, and whilst the landscape movement which these sentiments presaged made no impact on the everyday essentially subsistence plots that represented gardens to the majority of the population, it certainly did on the landed gentry. Only 16 years later – nothing in the life of a great garden – the delightfully named Batty Langley was asking 'Is there anything more shocking than a stiff regular garden?' (Langley, 1728). The boundary walls went, replaced by the ha-ha, and the landscape all but lapped at the steps of the house.

The pivotal garden of the period was Stowe, where Charles Bridgeman (d. 1738), William Kent (1686–1748) and John Vanbrugh (1664–1726) in turn

FIG 8. Neat clipped lines and topiary became important in English gardens from the early Tudor period. Haddon Hall, Derbyshire.

remodelled the landscape (Fig. 9). It was followed by numerous others, all great, all grand, created by a succession of disciples, most notably Lancelot 'Capability' Brown (1716–83) (who worked at Stowe early in his career) and Humphry Repton (1752–1818). Repton was more cautious than his predecessors and was content to retain a flower garden, 'detached and distinct from the general scenery of the place', but in need of being 'protected from hares and smaller animals by an inner fence' (Repton, 1803).

These gardeners are remembered in equal measure both for what they created and for what they destroyed. For the landscape park was not an addition but a substitution. The formal gardens were to a greater or lesser degree swept away, the boundaries disappeared, formal water features vanished, rivers were dammed and the topography reshaped. It was an idealised landscape of trees, grass and water, a contemporary eighteenth-century view of a classical Arcadia and, ironically, apart from the occasional temple and folly, it was almost a temperate equivalent of a habitat then awaiting discovery by European eyes: the tropical African savannah (Fig. 10). A limited but important range of native and non-native trees dictated the overall appearance, the fallow deer *Dama dama* became the *sine qua non* among garden animals, and the landscaped park turned into a new, semi-natural habitat with a flora and fauna uniquely its own. The

FIG 9. Stowe was the pivotal garden of the English landscape movement where Charles Bridgeman, William Kent and John Vanbrugh in turn remodelled the landscape. The artificial ruins were probably modelled by Kent.

FIG 10. The English landscape garden is, paradoxically, reminiscent of another landscape its creators never saw – the tropical African savannah.

word parkland passed into the currency of the English language with a meaning understood by all, and it is as familiar in field guide habitat descriptions today as sand dune, swamp and moor. I shall refer again to the characteristic wildlife of this remarkable and intriguing habitat, one that has been described, perhaps a trifle unfairly, as the only uniquely English contribution to garden style.

The kitchen garden, meanwhile, offered challenges of its own in an ever-growing obsession with the cultivation of the tender and exotic. Cucumbers, melons *Cucumis melo* and above all pineapples *Ananas comosus* demanded the finest and most inventive horticultural skills from gardeners at great houses everywhere. *Botrytis* grey mould and woodlice thrived as never before. And so it was as the century turned again and the Victorian age beckoned. Gardening and the garden environment were about to undergo their greatest revolution.

THE NINETEENTH-CENTURY GARDENING REVOLUTION

The number of plant introductions during the nineteenth century was greater than those of all previous centuries combined. South Africa and then Australia contributed annual flowers, China and other regions of the Far East contributed perennials and shrubs, as – on a large but much less well-lauded scale – did

Chile and other parts of South America. To take one example, where would modern British gardens and modern British whiteflies be without South American fuchsias? Over 4,000 *Fuchsia* species and cultivars are available to today's gardeners, yet apart from a brief eighteenth-century experience with a geographical 'outlier' – the Hispaniolan *F. triphylla*, grown by Philip Miller at the Chelsea Physic Garden – the majority did not reach Britain until well into the nineteenth century (Fig. 11). The first hybrid, 'Standishii', derived from *F. fulgens* and *F. magellanica*, did not appear until 1839. The impact on British gardening of what are, in most cases, tender plants, is hard to overstate. Quite apart from their almost endless summer flowering season, fuchsias are usually overwintered in a more or less actively growing condition in greenhouses, either as cuttings or mature stock plants, and thus provide year-round sanctuary and

FIG 11. Fuchsia species flooded into Britain in the nineteenth century from South America, but the origin of fuchsia rust *Pucciniastrum epilobii*, which also, as here, occurs on native species of *Epilobium* (willow-herbs), is uncertain.

a haven not only for whiteflies but for innumerable aphids (at least some of them native species) and vine weevils *Otiorhynchus sulcatus*. All these are non-host-specific pests and thus we have a situation in which one of the most popular flowers of the modern domestic garden is acting as a reservoir for three of its most significant insect pests.

In our warm summers, fuchsias are also a food plant for one of the most magnificent of European caterpillars, the increasingly common 8-centimetre long, eyed larvae of the elephant hawk moth *Deilephila elpenor*, and they are common hosts too for a fungus disease now generally known as fuchsia rust *Pucciniastrum epilobii*. It is a matter for speculation how common these organisms were in the past. Elephant hawk moths have a fairly catholic diet and, in addition to fuchsia, feed on species of evening primrose (*Oenothera*), willowherb (*Epilobium*), bedstraw (*Galium*), vine (*Vitis*) and bog-bean (*Menyanthes*). Fuchsia rust, however, like most rusts, is more conservative. It also occurs on native species of willowherbs which are in the same family as *Fuchsia* (Onagraceae), but its alternate host is spruce (*Abies*), not a native plant, and its natural geographical origin is uncertain, a situation compounded by the existence of several races, not all able to infect all hosts.

One of the least natural outlets for the nineteenth-century influx of tropical and subtropical annuals and tender perennials was the planting style that became known as carpet bedding. Although never a feature of small home gardens, it found much favour in the high Victorian country house garden and in the increasing number of municipal park flower gardens that became popular towards the latter part of the century. Carpet bedding was (and in few places such as seaside promenades, still is) the close planting of bedding plants chosen principally for their foliage and arranged in patterns to give the appearance of oriental carpets (Fig. 12). Sometimes the flowers are sheared off to enhance the foliage effects. Whilst no doubt heaven for slugs, carpet bedding did little for garden biodiversity, and when problems arose, they spread with the rapidity that is a feature of monocultures everywhere. With no species breaks, a host-specific pest or disease had ample freedom to roam.

But carpet bedding was an oddity, a rather short-lived curio, and a far more important gardening movement was to follow because, ironically, the century that saw the greatest number of exotic plant imports also gave rise to a style often referred to as 'a return to naturalism'. Although many horticulturists contributed to it, the name with which it is most usually associated is that of the Irishman William Robinson (1838–1935). He has been described (Allan, 1982) as the father of the English flower garden (partly because that was the title of his most successful book (Robinson, 1883)), but in truth, while he added many original

FIG 12. Victorian bedding schemes included many low-growing hardy and tender annuals as well as clipped foliage which was used for carpet bedding.

ideas, it was as its populariser that his contribution endures. He was a man '[who] to a considerable degree ... engineered the creation of his own myth' (Elliott, 1985). The style promulgated by Robinson and his colleagues, especially and most famously Gertrude Jekyll (1843–1932), was one of soft herbaceous plantings, of carefully blended colours and not a little use of native plants. It found immediate and more or less enduring favour in gardens of all sizes, although in the latter half of the twentieth century all-herbaceous plantings were modified by the inclusion of shrubs to give better year-round appeal and less labour input (p. 41). Neither Robinson nor Jekyll mentioned biodiversity by name – hardly surprising since the word did not appear until 1986 (Wilson, 1988) – but there is no doubt that they were familiar with its concept.

Robinson and Jekyll close the nineteenth century, open the twentieth and presage the dawn of the modern garden to which I devote my next chapter. But it is worth reflecting again on the changes in domestic horticulture wrought by nineteenth-century society. What made the pre-nineteenth-century garden a place largely in harmony with wildlife had little to do with the garden style favoured at any particular time. Whether formal courtyard, flowery mead or landscaped park, the historic English garden and its gardeners simply shared an empathetic way of life with the countryside around them, and whilst some exotic species had been grown here since the earliest times, gardening was still predominantly the cultivation of native or at least European plants. Three things changed all that. First, the coming of industry, its associated pollution and the development of poisonous pesticides and artificial fertilisers altered the natural history of the garden from the late eighteenth century onwards in a way from which only in the past decade or so has it been able to stage any serious sort of recovery; a theme to which I allude again in Chapter 3. Second, the expansion of the British Empire, the opening up of new areas of the globe to exploration and the activities of numerous plant collectors, led to an influx of alien vegetation into these islands to such an extent that our flora would never be the same again. Finally, and within our own lifetimes, the freedom of travel for all and the international movement of plants have brought the experience of exotic plant pests and diseases within the reach of every home gardener.

CHAPTER 2

The Modern British Garden

A NATION OF GARDENERS

EVERY YEAR, an organisation called The National Gardens Scheme publishes a volume known as *The Yellow Book*, formerly called *Gardens of England and Wales Open for Charity* (Anon, 2005a). (A comparable volume is published in Scotland by Scotland's Gardens Scheme.) The 2005 edition listed over 3,500 gardens of real horticultural merit, mainly private; and I do not for a moment doubt the number could be at least tripled without any loss of standards. I know I am on firm ground in saying that no other country in the world, and most certainly none of comparable size, could approach this. There is quite simply a greater depth and breadth of fine public and private gardens in Britain today than anywhere else. There are several reasons for this.

Our environment is amenable to the successful growing of a huge number of different types of plant – partly because there is almost certainly a greater range of solid geology and associated soil types in Britain than in any other country of comparable size (Stamp, 1946), and also because we have a cool temperate climate that for most of the national area lacks any regular extremes of temperature, precipitation or wind (Manley, 1952).

It is also significant that we have a land-owning tradition; that by general inclination we are owner-occupiers, not tenants, and with that land ownership comes an added wish to care and a wish to embellish (Fig. 13). This might seem a surprising statement because by marked contrast with the horizontal land ownership (everyone having a share) in, say, the United States – a 'land-owning democracy' in which the country is subdivided among its population (far from

FIG 13. There is a tradition of land and garden ownership in Britain which brings with it a wish to care and embellish.

uniformly, but at least relatively equitably) (Linklater, 2002) – a feudal tradition of vertical land ownership (a few people owning the bulk) prevails in Britain. This is unarguable, and it is similarly unarguable that land ownership in Britain is far from either uniform or equitable. It has recently been shown that in England and Wales 0.28 per cent of the population owns 64 per cent of the land, and although between a third and a half of the land in England and Wales is unregistered, it is estimated that a mere handful, only 89,000 people, own 88 per cent of the total: and 99.7 per cent of the population lives on just 1.78 million hectares (Cahill, 2001). But that really is not the point. My concern is not with large tracts of land, much less with farmland or 'open countryside'. My concern is with what I call domestic land, and my argument is that a large proportion of the population owns something attached to the building in which they live, no matter how small, and has done so for at least 100 years. The proportion of owner-occupied households in England rose steadily through the twentieth century. It had reached 57 per cent in 1981, 68 per cent in 1991 and 70 per cent in 2001–2 (Anon, 2003b). It is not the highest in Europe, but is close to it. Not all, of course, are houses with gardens, but of a total of approximately 24.5 million dwellings in Britain (Anon, 2003b), there are probably between 15 and 20 million with an associated garden. (These figures, and especially the comment that there are 20 million gardens in Britain, are commonly quoted, and although there seems to be no authoritative basis for it, everything points to it being reasonably accurate.) Even the tenant population occupies a higher proportion of houses with associated gardens/land than is the case in most other countries of western Europe, and it has often been pointed out to me that some of the best tended and most loved gardens in Britain are associated with local authority-owned tenanted houses.

With no real statistics on the number of gardens, there is ipso facto no information on average garden size, although from time to time, members of the horticultural trade in particular – who have a vested interest – try to gauge this. Thirty years ago, Hessayon & Hessayon (1973) claimed there were 14.5 million gardens in Britain and that 80 per cent of private households had a garden, although they did not indicate the proportion that was owned. They also stated that the average size of a British garden then was 186 square metres, 'less than half the French, German, Scandinavian or Belgian figure'.

An appealingly individual viewpoint was provided by Paskett (pers. comm.) who collected data for the lawnmower industry. He estimated that as most gardens had at least a bit of grass, there are not only about 20 million gardens, but also about 20 million lawns. He arrived at an average lawn area of about 100 square metres. This equates to 2,000 square kilometres of domestic lawn spread through Britain. The largest National Park is the Lake District (2,300 square kilometres), followed by Snowdonia (2,140 square kilometres). 'As these are either largely water or mountain', Paskett said:

> ... it means that 'the National Gardens Park' combines into the third largest National Park, ahead of the Yorkshire Dales (1,700 square kilometres) and the Peak District (1,400 square kilometres).

Paskett himself is perfectly well aware that isolated bits of lawn are very different from a continuous area of land, but the statistic is a helpful and entertaining one to grab the public's attention (Fig. 14).

If there are now around 20 million gardens in Britain and the average size is about twice the area of Paskett's average lawn, or slightly bigger than Hessayon & Hessayon estimated 30 years ago, we arrive at total of 4,000 square kilometres, desperately close to 'an area the size of Somerset' (actually 4,171 square kilometres) which is commonly invoked when environmentalists are seeking to make a point about the importance of gardens as habitats. But the differences between scattered bits and a unified county are so enormous that to read any serious scientific meaning into this is really rather pointless and I shall refer to this again later (p. 109). I also believe that not enough interest has been attached to the importance of gardens in relation to territories, particularly of birds and mammals (p. 245); and even less to the size of gardening communities rather than individual gardens. The total area of contiguous gardens in, say, an urban street or a housing estate, is of considerably more relevance to a robin, a bat or a fox than that of any individual plot.

Another collection of data undertaken for the horticultural industry and made available to me is contained in a survey for a garden equipment manufacturer (Electrolux Outdoor products/NOP 2003; pers. comm.). In a sample of 1,001 persons over the age of 15 throughout Britain, 85 per cent said they had the use of a garden; 70 per cent of those with the use of a garden said they did some gardening; 55 per cent said they spent over three hours a week doing so; and while 38 per cent said they 'enjoyed' gardening, 20 per cent found it a chore and only did the bare minimum.

More recently, detailed information on the potential that gardens offer has come from a project by a group at the University of Sheffield to which I shall refer again (p. 107). In an intensive study in Sheffield, the group estimated that the city contained 175,000 domestic gardens covering around 3,000 hectares. These gardens contained 25,000 ponds, 50,000 compost heaps and 360,000 trees over 2 metres high, as well as 45,000 bird nest boxes.

The area given over to gardens can be looked at in another way using the data of Countryside 2000, 'a partnership between several Government Departments,

FIG 14. Thousands of isolated bits of lawn are very different for wildlife from a continuous area of land of the same size.

Agencies and the Natural Environment Research Council', which 'repeated and extended previous surveys ... and provided measures of the current state of the countryside and indicators describing the changes which have taken place' (www.cs2000.org.uk). It gave 'a first look at the results for the Broad Habitats that are used as the framework for the UK's Biodiversity Action Plan'. The Country-side 2000 results revealed that 1,331,000 hectares or 5.8 per cent of the land area of Great Britain were classed as 'built-up and gardens' (areas that were more than 75 per cent built up were excluded). (Figures for Northern Ireland were unavailable and the breakdown was 7.7 per cent for England and Wales and 1.9 per cent for Scotland.) Of the total, around half (707,000 hectares) was classed as residential and this gives the best indication therefore of the importance of gardens in the national environmental context. The survey was based on data collected in 1998, and by comparison with figures for 1990, there had been an increase of around 4.9 per cent overall in the 'built-up and gardens' area and an increase of 18 per cent in the 'residential' component. Although, unfortunately, there is no indication of how much of this was due to residential buildings, it is a fair assumption that both buildings and gardens are on the increase and therefore that gardens are accounting for ever more of our national land area. This is good for the gardening industry certainly, which is expanding at the rate of around 20 per cent per annum and in 2004 had a retail value of around £5 billion. And if gardeners really are now as environmentally aware as many

FIG 15. New houses and gardens mean a decline in many kinds of habitat.

people believe, the instant inference might be that this is good for wildlife and biodiversity too. But as with all statistics, it pays to look beneath the surface and the increase obscures a wider and more worrying truth.

New houses and gardens do not materialise from thin air, and coincident with their increase were declines in the areas of several other landscape categories, including improved grassland, coniferous woodland, bog, calcareous grassland (an 18 per cent loss), inland rock, acid grassland (a 10 per cent loss) and boundaries (which includes hedges) (Fig. 15). It is true that the area of some habitats had increased – fen, marsh and swamp for example had gone up by 27 per cent, presumably through conservation activities – and that the interrelationship between rises and falls in the areas of different habitats is undoubtedly complex. Nonetheless, it is certain that not all new houses and gardens were built on 'unsurveyed urban land' and 'other land' – what are commonly called 'brownfield' sites – and other habitats must clearly be suffering at the expense of the rise in home and garden ownership. Equally worrying is the recent revelation that since 2000, 'brownfield' sites officially include former residential land and old gardens. Moreover, it has been pointed out that even traditional 'brownfield' areas such as abandoned factory sites and railway yards can themselves be biodiversity-rich habitats.

Political will is all very well:

Much of the need for new homes has hitherto been in areas such as the south east of England. It is unlikely that this pressure will diminish in the short term. Government policies are to direct as much housing development as possible towards brownfield sites, but the area of previously developed sites is limited. It is likely, therefore, that some greenfield development will also be needed in the future, but Government policy is to restrict the level of greenfield development considerably. (Defra, 2002)

But politicians' intentions do not always translate into practice:

During Labour's first term, Mr Prescott promised to cut back on building on 'greenfield' sites, to make more use of 'brownfield' land that had already been developed, and to concentrate on reviving towns and cities. The Government achieved its target of building 60 per cent of new houses on brownfield sites. However, planning studies, commissioned by the Government, show that the vast bulk of new housing in three of the four areas will go on greenfield land over the next 30 years. A total of 29,000 houses will be built in open country around Ashford, between 123,000 and 197,000 in the M11 corridor around Stansted, and 250,000 around Milton Keynes. Only in the Thames Gateway area will most houses be built on brownfield sites, but even here some 40,000 will be in the countryside, according to calculations from the Council for the Protection of Rural England (CPRE). (Lean, 2003)

And the trend continues:

Half a million new homes, part of the Government's plan for a massive building programme in the South East, were given the go-ahead yesterday. Planners gave the green light to 478,000 houses to be built in Bedfordshire, Cambridgeshire, Essex, Hertfordshire, Norfolk and Suffolk by 2021 ... Forty per cent of the new development will take place on undeveloped greenfield land ... (Fleming, 2004)

It seems that new home owners will have to be environmentally friendly indeed to make up for what has been sacrificed to provide them with gardens, although some authorities appear to believe that Government policy on new housing is tailor-made for the enhancement of biodiversity. Somewhat bizarrely, English Nature, 'the Government funded body whose purpose is to promote the conservation of England's wildlife and natural features', was reported to have said in 2003 that 'building thousands of new homes in the South-east would be good for the environment and could halt the decline in butterflies and other threatened wildlife' (Highfield & Clover, 2003). 'Low density housing, with large gardens, hedgerows, woodland and open spaces would help farmland birds, such as song thrushes and skylarks and butterflies', it was claimed. Members of Parliament and the Campaign to Protect Rural England were among those to pour scorn on the idea, and whilst I would be the first to suggest that gardening can and should be done with an empathy for the environment and to the benefit of wildlife, even I would be hard pressed to claim that gardens are better in this regard than properly managed lowland farms. English Nature rather unconvincingly went on the defensive:

English Nature believes that both development and agricultural policy and practice need to be sustainable. We are not calling for unconstrained development nor are we saying that housing development is better for the environment than sustainable managed agricultural land use. However, our agricultural policy of the last 50 years has led to major environmental damage. In some areas most of the once common wildlife has been lost through intensification of production of crops and livestock or the specialisation of agriculture and the loss of extensive livestock or mixed farming systems ... (English Nature, 2003)

FIG 16. Old terraced houses often have small but attractive gardens yet are commonly demolished to make way for modern estates.

In 2005, in a rare Government comment on the importance of gardens for home owners, Yvette Cooper, the Minister for Housing and Regeneration, reportedly claimed the absence of a garden as a justification for pulling down old terraced houses and replacing them with far more costly new ones, rather than undertaking renovation (Fig. 16) (Clover, 2005). She did not, however, indicate just how many terraced houses really do have no garden – my view is probably not many.

ALLOTMENTS

Home gardening in Britain does not begin and end with the garden that adjoins the house. There is another garden, the allotment, that by its nature is always tenanted. Whilst collectively allotments are not invariably visions of loveliness, at least they are used by people who genuinely want to grow plants – no-one is forced to have an allotment – and they are an important although not uniquely British part of the horticultural landscape. Like gardens overall, their role in our national biodiversity has been neglected.

Allotments in their present form date from the Allotment Act 1877, or to give it its full title, 'An Act to facilitate the provision of Allotments for the Labouring

Classes' (Fig. 17). If six or more registered parliamentary electors or ratepayers asked for it, a local authority was bound to determine if there was a demand for allotments, and if so, to provide them. The whole was littered with legal provisions and stipulations ('No building other than a tool house, shed, greenhouse, fowl house, or pigsty shall be erected on any part of any allotment …') but apart from allowing tenants to remove their plants at the end of a tenancy, there were almost no horticultural requirements, although local authorities generally enacted their own regulations and bylaws to try and ensure that the land was kept tidy, productive and non-commercial. The problem with a tenanted plot at some distance from a dwelling really arises when it becomes untenanted and no-one's responsibility, although it has often seemed to me that the allotment gardens' greatest contribution to biodiversity (not necessarily entirely desirable) comes when they *are* neglected – a sort of domestic set-aside.

By the First World War, demand for allotments was increasing considerably, and this continued well into the interwar years. Between 1936 and 1939 the total allotment area was just over 51,000 hectares, and by the early part of the Second World War in 1942, according to one estimate, it had reached well over 72,000 hectares (Simmons, 1998). It is cause for some thought that the national allotment area then was equal to roughly one-tenth of the total 'built-up and gardens' area of the United Kingdom only 56 years later. Adding home gardens

FIG 17. Allotments are hugely important assets for people with no home garden and date from the Allotment Act of 1877.

to allotments gives an even more formidable statistic of food production: 'In 1944, 120,000 hectares of allotments and gardens produced 1.3 million tonnes of food, about half of the nation's fruit and vegetable needs ...' (Pretty, 2001). The wartime expansion of the area of allotments and of home kitchen gardens was driven by one of the most remarkable and remarkably successful of all Second World War initiatives, the 'Dig for Victory' campaign. It was launched within a month of the outbreak of war and supported by a steady flow of posters and leaflets encouraging the home growing of produce. The claim that in 1944 over one million tonnes of vegetables were being grown in home gardens and allotments (Pretty, 2001) is a figure that it is impossible to substantiate, as is Pretty's belief that 'today, there are 300,000 allotments on 12,150 hectares, yielding 215,000 tonnes of fresh produce every year'. Cruder estimates are possible, however, and it is undeniable that the modern home garden plays a much smaller but nonetheless significant role in the growing of produce. When I was engaged in horticultural research in the 1970s, we used to believe that around one third of fruit and vegetables was grown by home gardeners; today, I am told, it is generally reckoned to be under 10 per cent. The incentives for home production have changed, however. The momentum of the Dig for Victory campaign continued well after 1945 but began to decline as the ready and relatively inexpensive availability of fresh produce in supermarkets rose. Home vegetable growing took a further severe knock in the two consecutive drought years of 1975 and 1976 when much time, cost and labour were expended on crops that failed. It has risen again, however, for a different reason. The increased appeal of organically grown crops and their relatively high price in shops (partly because of the higher production costs) has encouraged many gardeners to grow at least a few of their own. Supporting data are available from major seed companies (Sharples, pers. comm.). Shortly after 1945, sales of packeted seed in the United Kingdom were estimated to be between 70 and 80 million packets a year. The ratio of vegetables to flowers was around 3:1, but the trend away from vegetables resulted in more or less equal sales by the late 1950s. By the 1970s, flowers were well ahead; one major company reckons by 2.5:1, another by as much as 3:1. In the mid-1990s, the swing back to vegetables, however, was well under way, and by 2004 the ratio of vegetable to flower seed sales was around 1.75:1. Interestingly, the allotment has seen something of a comeback too, with the initiative launched by the National Society of Allotment and Leisure Gardens in 2002 of Britain's first National Allotment Week.

The allotment and the home vegetable garden are essentially short-term entities. Most vegetables are grown as annuals, or at most biennials, and it is in the nature of their production that the soil is constantly tilled and disturbed. It is

FIG 18. The hanging basket contains a disproportionately minute number of species and contributes an infinitesimally small benefit to the nation's biodiversity.

an environment conducive to the proliferation of a small number of garden pest species and horticultural weeds, but not to a great deal else. The same may be said of the annual flowerbed, although the area is almost always smaller than that given over to vegetables, and in modern gardens, annuals tend commonly to be grown in small groups within perennial plantings or in containers to which, peculiarly, vine weevils have adapted, but which are otherwise generally fairly barren habitats. That most bizarre of horticultural container creations, the hanging basket, is the garden equivalent of the Sitka spruce plantation in containing a disproportionately minute number of species and contributing an infinitesimally small benefit to the nation's biodiversity (Fig. 18).

LAWNS

One habitat that has undeniably increased in gardens and one of the few that
is almost entirely artificial with no natural parallels is the area of close-cropped
grass generally called a lawn. Close cropping of grass is not itself new. It was a
feature of the ancient forest clearings naturally browsed by deer and later still
by the more or less enclosed areas – parks – artificially maintained for hunting.
Rackham (1986) estimated that in the heyday of parks around the year 1300, there
were about 3,200 in England. But it is only necessary to walk through a grazed
pasture today to realise that it is not the same as a lawn. It is not cropped as
closely, it is heavily manured and the plant life (grasses included) is different.
I shall refer later (p. 109f) to the nature and significance of the species
composition of lawns.

The artificial close cropping of areas of grass for ornamental effect probably
began in Roman times and continued more or less unaltered until the early years
of the nineteenth century, the grass being shaved with scythes. It was a time-
consuming and laborious task, requiring great skill if bare patches were not to
be created, and extremely sharp scythes if the grass was not simply to be pushed
aside. Whilst these scythed areas became important features of country house
gardens, proper lawns did not intrude into home gardening until after 1830 when
a Gloucestershire engineer, Edwin Budding (1794 –1846) obtained a patent for a
machine based on that used for taking the nap from cloth. Budding's machine
involved a set of blades attached to a rotating spindle which moved against a
single blade and so operated in a scissor fashion, slicing the grass. Despite the
addition of petrol engines and other innovations, the essential features of the
lawnmower remained unchanged for well over a century (Fig. 19). Although
electric power and rotary cutting (slashing rather than slicing) were all tried in
the 1920s and 30s, they did not become popular until the 1960s when hovering
versions of the rotary mower soon followed.

At a stroke, Budding single-handedly created a completely new ecological
habitat that is now taken for granted but that (apart from golf courses and
bowling greens) is unlike anything beyond the garden environment. A number
of native plant and animal species have adapted to it and some have made it
essentially their own (p. 205ff). In turn, the desire for lawns in home gardens
led to the development of an entirely new industry providing not only lawn care
machinery and chemicals, but also the lawns themselves in the form of grass
seed mixtures and, more especially, grown turf. Digging up pieces of established
grass and transplanting it is centuries old (p. 11) and in my own childhood I can

FIG 19. All cylinder lawnmowers still embody the same principle as Edwin Budding's original machine of 1830. This is Green's Multum in Parvo model from 1880.

remember selling one's meadow as lawn turf being described as the final throw of the desperate farmer. Over the past 30 or so years, however, the sowing of specially selected grass seed mixtures and the subsequent highly automated harvesting of the turf has become a big commercial enterprise. Specially grown turf is now available throughout Britain and precisely matching rolls are delivered fresh to the point of use (Fig. 20). The grasses used are mainly selections and hybrids chosen for their durability, uniform appearance and reluctance to produce flowering stems, while being robust enough to withstand being walked and played on. Although relatively few different types of turf are available, the grass seed companies have really gone to town; one, for instance, currently offers different seed mixtures for 'fine ornamental lawns', 'premier lawns', 'universal lawns', 'prize lawns', 'front lawns', 'back lawns', 'shaded lawns', 'low maintenance lawns' and 'drought tolerant lawns'. Among the more important grass species that contribute to the blends are various red fescues *Festuca rubra* s.l. including Chewings' fescue *F. rubra* subsp. *commutata*, common bent *Agrostis capillaris*, brown bent *A. vinealis*, smooth meadow-grass *Poa pratensis* and perennial ryegrass *Lolium perenne*. The botanical nature of the grasses involved seems, however, to matter little to the wildlife that has adopted the lawn environment as opposed to the traditional meadow or grassland. Because lawns

FIG 20. Precisely matching rolls of turf enable lawns to be created instantly. Transplanting turf has been carried out for centuries.

are constantly being mown, its inhabitants hardly have a chance to feed on the foliage and either use the sward simply as cover or eat the roots. Whilst I am unaware of any detailed studies in Britain of the lawn as a wildlife habitat, a fascinating investigation in California (Falk, 1976) revealed suburban lawns to be 'ideal foraging sites for open area adapted flock-feeding species of birds' and showed 'food utilization by suburban birds considerably exceeded natural grassland bird utilization'. The study also revealed the suburban lawn (presumably a well-fed one) to be an extremely productive environment (1,020 grams of fresh plant material per square metre per year compared with 1,066 grams per square metre per year for a cornfield). I shall refer again to Falk's study in relation to the lawn fauna (p. 211).

ROCK GARDENS

One of the largest sections at many garden centres in respect of number of plant species is that of alpines or rock garden plants. They are mostly exotic, almost by definition, as although alpine plants never did come solely from the Alps, at least most of them came originally from mountains higher and more extensive than any in Britain. Today, they comprise a motley assortment of small perennials of miscellaneous origin that are grown in more or less the same way – in a free-draining compost embellished with pieces of rock. The genuine rock garden is now less common in British gardens and contributes little more to biodiversity than did its forebears. Alpines are more usually grown today in some form of container, often stone or replica stone troughs which supply a novel habitat for lichens as they tend to stay, unmoved, for many years in the same place (Fig. 21). Indeed gardening books offer recipes for encouraging what is generally referred to simply as 'growth' or 'weathering' by the expedient of painting the surface with cow manure, yogurt or both. Gilbert (2000) illustrated such a trough, but made no mention of it as a lichen habitat (p. 222). Enthusiasts grow alpines in alpine houses – greenhouses with no heat and extra ventilation – but all are attempts to emulate their natural habitat in regions with high rainfall, free drainage, extremes of temperature (exposed mountain tops become very hot as well as very cold) and above all, low humidity. It is the cold, clinging damp of British winters that is the enemy of alpine garden plants, not anything do with temperature.

The beginnings of rock gardening followed the beginnings of the British obsession with mountains and mountaineering. Mont Blanc was first climbed in 1786, and the pioneering mountaineers who followed wanted to take a little of it

FIG 21. Replica stone troughs are passable imitations of the real thing and are valuable for growing alpines but incidentally provide a wonderful habitat for lichens too.

home with them. Early rock gardens created at the end of the eighteenth and into the nineteenth century were therefore often fanciful re-creations of the Alps, topped with alabaster 'snow' and, in grand gardens, visitors were sometimes provided with telescopes to view the flora. These later evolved into a more 'traditional' style of rock garden that was, at its best, indistinguishable from a natural rock outcrop and provided a fine habitat for lichens, mosses, ferns and small invertebrates. More commonly, however, it was merely a pile of soil surmounted by stones and picturesquely maligned as an 'almond pudding' by the Yorkshireman Reginald Farrer who popularised and almost invented modern rock gardening in Britain during the late nineteenth and early twentieth centuries (Farrer, 1907). As such it contributed little to garden biodiversity, although it was (and is) a notorious trap for perennial weeds such as common couch *Elytrigia repens* (p. 108).

PAVING AND DECKING

The gradual demise of tarmac or poured concrete – the most hideous and generally barren garden materials – for paths and larger areas, and their replace-ment by some form of paving slabs has been of immense value in increasing the potential space for colonisation by crevice-inhabiting plants, bryophytes and animals, although perversely, gardeners see this as having created a rod for their own backs. Most of the plants (dandelions *Taraxacum* spp., pearlworts *Sagina* spp., plantains *Plantago* spp. and so forth) that most readily colonise cracks are perceived as weeds to be controlled by persistent herbicides or more general biocides, while among the commonest animals are ants which undermine the slabs by tunnelling in the favourably dry, friable layers beneath. The importance of what is now called 'hard landscape' in the modern garden is of course a mixed blessing, because no matter how interesting cracks and crevices are to the naturalist, they are not necessarily an adequate substitute for the loss of open soil beds. Saddest of all has been the consequence of the popularity of television makeover programmes that peddle the fantasy that a garden can be created in a weekend, and make extensive use of even less environmentally acceptable materials in the shape of stone chips or gravel laid over water-permeable membrane and, horror of horrors, wooden decking. It is perfectly understandable why they should do so. Given a few hours to transform an unsightly plot into something neat and tidy, they offer a perfect solution. That they are biologically almost sterile is clearly of no concern, although in due course, decking will attract a film of unicellular algae and with any luck might, if not too much timber

FIG 22. Replica oriental garden in a Herefordshire village.

preservative has been used, eventually support the growth of wood-rotting basidiomycete fungi.

GREENHOUSES AND CONSERVATORIES

In Chapter 1, I mentioned the repeal of the Glass Tax in 1845 and the impetus this gave to greenhouse gardening. It was a trend that has continued to the present day, although in the modern garden, the large greenhouse has given way to the conservatory that has more to do with lifestyle than the growing of plants. It is estimated that the conservatory market was worth £423 million in 2003, which represented a growth of 5 per cent on the previous year and 32 per cent on the preceding five (source: Mintel, January 2004). The seriously committed gardener with a greenhouse including some heating and devoted to plant raising, tomato production or to the overwintering of tender plants – and the provision of a safe haven for pests and diseases – is in the minority, although the types of greenhouse available have never been greater. Wooden frames have largely given way to aluminium and, while glass remains the best covering material, the use of polycarbonate and other plastics has brought down costs. However, the practicality of some of the small structures readily obtained at DIY outlets and which are little more than vertical cold frames is highly doubtful. Partly because there is some difficulty in defining exactly what does constitute a greenhouse today, accurate data are elusive. An indication can be gleaned from Hessayon (1983), who believed then that 14 per cent of gardens had a greenhouse, that each year one in every 150 households bought one, about half were heated and that whereas the most popular size had been 10 × 8 feet (3 × 2.4 metres), this had shrunk to 8 × 6 feet (2.4 × 1.8 metres).

THE HERBACEOUS BORDER

I left the last chapter in the early twentieth century with the gardens of William Robinson and Gertrude Jekyll and mentioned the gradual replacement of the Jekyllesque herbaceous border with mixing plantings of perennials and shrubs. This was a response to two related features of home gardening: a smaller garden area and the gradual disappearance of gardening labour. The herbaceous border is visually a wonderful creation for a few months of the year (Fig. 23). In the winter it yields nothing, and whilst in large gardens this is no disadvantage as there will always be space to create other areas of seasonal interest, this is impractical in the limited confines of the modern home garden. A skeletal or,

FIG 23. The herbaceous border reached its peak late in the nineteenth century and, visually, can be one of the great glories of the English garden.

as it tends to be called, structural planting of shrubs around which herbaceous perennials and some annuals are planted, makes more sense. Shrubs have a head start in the spring and so, together with bulbs, provide appeal early in the year. It is a garden that is probably better for wildlife too. The presence of all-year round shrubs and some small trees offers a food resource in the form of seed heads, buds and associated insects.

The herbaceous border is also undeniably labour intensive. Annual tying up and staking, dead-heading and cutting back and periodic division all take time. The owner of every garden worthy of the name a century ago employed at the very least one man and a boy, full time. In bigger, more complex or densely planted gardens, there were more, sometimes many more. The celebrated gardener Ellen Willmott (1858–1934) who is commemorated in the fine sea-holly *Eryngium giganteum*, sometimes known as 'Miss Willmott's Ghost', and in the many cultivars called 'Willmottiae' or 'Willmottianum', lived at a house called Warley Place in Essex where she employed 104 gardeners, all in uniform. Admittedly the garden was fairly large – around 6 hectares. It had been laid out between 1649 and 1655 by John Evelyn and interestingly is now a nature reserve managed by the Essex Wildlife Trust. The descendants of some of Miss Willmott's bulb and perennial plantings survive '… mingling with indigenous species', but predictably, one of the Trust's continuing tasks is 'controlling the spread of sycamore and other invasive plants …'.

Judging by the rack after rack of bedding plants on sale at garden centres in the spring, a visitor from Mars could easily be forgiven for imagining that the growing of annual plants (either hardy annuals or, more usually, half-hardy or tender types) was essential for every modern garden. In reality, those many millions of plants disappear into relatively few gardens and occupy relatively little space; at least when grown in open ground beds. In large measure, the acres of bedding plant trays are there to satisfy the hunger of the modern plant container. For whilst traditional 'bedding out' is now a recreation for the minority, the planting of tubs, window boxes, hanging baskets and other containers has become a feature of life for many home owners. It is almost instant gardening; and it is throw-away gardening too, the containers being emptied at the end of the summer season, commonly to be replanted with one of the great horticultural creations of the past 30 years, the winter flowering pansy *Viola × wittrockiana* (Fig. 24). The annual plant container is a transient habitat, of almost no biological merit other than as a nectar and pollen source for some insects, and even that depends on the choice of plants (p. 238f).

Today, garden 'help' for a day a week is about as much as all except the most wealthy garden owners can manage; and that too may be better for the other

FIG 24. Over the past 30 years, the winter-flowering pansy *Viola × wittrockiana* has brought colour to gardens in the coldest months.

garden inhabitants. For biodiversity, the less assiduously tidying up and clearing away is performed, the better. But in twenty-first century Britain, we have the curious paradox of more people owning gardens, more people spending more money on their gardens and more people claiming to enjoy gardens, but very commonly wishing to have to undertake less work in them. One of the most obvious consequences has been the inexorable rise and rise of plants that grow ever lower and lower – the advent of the labour-saving 'ground cover'. I have been unable to trace the origin of the expression (the OED does not venture an opinion) but I suspect it first appeared or at least gained widespread under-standing in the 1960s. Today, the ground cover section is one of the largest in the shrub area of many a garden centre. The theory is ecologically splendid, but reality seldom matches the expectation. The weeds will still grow whilst the infant slow-growing plant takes its many years to reach maturity, whereas the faster-establishing and maturing species are at least as likely to subjugate, along with the weeds, the other garden plants whose wellbeing they are intended to aid.

There is no denying that the impact of the garden on modern British life is huge. It impinges on our use of and attitude towards the wider environment and our approach to the natural world. What we buy for our gardens and why says much about our overall lifestyle and our perception of design. It is also quite clearly now recognised as a social phenomenon worthy of intensive academic study. Most of this falls outside my scope, but an extraordinary paper by Bhatti & Church (2000) tells it all.

CHAPTER 3

The Operations of Gardening and their Impact upon the Environment

G ARDENING IS 'The act or occupation of laying out or cultivating a garden; horticulture' (OED). I suppose that is all right for a general audience, but I think I can do slightly better; not least because a one-line definition makes it all rather too easy. Gardening or cultivation is not a single operation on a par with bird-watching or clog dancing. Rather it is a multitude of different, often seemingly quite unrelated and disparate skills and tasks that place huge demands on the perpetrator and huge demands on the environment of their garden. This is why great, as opposed to merely good or competent, gardeners are rare creatures; and why great gardens are not ten a penny.

I find it useful to divide the basic skills and tasks of gardening into two categories: physical (digging, hoeing, pruning and so forth) and chemical (fertilising and pest control), although there is a degree of overlap in some areas. Both embrace operations directed mainly at plants (like pruning and pest control) and those mediated mainly through the soil (like digging and manuring), although, of course, ultimately all are destined or intended for the plants' benefit.

PHYSICAL GARDENING

Digging

Digging is the most fundamental of all gardening operations and is the one that has the greatest impact on the greatest number of organisms, albeit most of them rather small (Fig. 25). You cannot put a plant in the soil without digging some sort of hole. You cannot remove other than a small plant except by digging it up.

FIG 25. Digging is the most fundamental of gardening operations and has the greatest impact on the greatest number of organisms.

You certainly do not need to dig larger areas in order to garden, but you will not grow very good vegetables if you do not, your annual flowers will struggle and your perennials will decline relatively quickly.

I once a defined a gardener as someone who is not satisfied with what nature has given him. This dissatisfaction can be apparent in many ways, but most importantly, I think, in relation to soil. If the pH is low, then gardeners want to grow plants that require high pH. If it is high, they want to grow rhododendrons and azaleas. If it is free draining, they complain because they cannot grow roses. If it is wet, unyielding clay, they just happen to adore Mediterranean plants; and of course, they want to be able to dig and cultivate it on any day that they, rather than the weather, choose. There is no real evidence – but it does not take much knowledge of soil biology to speculate – on the changes that take place in the soil flora and fauna in response to gardeners improving aeration and altering crumb structure by digging. There are some data from studies of agricultural soils (although not as extensive as might be expected) that suggest that tillage operations can reduce the populations of soil organisms, either directly by injury or disturbance, or indirectly by increasing oxidation losses of the soil organic matter on which these organisms depend (see for instance Stewart & Salih, 1981; Aarstad & Miller, 1978). Digging also helps limit the growth of perennial weeds, just as hoeing helps limit the growth of annual weeds, moss and fungi. It is also in combination with digging that organic matter (manure, compost or leaf mould) is often added to the soil (see below).

Hedge clipping

Clipping of hedges limits bird nesting sites and, more importantly, disturbs birds already nesting if not timed carefully. I doubt if data are available on the losses of eggs and nestling garden birds through nest abandonment following disturbance by gardeners, and I suspect that in any event it would be almost impossible to separate such losses from those due to cats and other factors; but I do not doubt the numbers are huge. Annual or biannual hedge clipping initially limits the food available for leaf-eating creatures, although its encouragement of new, soft, tender growth ultimately increases what is available to them and also provides hitherto unavailable food resources for sap-sucking creatures such as aphids and fungal pathogens that are limited in their ability to attack more mature tissues. Anyone with a box or beech hedge will see every year how aphids flock to the tender new growths (Fig. 26). These new shoots are also vulnerable to late frost damage, the frost injured tissues in turn providing substrate for weaker pathogens that are only able to invade already injured foliage. More directed pruning of ornamental flowering plants and fruit trees will also initially remove some potential food material for leaf- and wood-eating creatures. However, the cut surfaces of the pruning wounds themselves provide entry points for decay and canker-forming pathogens, and any excised shoots left lying in the garden will be the raw material for saprotrophic fungi. Done properly, pruning will in due course encourage more bud, flower and fruit production and thus provide a bounty, in turn, for the likes of bullfinches *Pyrrhula pyrrhula*, aphids, *Botrytis* grey mould, countless decay fungi, wasps, blackbirds *Turdus merula*, starlings *Sturnus vulgaris* – and even such garden exotica as waxwings *Bombycilla garrula* which flock south from the Arctic each winter to feast on the produce of ornamental and fruiting trees.

FIG 26. Beech aphids *Phyllaphis fagi*. Regular clipping stimulates soft new growth, prone to aphid attack.

Mowing

I shall have more to say about lawns later, but the ways gardeners maintain these most peculiar and distinctive garden habitats have an inevitable impact on their fauna and flora. Whilst much of the impact is through the use of chemicals – fertiliser and weedkillers especially – mowing, raking and scarifying are significant too. Regular mowing removes much of the substrate for grass leaf-feeding animals and fungi (Fig. 27), while scarifying and raking remove most of the lawn bryophyte flora and make wholesale inroads into the world of countless invertebrates which depend on the mass of moss and dead grass for shelter. The ephemeral nature of fungal fruiting bodies means they are much less affected – they may have come and gone between the weekly outings of the lawnmower. It is chemical fertilisers that are their downfall (p. 244). Ironically, the mulching mower which chops the grass into smaller pieces and then forces them back into the lawn surface rather than spraying them into a grass collector is probably even more damaging. Although promoted by manufacturers as environmentally more desirable in lessening the need for fertiliser, no mention seems ever to be made of the fact that the ensuing carpet of wet mulch smothers much soil surface life.

The alternative to leaving the mowings on the lawn is to cart them off, with other garden 'debris', to a compost-making facility, often erroneously called a heap, but in reality needing to be at least partially enclosed in order to do the job properly and more accurately, therefore, a bin. Compost making is widely judged the *sine qua non* for an organic gardener, but in the garden industry survey to which I referred in Chapter 2, the sample of 1,001 persons approached offered the following response to the question: in which one of these ways, if any, do you dispose of your garden waste? (Table 3).

TABLE 3. Survey on the disposal of garden waste.

HOW DO YOU DISPOSE OF MOST OF YOUR GARDEN WASTE?	PERCENTAGE
Place it straight into the compost bin or heap	20
Shred it and then put it into compost bin or heap	6
Put it straight into bags to be taken by the dustmen with the household waste	25
Shred it and then put it into bags to be taken by the dustmen with the household waste	4
Put it straight into bags to be taken to the general household waste dump	18
Shred it and place it into bags to be taken to the general household waste dump	5
Shred it or put it straight into special bags provided by the council for composting in a special council compost area or take it to the council compost area	14
Other (burn it)	6
No waste	1
IF YOU MAKE COMPOST, DO YOU EVER USE THE COMPOST YOU MAKE IN YOUR GARDEN?	
Yes	74
No	26

With only one quarter of gardeners having their own compost facility, compost making cannot be said to be a major pursuit, and the fact that only three-quarters of those who do make compost actually put it to any use, suggests that the compost bin or heap is widely perceived more as a convenient waste depository than any serious horticultural or environmental undertaking. I suspect that for many people, it is merely a means to avoid carting the debris

FIG 27. Regular mowing removes much of the substrate for grass leaf-feeding animals.

FIG 28. Local authorities provide purpose-made containers for the collection of 'green' waste.

elsewhere. I discuss the conservation value of compost bins later, but suffice it to say that, ironically, their greatest value for wildlife enhancement probably comes when they are not functioning properly (p. 252)!

CHEMICAL GARDENING

Composting

When compost is put to practical use, its value is three-fold – for the improvement of soil structure, as a moisture-retaining and weed-suppressing mulch, and as a fertiliser – and this leads me neatly on to a consideration of the wider topic of chemical-based gardening tasks. It is a gardening maxim that plants must be fed artificially; or at least, that the natural supplies of mineral nutrients in the soil must be artificially supplemented. Without this supplement, the expectations that gardeners have of their plants in respect of flower and fruit production or yield would be largely unfulfilled, and the plants would appear little different from their wild counterparts. That organic matter added to the soil would enhance plant growth has long been known (Fig. 29). Roman gardeners did this, and Palladius and medieval writers describe the use of dung, domestic refuse and other organic matter for the purpose. Landsberg (1995) mentioned the provision of channels to collect liquid effluent from

FIG 29. The benefits of animal manures for soil improvement have been known for centuries.

dovecotes in medieval gardens and gardening writers down the centuries have made ample reference to the many and varied concoctions that individual gardeners have used to enhance their efforts. The quantities of organic matter required to provide adequate nutrient supplements for common crops are considerable (Tables 4 & 5).

It is evident from these tables that even the most nitrogen-rich manures such as chicken or pigeon contain only a small proportion of the requirements

TABLE 4. Nutrient content of some commonly used organic manures and composts.[1]

MANURES	N PER CENT	P PER CENT[2]	K PER CENT[3]
chicken	2.0	1.8	1.0
cow (with straw – fresh)	1.2	0.4	0.5
cow (with straw – old)[4]	0.4	0.2	0.6
dog	0.4	0.2	0.1
horse (stable)	0.7	0.5	0.6
pig	0.6	0.6	0.4
pigeon	3.4	1.4	1.2
rabbit	0.5	1.2	0.5
sheep	0.8	0.5	0.4
COMPOSTS			
bracken	2.0	0.2	0.5
garden compost	0.7	0.4	0.4
leaf mould	0.4	0.2	0.3
mushroom compost	0.6	0.5	0.9
sawdust	0.2	0.1	0.1
seaweed	0.6	0.3	1.0
silage waste	0.2	0.1	0.6
soot	3.6	0.1	0.1
spent hops	1.1	0.3	0.1
straw	0.5	0.2	0.9

[1] attributes of manures vary with the types of bedding used for the animals and with other variations in the conditions in which they have been kept. Nutrient contents also vary with the age of the material and the conditions in which it has been stored.

[2] as P_2O_5.

[3] as K_2O.

[4] stored under cover for six months.

TABLE 5. Approximate nitrogen requirements of common garden vegetables.

CROP	NITROGEN REQUIREMENT (GRAMS/SQUARE METRE)
beetroot	19
broad bean	9
Brussels sprout	25
cabbage	25
calabrese	13
carrot	2
cauliflower	19
early potato	15
French beans	13
leek	15
lettuce	11
maincrop potato	19
onion	11
parsnip	9
pea	0
radish	2
spinach	19
swede	9
turnip	13

of basic garden vegetable crops. Pig manure, for instance, contains on average 0.6 per cent by weight of nitrogen. If a cabbage crop requires about 25 grams per square metre of nitrogen throughout its life and if pig manure alone is relied on, 4 kilograms of manure per square metre of cabbage bed will be necessary. Even allowing for the fact that in past centuries, vegetable varieties were innately lower yielding and the expectations of growers were less, nonetheless, over the centuries, vast quantities of additional organic matter will have been loaded onto the soil of intensively gardened land. The effects of this on the wildlife of the soil must have been considerable because, apart from any other effect, every gardener knows that as they put organic matter on the soil, the population of earthworms builds up. The effects on other animals and on microbial soil life have been investigated in some detail for agricultural soils and there is no reason to suppose that the situation in home gardens is any different. Russell (1973), for instance, commented that high soil organic matter levels tend to be correlated with large populations of soil flora and fauna.

But even today, the distinction between the importance of soil amendments as plant nutrients and their value in improving soil structure is often misunderstood. Much of the value of applying organic matter to garden soil derives from the formation of a good crumb structure and porosity and consequent improvement of aeration and drainage. Over past centuries, although rather little in home gardens today, marl and other mineral materials have been used to similar purpose. It is highly improbable that down the centuries any of these practices had a significantly detrimental effect on wildlife, and undoubtedly, then, as now, the extensive addition of organic matter to the soil would have enhanced rather than depleted the populations of earthworms and other soil animal life and of bacteria and fungi.

Chemical fertilisers

Arguably the biggest changes in gardening practice, as in commercial growing, came with the introduction of artificial chemical fertilisers in the second half of the nineteenth century, although for many years, most were not strictly artificial. Superphosphate was manufactured specifically as a fertiliser using the process developed by Lawes of Rothamsted (Russell, 1957) and ammonium sulphate was produced as a by-product of the gas industry, but the vast quantities of sodium nitrate used were dug from the ground in Chile. By the first quarter of the

FIG 30. Fish, blood and bone, despite its name, is only organically based because potassium sulphate is added to augment the animal products.

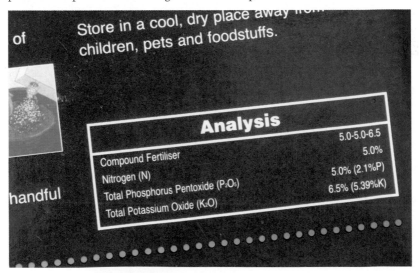

twentieth century, an increasing proportion of chemical fertiliser was, however, being produced artificially, and the gardener going into a garden centre or shop today will find a considerable array of blends, often tailored (quite unnecessarily for most garden purposes) to the needs of particular plants. Even that general stand-by of many organic gardeners, fish, blood and bone, is only organically based, and contains potassium sulphate as an addition because the potassium content of pure dried blood, fish meal and bone meal is almost nil (Fig. 30).

Watering

Watering is an even more integral part of gardening activity than fertilising. Even gardeners who seldom if ever feed their plants realise that additional water is almost always desirable and often essential if their plants are to survive. In small gardens, with a disproportionate reliance on containers, the problem is magnified. The reason is not hard to find. Whilst a plant starved of fertiliser will slowly and gradually display the painful consequences, it will be an extremely starved plant that dies. A shortage of water, however, is all too soon apparent, and with climate change overall providing Britain with summers that are both drier and warmer, the effects of water shortage are becoming ever more apparent. This is a fact of which gardeners have become more conscious too since the enactment of the Water Act 1989, when the ten public water authorities became private companies. The Act was a huge slab of legislation which impinged on every aspect of our national water supply and use and *inter alia* it required:

> ... the Secretary of State, the Minister, the Director and every relevant body ... to take into account any effect ... on the beauty or amenity of any rural or urban area or on any such flora, fauna, features, buildings, sites or objects ... [and] generally to promote ... the conservation of flora and fauna which are dependent on an aquatic environment.

These provisions were presumably intended to conserve and protect the flora and fauna from the consequences of water abstraction, treatment and delivery rather than to have any impact on the domestic water consumer. Nonetheless, there has been a considerable, indirect effect on the wildlife of gardens through the Act, its subsequent amendments and related legislation imposing require-ments and constraints on gardeners. These include the still little appreciated requirement of the Water Supply (Water Fittings) Regulations 1999 for taps to which hose-pipes are attached to be equipped with a suitable backflow prevention device so contaminated water is not siphoned back into the mains; and the even less appreciated need for garden ponds to have impervious linings and be watertight. How many gardeners realise that if their pond leaks, they are committing an offence (Fig. 31)?

A much more obvious and practical consequence of the new legislation, however, has been the charging for water as a distinct commodity. Earlier generations, especially those in the period after the Second World War, had grown up believing the supply of clean water for the home and garden was a divine right; and moreover, because the cost was concealed in the small print of the annual domestic rate statement, tending to imagine that it came more or less for nothing. Having a quarterly water bill was a rude change, but even ruder was the introduction to domestic customers of a metered supply. Possibly nothing since the repeal of the Glass Tax in 1845 has more affected the way British gardeners garden than the necessity of paying for their water by the litre.

The introduction and management of water metering has varied between water companies. Some initially charged for meter installation, others did not. Some have it as an entirely voluntary option for all customers, others require it only if unattended garden hoses and sprinklers are to be used. In 2004, only about one quarter of domestic customers received a metered supply, most still paying a flat rate charge (source: Water UK, www.water.org.uk).

According to one source, in the 15 years between privatisation in 1989 and 2004, the average domestic water bill in England and Wales increased by around

FIG 31. Artificial ponds are a feature of many modern gardens – but it can be illegal to allow them to leak.

20 per cent, although water costs now vary hugely from one water company to another. In 2004, the average annual water and sewerage bill in the South West Water area was around 40 per cent higher than that in the Thames Water area (source: Consumers' Association *Which*). It would be a folly to believe these issues do not influence the way gardeners garden and, less obviously but no less importantly, the types of gardens they have and the types of environment they create. Although *average* UK 'outdoor water use' (gardening and car washing) accounts for only about 6 per cent of annual domestic water consumption, on 'hot summer evenings', 50 per cent or more of the water supply may be used for garden watering (Anon, 2002*b*). In evidence to the Parliamentary Select Committee on Environmental Audit in 1999, the Managing Director of Severn Trent Water Ltd said:

> We do not believe that we should discourage people from using water in their gardens if they want to pay for it. If they use a sprinkler they have a meter. The odd watering can of water does not create an excessive demand on our system. I have to listen to the arguments of my customers who say that if they have invested £25 in a plant, because the climate will now sustain more exotic plants, they are going to water it anyway ... (Anon, 1998*a*)

Many statutory, voluntary and environmental bodies issue guidance on effective garden water management and the Environment Agency leaflet cited above (Anon, 2002*b*) contains a representative sample of the advice. Perhaps the most obvious and sensible of its suggestions was for the widespread installation and use of water butts to collect rainwater (Fig. 32). I have frequently counselled gardeners against using water from rain butts on young seedlings, especially in the warmth of greenhouses, because of the likelihood that among its inhabitants will be the spores of pathogenic fungi, but this should not in any sense detract from their overall value. Apart from anything else, the rainwater butt is a significant but unappreciated garden habitat. However, even John Clegg, perhaps the outstanding authority on British freshwater life of recent times and one of the finest British naturalists never to contribute a New Naturalist volume (mainly I suspect because he worked for a rival publisher), barely recognised this. Water butts are not mentioned in his standard work (Clegg, 1965), perhaps because he considered them among the waters 'which contain large quantities of decaying animal and vegetable matter or other forms of pollution' and which he thought the pond-hunter could safely ignore 'unless he is in search of certain aquatic worms or the larvae of one or two insects, such as the Rat-tailed Maggot, all of which are well adapted for living in the black mud at the bottom of these

FIG 32. Rainwater butts are increasingly used to overcome garden water shortages and restrictions.

unwholesome waters'. In reality, whilst rat-tailed maggots (the larvae of the syrphid *Eristalis tenax*) are common in butts, even those that have a close-fitting lid, there is altogether a more rich and diverse flora and fauna there that would repay close investigation. There may be a PhD in it for someone.

In addition to recommending the installation of rainwater butts and the use on 'most non-edible' plants of what is unappetisingly referred to as 'grey water' from baths and showers, the Environment Agency's publication offers more straightforward horticultural information. In general I would support its advice to ignore lawns when watering the garden:

> *Letting the grass grow longer helps shade the soil and reduces the need for water. If you must water your lawn, remember that infrequent soaking is far more beneficial than regular sprinkling as it encourages roots to search for water stored deep in the soil's surface ... Some varieties of grass are particularly suited to dry conditions, such as fescue grasses and smooth stalked meadow grass.*

In reality, even the brownest of lawns will rapidly spring back to life within a short time of the first post-drought rain shower. But in common with other well-intentioned advisors (and alluded to in the evidence to the Environmental Audit Committee cited above), the Agency then suggested having 'a Mediterranean-style garden' and offered a rather bizarre assortment of plants including *Agapanthus, Alstroemeria, Buddleja, Ceanothus, Cistus, Dianthus, Dimorphotheca, Eremurus, Eschscholzia, Kniphofia, Lavandula, Lonicera, Nepeta, Oenothera, Olearia, Rosmarinus, Thymus* and *Tulipa*, not all of which by generous stretch of the imagination can be described as Mediterranean or even of Mediterranean style (Fig. 33).

FIG 33. The Californian poppy *Eschscholzia californica* is one of many plants now officially recommended as drought tolerant.

Distinctly more profound and carefully thought-out advice came in the important document *Gardening in the Global Greenhouse* (Bisgrove & Hadley, 2002) to which I have referred elsewhere (p. 299). This summarised a report commissioned by the Oxford-based UK Climate Impacts Programme, although it was accompanied rather disarmingly by a note headed 'Should I trust this article?' explaining why it had not been peer reviewed. Yet on balance the emphasis of the report's concern was rather more on increased temperatures than on a decline in summer rainfall, and relatively little was said about changes in gardening practices. However, it was pointed out that working in the garden in summer would increasingly represent a health hazard from sunburn, dehydration and other factors. The report offered a more interesting list of plants likely to perform better in a warmer (and by implication drier) climate; a list that included *Aeonium, Agave, Aloe, Canna, Carpobrotus, Cordyline, Crassula, Leucodendron, Musa, Olea, Phoenix, Protea, Puya, Restio* and *Yucca* (Fig. 34). If this analysis and prediction prove to be correct, and current evidence makes this appear increasingly likely, then, other things being equal, it is reasonable to

FIG 34. South African Proteas may yet be seen in English gardens as summers become warmer.

assume that the growing of species increasingly distantly related to native vegetation and increasingly adapted to quite different ecosystems will be less attractive to native animals.

But even in this document, almost no mention was made of the impact on garden wildlife of climate change. There was brief reference to the effect it will have on some garden pests such as cabbage root fly *Delia radicum* and cabbage aphid *Brevicoryne brassicae*, and fungal pathogens such as *Ciborinia camelliae*, the cause of *Camellia* petal blight. Roe deer *Capreolus capreolus* and grey squirrels received a passing mention because 'warmer winters will increase their survival rates' and it was pointed out that as grey squirrels are fond of beech *Fagus sylvatica*, which is also highly sensitive to drought, the combined effects of drought and squirrels could be serious for beech trees. There was, however, nothing on the effects of increased dryness on non-pest species in the garden habitat, nor was there anything on the consequences for wildlife of the adaptations gardeners may have to make to facilitate gardening in drier summers.

Garden watering is big business and it seems that gardeners will water regardless of weather conditions (Fig. 35). In 2002 (the latest year for which results are available), the turnover of the leading British manufacturer of garden watering equipment rose by 8.5 per cent over 2001 (source: FAME), yet it was a relatively wet season – the total average annual rainfall in England and Wales in the same year, 2002, was 1,117.8 millimetres, 15 per cent higher than in 2001 (source: The Met Office Climate Research Unit, University of East Anglia). I suspect that, cost notwithstanding, garden watering will in the short term become more frequent and the summer garden, or parts of it, might actually become wetter. Thereafter, garden watering probably will become less significant; or at least less frequent and/or more erratic. After all, it took only two dry summers, 1975 and 1976, for water-dependent home garden vegetable growing to take a fall in popularity from which it has never really recovered (p. 33). The increasingly dry garden habitat might please gardeners wanting to see fewer slugs and snails, but it will also mean fewer amphibians, fewer earthworms and other moisture-dependent invertebrates and fewer of the creatures, such as hedgehogs *Erinaceus europaeus* and birds, that rely on them as food.

Anyone who has spent a leisurely summer afternoon watching a garden sprinkler doing its work will have witnessed the magnetic attraction garden water has for birds wanting a shower, a drink and the opportunity to find live food. So-called 'water features' such as ponds and fountains will probably remain as popular as ever – and might even become more so because of the increased attraction of the sound of moving water on hot summer days. But whilst garden

FIG 35. Garden watering is big business and garden watering systems are increasingly sophisticated – but these are of no use during hose-pipe bans.

water as an aquatic habitat and even as a source of drinking water for vertebrate wildlife may not diminish, water available as moisture in the soil and as an aid to attracting food for them certainly will.

Chemical pest control

In the garden industry survey to which I referred earlier (p. 27), 1,001 persons were asked about the methods they used to clear their gardens of weeds and pests. Table 6 summarises their responses.

I have nothing similar from a century or so ago with which to compare these responses, although it is interesting that we tend perhaps too easily to think of organic gardening as new and the past as a time when all pesticides were diabolic. A copy of *Amateur Gardening* magazine on my desk is dated 11 March 1893, yet it contains advertisements for 'Fir-tree oil soluble insecticide – the most pleasant and reliable of all insecticides' and 'Lemon oil insecticide – the safest and most effective liquid insecticide', although admittedly alongside promotions for various anonymous weedkillers and a large advertisement offering insurance against garden accidents!

It is moreover undeniable that some quite astonishingly toxic and noxious chemicals have been used for agricultural purposes, and a fair number found their way into gardeners' armouries too. It was the increasing and largely

TABLE 6. Preferred methods of pest, disease and weed control.

METHOD	PERCENTAGE
chemical control methods	48
natural/organic methods	47
don't try to control	15
don't have any	5
don't know	2

uncontrolled use of some of the persistent organochlorine insecticides that led the American writer Rachel Carson to publish her profoundly disturbing book *Silent Spring* in 1962. Since then, the use of agrochemicals of all types has been much more carefully regulated, the number of products gardeners can buy has dropped year by year, and those available for garden use today are few indeed.

In July 2003, a further large nail was hammered into the coffin of garden pesticide usage when a range of products including those containing the insecticides chlorpyriphos, chlorophos, dimethoate, lindane, malathion, permethrin, pirimiphos-methyl, resmethrin and pirimicarb, the fungicides carbendazim, triforine and bupirimate, the weedkiller dichlorprop and all tar oil-based products were withdrawn. Additional withdrawals in 2004 and 2005 were weed or moss killers containing dichlorophen, atrazine, simazine or paraquat. None of these products was removed for safety reasons and the action was not, or only obscurely, related to their effects on wildlife. It was simply a response by manufacturers to new and more stringent British and European regulations. The British Government required a reappraisal of some insecticides because of concerns over their effects on human health, and manufacturers determined that the costs could not be justified. Similarly, chemicals approved for use in the EU prior to 1991 were required to undergo additional testing and here too, the costs of these tests in some cases were prohibitive.

The proportion of overall national pesticide production that ends up in home gardens is small compared with commercial consumption (Table 7) but it is significant in two respects. First, it is increasing proportionately at a much higher rate than in any other market sector – despite the widespread publicity given in the gardening press and broadcasting media to the merits of organic gardening. To be fair, organic gardeners do not eschew the use of pesticides. They simply choose from a more selected range and so their consumption does contribute to these data (see below). But second, it is a use that the public can see

TABLE 7. Total sales in the UK of active ingredients (tonnes) of chemicals for garden and household use in 2001, compared with other markets.

YEAR	HOME AND GARDEN	AMENITY AND INDUSTRY	AGRICULTURE AND HORTICULTURE	TOTAL
1997	2,285	745	22,205	25,236
1998	2,772	952	21,510	25,234
1999	3,656	882	21,889	26,427
2000	4,306	1,118	18,469	23,893
2001	4,893	1,281	20,176	26,350
five year percentage change	+114	+72	−9	+4

Source: Crop Protection Association, 2002.

for themselves. Reading about environmental concerns because of the national usage of insecticide does not mean as much as looking in your garden shed and seeing bottle after bottle of the stuff; or of smelling it when you spray your roses.

A further breakdown of the 2001 total into constituent product groups is revealing (Table 8).

The fluctuating trends for the garden sector continued. Following improvement in 2000, there was a decline in 2001 with sales decreasing by 9 per cent to £46.6 m. The volume of products used in gardens increased by 14 per cent, but this was due to increased sales of ferrous sulphate (for moss control in lawns), sodium chlorate (for weed control) and some fatty acids (for disease control). (Crop Protection Association Handbook, 2002; Peterborough, Crop Protection Association, 2002)

Probably no other pesticides still available for garden use have provoked as much debate about their possible impact on wildlife as those employed for slug control (Fig. 36). In Britain, two have been widely used: the carbamate methiocarb and, most extensively, metaldehyde (2,4,6,8-tetramethyl-1,3,5,7-tetraoxacyclooctane), variously available in liquid, pellet and tape form for slug and snail control. Methiocarb slug controls have recently been withdrawn, but even though the chemical had long been known to be 'toxic to terrestrial mammals', 'very highly toxic to birds on an acute oral basis', 'highly toxic to coldwater ... fish, and very highly toxic to aquatic invertebrates' ... and 'highly toxic to honey bees' (www.epa.gov/docs/REDs/factsheets/0577fact.pdf), the greatest

TABLE 8. Sales in the UK of active ingredients (tonnes) of different groups of chemicals for garden and household use in 2001, compared with other markets.

TYPE OF CHEMICAL	MARKET AND ANNUAL CHANGE IN CONSUMPTION					
	Agricultural and horticultural	Per cent change on previous year	Industrial, amenity and forestry	Per cent change on previous year	Garden and household	Per cent change on previous year
Herbicides	11,817	24	1,067	25	853	-1
Fungicides	3,628	-16	94	-7	11	-11
Insecticides	857	14	11	-13	193	4
Seed treatments	341	21	NA	NA	NA	NA
Molluscicides	409	-20	NA	NA	NA	NA
Growth regulator	2,399	-2	NA	NA	NA	NA
Ferrous sulphate-based products	NA	NA	NA	NA	3,440	26
Other	725	18	109	-29	396	-23
Total	20,176	9	1,281	15	4,893	14

FIG 36. Slug pellet use is often frowned on by conservationists, and may become unnecessary as drier gardens have fewer slugs.

attention and concern had nonetheless always attached to metaldehyde. (Interestingly, despite its dubious attributes, methiocarb is still available in combination with imidacloprid as an aerosol for the control of airborne garden pests.)

Metaldehyde is undeniably effective as a slug killer:

Excess mucus production is the first sign of poisoning in both slugs and snails. This reaction depletes the slugs' energy reserves and weakens the slug. Subsequently, cell membranes are ruptured and mucus cells irreversibly destroyed after which death is inevitable. These effects occur at temperatures as low as 2°C and slugs cannot recover by taking up ambient water. (www.metaldehyde.com/meta/en/mode.html)

It has often been suggested that metaldehyde may have an impact on birds and especially on hedgehogs if they feed on dead or dying slugs or snails that have ingested the chemical. *Gardening Which?* reported in August 1988 that a hedgehog would have to eat 2,000 slugs poisoned with metaldehyde in one night to be killed, but as usual with that publication, there were no supporting data. It stated:

> *The blue colour of the pellets is also claimed to deter birds from eating them. If you are still worried, then there are slug-pellet containers that children and animals cannot reach into, or you can use a liquid formulation. Liquids penetrate to slugs underground, but they are shorter-lasting than the pellets.*

Pet owners commonly express concern about the use of metaldehyde (or at least, of slug pellets), and there is evidence that dogs are positively attracted to it. Dogs certainly can be and have been killed by metaldehyde; an incident at Thirsk, North Yorkshire in September 1998 resulted in a dog dying after being walked near a potato field. Slug pellets had been spilled, and the owner of the field was later fined £4,500 plus £4,000 costs at Northallerton Magistrates Court. Genuine examples of pets having been harmed by metaldehyde picked up in gardens are, however, elusive, as is real evidence about its impact on wild animals. General statements are often contradictory. Pesticide Action Network UK (Pan UK), an organisation 'working to eliminate the hazards from pesticides' and dedicated to providing 'information on pesticide problems and alternative developments', has stated that metaldehyde is 'harmful to fish and other aquatic life' (www.pan-uk.org/pestnews/homepest/slugs.htm). By contrast, Extoxnet, 'a pesticide information project of … Cornell University, Michigan State University, Oregon State University and University of California at Davis', could equally emphatically say 'Available data suggest that metaldehyde is practically non-toxic to aquatic organisms' (pmep.cce.cornell.edu/profiles/extoxnet/haloxyfop-methylparathion/metaldehyde-ext.html), citing US Environmental Protection Agency (EPA) (1988).

There is now no way of knowing what effects garden pesticides of the past may have had on wildlife, but with nicotine and arsenical compounds such as Paris green (copper aceto-arsenite) and lead arsenate widely available, it is tempting to conjure a vision of widespread environmental contamination stemming from gardens. In practice this seems improbable. The historical non-commercial buyers of such pesticides would have been the gardeners of the great houses, generally for use in their greenhouses, not the man in the cottage trying to protect his vegetable plot (Fig. 37). Historical garden pesticide contamination

FIG 37. In the past it was gardeners of the great houses who used pesticides.

and effects would pale alongside the impact of the events of the mid-twentieth century when the first choice for insect control in many gardens was DDT; but even then, some circumspection is needed.

It is beyond my scope to examine the impact of the type of commercial pesticide use that impelled Rachel Carson and for which there are plenty of unpleasant data. Almost all the evidence about the harmful effect of modern pesticides on wildlife in gardens or arising as the result of pesticide usage in gardens however appears to be anecdotal. Evidence of pets and wild animals being poisoned by careless use of pesticides on farmland certainly does occur from time to time, but misuse of pesticides in gardens is most infrequent, and instances of wildlife being proved to have suffered in consequence even rarer. In what appears to have been just such an isolated incident at Harlington, Bedfordshire in September 1998, a grey squirrel was seen in a distressed state in a residential garden. A rodenticide treatment to control squirrels had been carried out and it was suspected that a bait not approved to control squirrels had been used. Laboratory analysis confirmed that the bait contained difenacoum (only warfarin, in specified circumstances, is approved for grey squirrel control). Subsequently, at Luton Magistrates Court on 14 July 1999, a 'professional pest controller' pleaded guilty to using a pesticide and failing to follow the conditions of approval. He was given a 12 month conditional discharge with costs of £500 (Anon, 2000b).

In the most recently available annual report of the Environmental Panel of the Advisory Committee on Pesticides (Barnett *et al.*, 2002), there was no reference to poisoning of wild animals by any pesticides that had been used in gardens. There were some reports of domestic and wild animals (especially foxes and raptors) having been poisoned by chemicals that are *available* to gardeners, but the source of the material was commercial use, illegal activity (that is, deliberate poisoning) or unknown. None of this advocates the use of pesticides in gardens but, conversely, employing garden pesticide usage as an explanation for the decline in populations either of wildlife in general or of individual animal species, does seem at present to be fallacious.

No pesticide has been withdrawn from garden use solely because it posed an unacceptable threat to wildlife. Before the 2003 'legislative' withdrawals (see above), most commonly, as in perhaps the two most high-profile instances in recent years, it has been because of a proven or perceived threat to human health. When approval for the use of the proprietary product Roseclear was withdrawn

FIG 38. More pesticide and fungicide is probably bought for use on roses than on any other garden flower.

in 1996, it was because it posed a 'hazard of accidental eye damage which is unacceptable in an amateur garden pesticide'. Roseclear contained the insecticide pirimicarb and the fungicides bupirimate and triforine. Ironically, as the manufacturers pointed out, the 'advantage of Roseclear had been its lack of adverse effects on a number of beneficial insects including bees and ladybirds' although whilst pirimicarb was often promoted as 'environmentally friendly' and specific to aphids while leaving beneficial insects unharmed, it was nonetheless considered sufficiently hazardous to require it to be labelled 'dangerous to fish or other aquatic life'. Indeed in 1995 the then Ministry of Agriculture, Fisheries and Food (MAFF) was requesting 'further data of effects on aquatic vertebrates in the field'. Subsequently, the manufacturers, who stressed throughout that the eye hazard was limited to the concentrate and that pack labelling stated this clearly, reformulated the product.

Weedkillers

The range of weedkillers available to gardeners has always been smaller than that of fungicides and insecticides and there is even less evidence for their adverse effects on wildlife – apart of course from their lethal impact on plants! Most modern garden weedkillers have effects of relatively short duration and indeed their merit is that planting or seed sowing can take place soon after their application because they are degraded in the soil. There has never been much justification for using weedkillers in home gardens other than for the initial clearing of weed-ridden plots or for eradicating persistent and highly competitive perennial weeds such as common couch. Ironically, the rapidly degraded but highly effective translocated weedkiller glyphosate (N-(phosphonomethyl) glycine), which is still available to gardeners, is often an essential precursor to establishing a wildlife garden as it provides almost the only certain way of clearing a plot of aggressive perennial weeds to enable more choice native plants to establish.

One of the commonest misconceptions among gardeners is that organic products (in the horticultural sense; that is, products derived from some animal or plant origin) are inherently safer in the environment. In reality, the spectrum of toxicity of some is wide and their potential for killing wildlife considerable. Rotenone (derris) is a widely used organic insecticide derived from the roots of various species of *Derris* or *Lonchocarpus* from Southeast Asia, Central and South America (Fig. 39). It is available worldwide in at least 118 formulated products from a large number of manufacturers. It is synergised by the addition of piperonyl butoxide (PBO), which is itself of natural origin, derived from Brazilian sassafras (*Aniba* sp., Lauraceae). Rotenone is expensive compared with synthetic

FIG 39. The South American plant *Derris elliptica* is the source of an important organic but wide-spectrum insecticide.

insecticides, but is moderately priced for a natural product, and is sold in the United Kingdom and approved for use in gardens against, *inter alia*, greenfly, blackfly, red spider mite and caterpillars on 'all edible and ornamental plants'. It is generally said to be non-toxic to syrphids and honeybees. It is, however, toxic to ladybird beetles and predatory mites as well as birds, and acutely toxic to fish. Indeed, it has been used in South America as a fish poison by native peoples who threw the crushed roots of *Lonchocarpus nicou* into streams and pools. The chemical in the roots stunned the fish and caused them to float to the surface, from where they were easily collected. *Derris elliptica*, which also contains rotenone, was used as an arrow poison.

There is an increasing realisation that just because such natural products originated in the environment, they are not automatically safe to use in it (although curiously this is still not widely enough appreciated among organic gardeners themselves). For this reason, pesticide manufacturers have gradually sought other, less widely damaging products for garden use. Currently, products containing 'natural soaps' and 'rapeseed oil' are widely promoted (Fig. 40). Canola oil, also known as low erucic acid rapeseed (LEAR) oil, is the fully refined, bleached and deodorised edible oil obtained from certain varieties of *Brassica napus* or *Brassica campestris* of the family Brassicaceae. It contains no more than 2 per cent erucic acid. The name canola appears to have been coined in Canada ('Canada oil') for the products of genetically modified rape, presumably on the basis that it is a more appealing name than rape itself and avoids the emotive genetically modified (GM) tag. The human toxicity of canola oil is said officially to be negligible, and indeed it forms a part of many human foodstuffs and is readily metabolised in humans. However, several health and environmental pressure groups have attributed a considerable number of effects to it, ranging

FIG 40. Aphids are fairly effectively killed with natural soap-based products and rapeseed oil – but so are many beneficial insects too.

from glaucoma to 'mad cow disease'. It certainly has a wide spectrum of activity against pests. In October 1998, the American Environmental Protection Agency conceded that it did not have 'toxicity test results for non-target insects, fish, and other wildlife directly exposed to canola oil' and 'ecological effects data for terrestrial and aquatic animals, and non-target plants for canola were waived ...'. There seem to be no data available from Britain on the environmental effects of insecticides containing canola oil. However, there does appear to have been an unfortunate trend towards the marketing of pesticides ostensibly with low mammalian and/or avian toxicity, but which coincidentally have relatively little selectivity against pests and are therefore potentially harmful to enormous numbers of invertebrate species, pest or not.

Relatively few modern garden fungicide products have been withdrawn for reasons other than considerations of marketing or mammalian toxicity, although the widely used systemic fungicide benomyl (methyl 1-(butylcarbamoyl) benzimidazol-2-ylcarbamate), hailed in the 1970s as the agricultural product of the decade, was arguably the most significant. It was introduced to the UK in 1971 and became available to gardeners shortly afterwards with approval for use against a wide range of plant diseases. It has the merit of remarkably low mammalian toxicity; it was said that its toxicity was so low that it proved impossible to administer large enough doses to establish an LD 50 (the dose required to kill 50 per cent of a population of test organisms). It was withdrawn from the garden market in the late 1990s (and in 2001 its manufacture for all purposes was discontinued) following clinical concerns, most notably an alleged link first voiced in 1993 between exposure of pregnant mothers to benomyl and their children being born without eyes (anophthalmia) or with related syndromes including reduced eyes and blindness due to severe damage of the optic stem. Its acute toxicity to earthworms had for some time also been a matter of concern and was probably an additional consideration (Sorour & Larink, 2001). Benomyl indeed subsequently became a reference standard in tests for the evaluation of pesticides on earthworms (Heimbach, 1997).

Earthworm toxicity was a property shared with other benzimidazole compounds, including thiophanate-methyl (diethyl 4,4-(o-phenylene)bis (3- thioallophanate)) and carbendazim (methyl benzimidazol-2-ylcarbamate). Carbendazim was withdrawn as part of the wholesale culling of approved products in 2003 (p. 63) but thiophanate-methyl remains available to British gardeners as a root dip for treating brassicas against club root disease, a procedure for which I take the dubious credit (Buczacki *et al.*, 1976). In addition to the acute toxicity of the benzimidazoles, other, sublethal effects have been noted in treated worms, including reduced feeding, retarded growth rates, reduced cocoon production and spermatogenesis, and reduced nerve conduction velocity. Although the abundance of earthworms may be affected by relatively few turf pesticides, earthworm distribution and behaviour may be altered to a greater degree. Litter and surface soils treated with certain pesticides have a repellent effect on earthworms, and this reduces the breakdown and incorporation of organic matter into the subsurface horizons. Benomyl and carbendazim exhibit this repellent effect, which results in the avoidance of feeding in treated soils, and among the consequences for the plants are the reduction in the amount of available nutrients in the root zone, decreased porosity and aeration of the soil, decreased water-holding capacity and poor drainage.

Other widely used garden pesticides that have been restricted in the UK for human health reasons in recent years include vinclozolin ((RS)-3-(3,5-dichlorophenyl)-5-methyl-5-vinyl-1,3-oxazolidine-2,4-dione; 3-(3,5-dichlorophenyl)5-ethenyl-5-methyl-2,4-oxazolidinedione), a fungicide that can cause birth defects in the foetus, and chlordane (1,2,4,5,6,7,8,8-octachloro-2,3,3a,4,7,7a-hexahydro-4,7-methanoindene) (technical chlordane is a mixture of chlorinated hydrocarbons and contains heptachlor, which might contribute to the insecticidal properties of the technical formulation) which has a number of objectionable properties, most notably toxicity to birds and possible carcinogenic effects in humans. Chlordane is a persistent compound, with a half-life in soils of five to 15 years. In 1999, it was reckoned that 25–50 per cent of all the chlordane ever produced still exists in the environment. It was still being sold to British gardeners in the 1980s as a worm repellent, but was then withdrawn.

Carbaryl (1-naphthyl methylcarbamate), an insecticide used in orchards, amenity treatments and public health, which has relatively low toxicity to birds and fish, but is highly toxic to aquatic invertebrates, was withdrawn from sale in the UK in 2002 'because it was not supported by any agrochemical companies, when the relevant approvals were reviewed' (Hansard, written answer, 26 April 2002).

The corollary of the dangers to wildlife inherent in the use of wide-spectrum pesticides is that ever more biological control techniques are becoming available to gardeners (p. 249ff), although it seems probable that the control of garden pests will remain largely chemical-based for some time to come.

Finally, I should make a comment on pest control methods that have a particularly direct and visible impact on wildlife by putting a barrier in its path (like a fruit cage) or simply by frightening it (like a scarecrow) (Fig. 41). There is a small but defined market for mammal and bird repellents and scarers that enable gardeners to protect their plants from creatures they really do not want to kill (generally because they are big, have fur or feathers and remind them of their

FIG 41. A fruit cage offers valuable but harmless protection from birds and is essential in most gardens to obtain a crop.

pets) or are legally prevented from killing. The RSPB takes an interesting stance on the matter – it says that as a conservation body, it is 'not generally involved in deterring or scaring birds or other animals' but recognises 'that in some circumstances, people can have problems' and provides extensive information and advice on numerous deterrents and protective barriers to deter feral pigeons, magpies, gulls, sparrowhawks and herons, as well as cats, grey squirrels, slugs and snails. It reminds gardeners that:

> The operation of a deterrent must not trap, injure or kill a bird.
>
> A scaring device or barrier deterrent must not be set so that it prevents nesting birds access to their active nest.
>
> Scaring devices must not be used close to the nest of a Schedule one species, since any kind of disturbance of these birds at or close to their nest is strictly illegal.
>
> Before starting to deter birds from one site, make sure that there are alternatives for the birds to go to. Otherwise the deterrent will not have the desired effect, and will simply serve to distress the birds. (www.rspb.org.uk/gardens/advice/deterrents/index.asp)

CHAPTER 4

Gardens in the Context of the British Ecological Landscape

A GARDEN IS NOT a natural habitat; it is a folly to suppose otherwise. But it is an equal folly to imagine or pretend that its inhabitants do not obey the same natural rules, experience the same natural pressures and respond just as naturally as those living in places much less influenced by man. I have long believed that a real understanding of the operation of a garden can come most effectively and meaningfully through an appreciation of some of the basic principles of ecology; and to understand how a garden functions as a habitat, this is essential.

This is not the place to cover in more than a most simple way a subject that has been one of the great growth areas of biological science in the past century. But it is a sad truth that whilst the word ecology is in our newspapers every day and is heard if not used by everyone, its essential concepts are still alien to the general public and, sad to say, to most gardeners. Garden ecology itself is still an almost untrodden area. Apart from my own basic introduction written 20 years ago (Buczacki, 1986), and a chapter by Max Walters (Walters, 1993) in which he paid generous tribute to my own efforts, there is still almost nothing. Jennifer Owen's weighty tome *The Ecology of a Garden* (Owen, 1991) contained a mass of interesting and valuable data, largely the results of several years spent trapping insects in her own garden; though not strictly ecology in the sense I mean it here.

There is certainly no shortage of literature on ecology. At the last count, there were around 50 journals worldwide with an almost entirely plant or animal ecological remit, in addition to many that carry subjects of ecological interest in a wider botanical or zoological context; and indeed many more that stretch the definition to embrace such diverse areas of endeavour as conservation, environmental health, even 'environmental business'. Among the leading journals on 'proper' ecology and one that has certainly garnered the best title is the *Journal of Ecology*, published since 1913 for the British Ecological Society. Each bimonthly issue contains around 12 papers. It has three more recent sisters, the *Journal of Animal Ecology*, *Journal of Applied Ecology* and *Functional Ecology*. As far as I can determine, none of them has ever published a paper with the word garden in the title.

I am not naïve enough to imagine this means that there is nothing in the publications relevant to garden ecology, but even on closer scrutiny and analysis of the papers, there does not seem to be much. There is a good deal on grasslands and forests and species interactions, but, as I have suggested repeatedly, whilst gardens contain grass and trees, they are not grasslands and they are not forests. Plant and animal life in gardens is subject to a different spectrum of influences for different reasons. This absence of topics relevant to gardens is not a criticism of the journals, which can only publish what is submitted. It is partly a criticism of ecological researchers who are presumably ignoring gardens in the same way as are most other scientists. In Britain, the Centre for Ecology and Hydrology (CEH) is the designated Centre of Excellence for research in the terrestrial and freshwater environmental sciences. Apart from some undeniably important studies on the impact of invasive alien species on British habitats (p. 107), which have a peripheral importance and interest for gardeners, here too gardens are largely neglected. More significantly, therefore, the absence of publications on garden ecology must be a criticism of the bodies funding ecological research which appear not to be supporting work on garden ecology.

In Britain, the principal such body is the Natural Environment Research Council (NERC). In 2004, I approached the Council with two questions, the first of which was 'Are home gardens considered distinct and discrete environments by the NERC?'. They did not reply directly, but the view of an NERC-funded researcher to whom my query was referred was that they probably did not hold any particular position on this, although a general view prevailed that no given environment is necessarily distinct and discrete, but that they 'all form parts of what is essentially a continuum of environments' which can be divided 'in numerous ways for convenience and for the purposes of addressing specific questions' (Fig. 42). This is a contentious view that can be argued both ways, but my own position is that I believe gardens are subject to such distinct and unusual pressures and uses that they are clearly a case apart. To think of a 'continuum' is wrong. It brings me again to the 'area the size of Somerset' analogy (p. 26). The ecology of small areas is unarguably quite different from the ecology of large ones. Ecologically, gardens represent fragmented landscapes containing local

FIG 42. Gardens have been described officially as part of 'a continuum of environments'.

FIG 43. Individual habitats may be connected by strips of intervening land, such as roadside verges.

populations, with different consequences for different types of organism. It is a self-evident but frequently overlooked truth that while creatures such as badgers *Meles meles* and many birds of prey tend to be distributed across entire land-scapes, smaller animals such as voles are confined to restricted habitat types, and so for them, the wider landscape consists of suitable patches of habitat separated by bits that are unsuitable. It is also a well-recognised ecological feature that habitat patches may be connected by narrow strips of similar vegetation and ecology, and it is generally although not universally considered that these can serve both as corridors for dispersing organisms and as linear habitats for many plants and small animals (Fig. 43). It is exactly this situation to which I alluded when I stressed the importance of considering both individual gardens and garden communities (p. 27).

The response to my second question to the NERC: 'Is any research funding (current or recent) directed specifically at the science of home gardens and most specifically at garden ecology?' in part vindicates this position, because my attention was drawn to the fact that for two years to 2002, the Council funded what was perhaps the only serious British research study into garden ecology in recent times. It was inevitably given an acronym – BUGS – Biodiversity in Urban Gardens in Sheffield. The project had three interesting and complementary objectives – to determine the size of the resources that urban gardens provide for biodiversity, to determine which garden features were most important for diversity, and to determine which simple procedures would enhance biodiversity in gardens. Many of the findings are still unpublished, but I shall refer to some later. First, however, I need to examine the meaning of ecology, and especially ecology in a garden context.

Although the subject of ecology is now vast, embracing not only botany and zoology but disciplines as diverse as fundamental evolutionary theory and religion, my compass here will be simply that defined (in part) by the dictionary definition of the word itself: 'Ecology (formerly œcology), 1873 (Haeckel), from Greek, oikos- and -ology; after economy; that branch of biology which deals with the mutual relations between organisms and their environment' (OED), or, as my own ecology tutor Joyce Lambert put it most succinctly, 'the study of homes' and, even better, 'what lives where and why'. I shall therefore confine many of my remarks to what was once called plant sociology, a term devised by the pioneer Swiss plant ecologist Josias Braun-Blanquet (1884–1980), and introduce the concepts of plant communities, succession, climax, competition, colonisation and invasion.

LAND-USE HISTORY

If you set about establishing a garden in Britain today, you will begin to cultivate soil that has experienced generations of human influence (Rackham, 1986). Every gardener inherits both ancient and recent history in their garden, and to understand the lessons of the past is to appreciate the present and plan for the future. The key to this (and in truth, I believe to successful gardening in its entirety) is to grasp the concept of plant succession: the sequential changes that occur over a period of time in any plant community and the factors that influence them.

A simple example will illustrate the notion. In the Derbyshire Dales, close to where I was born, there is a stretch of limestone hillside that has been grazed for centuries by sheep and rabbits (Fig. 44). It has the appearance of other grazed hillsides in the predominance of plants with a creeping habit like wild thyme

FIG 44. The Derbyshire Dales, grazed for centuries by sheep.

FIG 45. The cowslip *Primula veris* resists animals' teeth by its sunken leaf rosette.

Thymus polytrichus and rosette-forming species like cowslip *Primula veris* with, respectively, basal or sunken meristems that are thus protected from damage by the animals' teeth (Fig. 45). A few years ago the owner of the land fenced off a small area, resulting in the exclusion of sheep and rabbits. The old grazed hillside is no longer recognisable. Everywhere there are small bushes of blackthorn interspersed with guelder rose *Viburnum opulus*, burnet rose *Rosa pimpinellifolia*, bramble *Rubus fruticosus* agg. and other shrubby and bushy species. Whilst seeds of blackthorn and the many other species now so obvious had been dropped or blown into this area of hillside for countless years, none had previously realised their growth potential because the livestock browsed away their tops. With the removal of the grazing pressure, that stretch of land has been taken over or colonised by a whole range of different species. Sheep do not usually graze gardens (although sometimes rabbits do) but there is a comparable grazing pressure that gardeners themselves impose. It is called hoeing and weeding, and if the pressure the hoe, the fork and the weedkiller impose is removed, the garden too will take on a completely different aspect. In this way, it is possible to see that changes in the composition of the vegetation do take place as a result of one's own actions; but how can information be gleaned about the changes that preceded present acquaintance with the land, and how is it possible to judge what changes may take place in the future?

The most obvious ways to discover facts about the recent history of a garden are to talk to the previous owners, to find out whether old photographs of the site exist or whether details of any kind are given in the deeds of the property. With luck, this might give information extending back for a hundred or so years. Generally there will then be a blank and the human, documentary sources will have been exhausted. To an expert with more enlightened interpretative skills, however, every plant habitat, whether garden, farm or bog, has its own, inbuilt documentation that provides clues to the history of the site and that may enable a picture to be drawn extending back many thousands of years. Many scientific techniques are now employed in the study of vegetational history, and the radiocarbon-dating method may allow a fairly precise age to be assigned to a fragment of plant tissue. Nonetheless, the simplest methods are still often the most rewarding, and the three tools that are especially valuable regarding the nature of the predominant species, as opposed to the age of their remains, are those extremely durable plant structures, wood, seeds and pollen. Yet again, however, I am frustrated by the lack of genuine garden evidence, and what follows is largely an extrapolation to gardens based on common sense. I can only agree with Murphy & Scaife (1991):

> There is no doubt that the various types of palaeoecological analysis now routinely used in studying aspects of archaeological sites are capable of yielding useful information on early gardens, horticulture and arboriculture. In practice, however, these techniques have not yet been extensively applied to the study of gardens.

Have we not heard that somewhere before? But here goes.

Whilst it is fairly easy to identify the species of a woody plant from microscopic examination of a small fragment of wood, unearthed from deep down in the ground, a sequence of annual rings is yet more revealing. Even if the plant died many years ago, the relative width of the rings and the size of their cells will indicate how growing conditions and climate varied in the past. Seeds and pollen, with their hard outer coats, can survive for long after they have lost their viability, and thus indicate the types of plant that grew in an area in ages past. Examined under the microscope, the characteristic differences between the pollen and seeds of different species can be seen (Fig. 46). First, therefore, let me take a very simple example. If you dig a vertical hole, or take a precise core of soil from your garden with an auger, and carefully dissect successive short lengths of the core, you will find seeds and other plant remains. Logic suggests that the further down the core a particular type of seed or pollen grain appears, the longer ago will it have dropped onto the ground. If you find wheat seeds some way below the surface therefore, you may conclude that at some time past, wheat grew on the site where your garden now stands. Unfortunately, the situation is greatly complicated by the fact that you and your predecessors have dug the soil and therefore mixed up the different layers. Moreover, below a certain depth, there will probably be no recognisable seeds or pollen grains in the soil, because, like most garden soils, it is replete with bacteria and other micro-organisms that degrade even durable seed and pollen coats after a few years.

If a comparable core is removed from a mud deposit, however, such as the silt of a lake bed, or from the peat of a bog where, in the poorly oxygenated conditions, decomposition is minimal, a vast fund of information can be obtained about the plants of the surrounding area. From such an analysis,

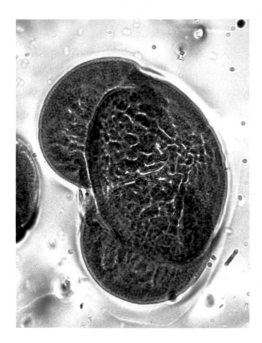

FIG 46. Fossil spruce *Abies* pollen grains.

a picture can be drawn of the changes in plant life that have occurred over many years, and it is apparent that quite specific sequences or successions of species take place in particular environmental conditions. Ultimately, a state is reached where overall change in species composition ceases. Individual plants of course grow and die, but the community as a whole is fairly stable. This is called a climax community, and over much of Britain, it is hardwood forest with some open areas. Today's gardeners are fighting the natural tendency of their garden to revert to some component community of that natural hardwood forest. This process cannot be arrested except by constant attention. Today there is a lawn; but if mowing stops, then by next year there will be a hay meadow, in a few more years, scrub (as on the Derbyshire hillside) and, ultimately, what today's gardener will bequeath to his successors will not be a garden but a wood.

ECOLOGICAL SUCCESSION

The earliest stages of the succession process are readily visible in many a town and village. If a house remains empty for a year or so, the garden becomes unrecognisable as such (Fig. 47). Sometimes, even the shorter period between a house sale being agreed and the new owners moving in can result in the garden that looked so neat and controlled at the first viewing or in the estate agent's

FIG 47. It takes only a year or so for a neglected garden to revert to a semi-wild state.

literature turning into what, in popular parlance, is called a 'jungle'. Examples over a longer timescale are rarer because in our overpopulated islands, land is unlikely to remain unoccupied and free from human interference for long enough, although some of the most striking instances are those of large, country house properties where the garden has been neglected or abandoned while the land remains in private hands. The sad catalogue of English country houses listed by Worsley (2002) that were abandoned and demolished in the twentieth century, most with lost gardens too, encompassed in excess of 1,200 properties, and the sites of many are being reclaimed by native vegetation. I mention elsewhere (p. 274) the garden of the naturalist Thomas Pennant, now a wood but once, I suspect, a rather fine garden. In 1987 I photographed the former garden site of a house called Seggieden in Perthshire which in the 1880s had been splendid enough to have inspired its owner to produce an album of wonderful flower paintings (Buczacki, 1988). Seggieden was progressively abandoned during the twentieth century and the house was burned and razed in 1970. By the time of my visit, the shape of the garden was barely recognisable and sapling trees were well established (Fig. 48).

The entire transformation from garden back to trees or wood is extremely uncommon, but a superb and well-chronicled example is the landscaped park designed by Coplestone Warre Bampfylde at Hestercombe, his Somerset home. He inherited the ancient estate in 1750 and set about creating a landscape garden after the fashion of the time (p. 17f). Although in 1904 the Hon Edward Portman, the then owner, commissioned a magnificent formal garden from Sir Edwin Lutyens with planting by Gertrude Jekyll, the landscape garden a few hundred metres away was gradually forgotten and neglected. By the mid-twentieth century, the eighteenth-century landscaped parkland had been clear-felled, and the site was being managed for commercial forestry. By the 1990s, when restoration began, the garden was all but unrecognisable on the surface, although clearing and careful archaeology have revealed its underlying structure (Fig. 49A–C).

The process can of course be reversed (as is happening at Hestercombe) although, as with so much in the natural world, this is not straightforward. Trees and shrubs can be cleared and removed, although interestingly, in many parts of the country (Statutory Conservation Areas in England and Wales), the trees may have acquired automatic legal protection. Any tree (including a fruit tree) in a Conservation Area that exceeds 75 millimetres in diameter at a height of 1.5 metres above ground level may not be felled unless its removal or lopping is required to improve the growth of other trees, when its diameter has to exceed 100 millimetres. There are exceptions, and the whole tree protection business covers several pages of the appropriate Acts and Regulations. Dead, dying or

FIG 48. The historic Perthshire garden of Seggieden has all but returned to nature since the house was razed in 1970.

FIG 49A–C. The Somerset landscaped garden of Hestercombe in the eighteenth century (A), overgrown in the mid-twentieth century (B) and then restored (C).

FIG 49B.

FIG 49C.

diseased trees are exempt, although it may be hard to prove any of these things
once it has been cut down. But natural ecological processes as well as the law
intervene to make the reclamation of a garden difficult. As any experienced
gardener knows, even one year of seed production by a weed population can leave
a legacy that will take many more years of careful work to remove. The old adage
that 'one year's seeding' leads to 'seven years' weeding' is probably true for many
garden species (p. 111ff).

EXOTIC PLANTS

I referred in Chapter 1 to the fact that many of our garden plant species are alien
or exotic, in the sense that they originate in other parts of the world. Many also,
therefore, originate in different ecological formations, and sit uneasily in our
deciduous summer forest environment; yet another reminder that gardening is
a highly unnatural process. Plants from many different environments are being
forced to compete with each other on unequal terms. In some instances, perhaps

many instances, it works surprisingly well; Himalayan birches *Betula utilis* var. *jacquemontii* and related forms as well as rhododendrons appear to live extremely harmoniously with a British oak wood, despite the wide disparity between the rainfall, temperature ranges, light intensity, seasons and other wildlife of their natural and adopted homes. Some species clearly have wide tolerances of conditions outside their optima. Others equally clearly do not, and the Siberian larch *Larix sibirica*, for example, despite tolerating in its native habitat some of the lowest winter minimum temperatures on earth, is quite unable to cope with our 'fits and starts' seasons which may expose it to a few mild days in January, trick its physiological processes into believing that spring has arrived and result in leaf buds bursting, only for them to be laid low by a return to frosty weather (Fig. 50). I discuss the significance of alien species in gardens for the indigenous wildlife in Chapter 7, but a little more should be said about the nature of competition between plants and of what makes a good competitor.

In essence, all plants are striving to help their offspring to survive and, to achieve this, they must grow to maturity and reproduce. They can do this only if they have adequate light, air, moisture and nutrients for their own unique blend of physiological processes to function efficiently. But all other plants in the surrounding environment are seeking the same resources and, clearly, there is finite physical space within any plant community that satisfies the blend of requirements needed by each species; what is often called its ecological niche. If two species have more or less the same requirements for environmental conditions, they will be in direct competition with each other, and any factor that can tip the balance away from one will be very important. This factor could be a pest or disease that suppresses its speed of growth, a slightly greater susceptibility to late frost, a lower seed production, which means there will be numerically fewer individuals, or any of countless other small variables. Within a single species, moreover, the natural variation generated by sexual reproduction will sometimes result in the production of mutants that are either more or less efficient than their normal parents. Chlorophyll-deficient variegated forms, for instance, tend to grow more slowly and are usually unable to compete as satisfactorily. It is because native plants have, through thousands of years of competition, each 'found' their own ecological niches, that they are so efficient at competing with the alien garden plants that are deposited in their environment. This is not to say, however, that all introduced or alien species are unsuccessful; some of the most successful weeds were originally aliens (p. 111ff).

Nonetheless, it is infrequently that an exotic species, newly planted in any particular ecological niche, finds itself more suited to that niche than the 'local residents'. This is why weeds usually triumph in a garden over the aliens if

FIG 50. The Siberian larch *Larix sibirica* cannot survive Britain's 'fits and starts' winters.

gardeners do not intervene to suppress them. Only occasionally does an artificially introduced plant, by chance, immediately prove a better competitor and more successful than the native species and, when this does happen, it is likely to oust the incumbents, a topic to which I return in Chapter 5.

CLIMAX VEGETATION

I have described the natural climax vegetation of much of Britain as typical of the European deciduous summer forest, although in the North of Scotland this gives way to the north European coniferous forest (Rackham, 1986). Yet there is little hardwood forest (and, indeed little natural coniferous forest) to be seen in Britain today. Where has it gone and what do the subsequent events mean for gardeners? In fact the forests over much of Britain have disappeared not once, but several times, the climax formations having been swept away in the ice ages and replaced temporarily in the interglacial periods by communities ranging from warm temperate or subtropical to those typical of the present-day northern tundra. Consequently, at different times, many plants have flourished in Britain that no longer exist here, but, more significantly, we have lost several major species that might be expected in our present-day native flora, but that never recolonised after the ice finally retreated (Godwin, 1975). Most notable among them were Norway spruce *Picea abies*, hemlock *Tsuga* spp. and silver fir *Abies alba*, although it will interest gardeners to know that other species that once grew wild in the British Isles include *Rhododendron ponticum* and the grape-vine *Vitis vinifera*. It is not necessarily fair to assume, however, that these will all be good competitors in the wild or will thrive well in gardens today, because whilst our soils and geology are more or less the same as they were then, the climate has altered and the associated vegetation is different. For instance, *Rhododendron ponticum* is a robust species that has certainly proved itself well able to thrive aggressively throughout modern Britain since its reintroduction around 1770 (p. 176f). It tolerates a wide temperature range, is a prolific seed producer that develops dense, light-excluding thickets, and has no obviously similar competitors for the same ecological niche. Norway spruce, probably reintroduced in the Anglo-Saxon period, also self-seeds freely and is naturalised in open ground, clear-felled areas and heathland throughout much of Britain (Preston *et al.*, 2002), but its ambitions may be limited perhaps by its rather more strict soil preferences, relatively lower seed production and the presence of several competing species. The grape-vine, by contrast, reintroduced by the Romans (p. 5), is much less widely naturalised today and then mainly in areas where it is close to cultivation. The reasons for its lack of success are less immediately obvious, as the true species self-seeds fairly freely. It may, however, be more demanding of higher summer tempera-tures and indeed the presence of *Vitis vinifera* pollen in deposits of the Hoxnian interglacial period in Suffolk (around 400,000 BP) has itself been taken as evidence that there was then 'a summer climate at least as warm, and probably warmer, and wetter than that predominant across north-west Europe today' (Turner, 1968). It is also significant that grape-vines are grown in gardens and commercial vineyards as selected cultivars, some producing few or no seeds and even more demanding of warm summers. It is only when these cultivars are grafted onto wild *Vitis vinifera* stock and that is in turn neglected enough to be allowed to sucker, flower and fruit that significant numbers of seeds will be liberated into the environment. It is also true that it will encounter some serious native competitors such as *Clematis vitalba* which require similar conditions – a similar ecological niche.

HUMAN INFLUENCE

The last ice age ended between 10,000 and 15,000 BP and the forests subsequently returned, only to disappear again, for the final time, at the hands of our ancestors. The key to this final demise lies first in the nature of the dominant species, principally oak *Quercus petraea* and *Q. robur*, beech, ash *Fraxinus excelsior*, birch *Betula* spp., elm *Ulmus* spp., lime *Tilia* spp., alder *Alnus glutinosa* and hornbeam *Carpinus betulus* (Fig. 51) in the hardwood forest, and Scots pine *Pinus sylvestris* in the coniferous forest (Fig. 52). Such trees yield timber, and for the past 5,000 years men have felled them to build their homes, fortresses and ships and to fuel their fires. But wherever trees grow and whatever their species, their size prevents man from indulging in another of his characteristic activities, agriculture – and its derivatives, horticulture and gardening. So forests were cleared to make land available for farms and, in consequence, for the first time, alien species were deliberately imposed on the British ecological landscape.

FIG 51. Hornbeam *Carpinus betulus* was once an important species in our native broad-leaf forests.

FIG 52. Scots pine *Pinus sylvestris* was the dominant tree of the northern Caledonian Forest.

Pollen and seed analyses of ancient peat and mud deposits show graphically the sudden occurrence of these aliens, the decrease of the trees, and, as an extremely significant consequence, the rise in importance of the many species that we now recognise as typical of disturbed ground. These are the weeds of cultivation, many of them fast-growing and fast-maturing annuals that compete for light, water and space very effectively with the less well-adapted crop species from alien ecological communities. A graphic example of the competitiveness of 'weeds' is that of the cereal rye, which seems to have originated in Central Asia and may have occurred as a weed among crops of wheat, barley and oats. Realising that

FIG 53. The Enclosure Acts of the late eighteenth century removed much natural vegetation but greatly increased the hedge habitat.

they were fighting a losing battle on poorer soils and in colder climates, the northern farmers turned to the weed instead of the crop and began cultivating rye to the extent that by medieval times it had assumed a predominant place in British agriculture. Only with modern methods of crop husbandry and improved varieties has wheat ousted it.

The final blow to our natural vegetation was dealt by the gradual enclosure of the land that culminated in the Enclosure Acts at the end of the eighteenth century (Fig. 53). These very demonstrably rendered unto the farmer that which was the farmer's, and enabled individuals to make their mark on the landscape in a particularly enduring way. As in all aspects of human interference with nature, however, there was, even here, some benefit to be derived from the creation of a novel habitat in the shape of the hedges and, to a lesser extent, the walls that provided the field boundaries. Indeed, whilst the present appearance of most of the British landscape is the result of the replacement of the natural climax plant formations with communities shaped by human influence, these do repay examination for, at least, they allow a gardener to see a very wide range of habitats and a large number of very different subclimax communities.

PLANT COMMUNITIES TODAY

Perhaps the most obvious way to appreciate the range of plant communities in modern Britain from which your garden may have been derived is to use the categories employed in the *Countryside Survey 2000* (p. 27f). There Britain's countryside is divided into improved grassland; arable and horticultural; neutral grassland; broadleaved, mixed and yew woodland; coniferous woodland; bog; dwarf shrub heath; acid grassland; fen; marsh and swamp; bracken; calcareous grassland; inland rock; montane; standing open water and canals; rivers and streams; built-up and gardens; boundary and linear features; and other land. This might be all right for conservation purposes and for information about gardens newly formed on relatively 'virgin' sites, but for a gardener, the often very important recent horticultural history is obscured in the two very wide categories 'arable and horticultural' and 'built-up and gardens'. I shall therefore opt for the older divisions used by the second Land Utilisation Survey in the 1960s. This magnificent but unfinished project resulted in maps at the scale of 1:25,000 for 15 per cent of England and Wales. The survey used 70 land-use categories printed in 11 colours, but the broad divisions I find especially useful are the major categories of arable land, market garden, orchard, grassland, woodland, heath and moorland, water, marshland and coastal habitats (in addition, of course, to industrial and other built-over areas).

Land for crops

Collectively the first four of the land-use categories – arable land, market garden, orchard and grassland – probably now occupy around 19 million hectares, an area slowly being depleted as housing and roads make increasing demands on the available space (p. 29). What is important, however, is that many gardens are now being created on land with a long history of growing crops, and even more of them are surrounded by old horticultural land with its attendant pollen, seeds and weeds. Interestingly, very few of the crops themselves have become so well adapted to our environment as to be listed officially as introduced components of the British flora, and although I consider the origin and ecology of some of them in the next chapter, there are certain features of such previously cropped land that are best discussed here.

The largest component crops of British agriculture are members of the grass family: cereals, and grass for grazing, hay and silage. Next in importance are potatoes, sugar beet, fodder crops such as swedes, turnips and kales, and the most recent introduction, oil-seed rape (Fig. 54). The remaining 250,000 hectares

FIG 54. Oil-seed rape has become one of the most extensively grown crops over the past 40 years.

are occupied by horticultural crops, and although this means principally vegetables and fruit, it is not synonymous with the old categories of market garden and orchard, for over three-quarters of our national vegetable production is now based on arable farms rather than smallholdings. The vegetable crop grown most extensively, by a long way, is peas, although the production is concentrated in a restricted area of eastern England. If your garden is derived from old vegetable-growing land, however, it is almost certain once to have borne brassicas, which are collectively the most important of our vegetables, and probably beans, bulb onions and lettuces too. Extensive areas of orchard occur principally in Kent, the Vale of Evesham and Herefordshire, with apples easily the largest crop. Nonetheless, one of the most conspicuous declines among British crops in recent times has been that of cherries, and there is a good chance that a new garden in Kent lies on the site of a former cherry orchard.

Almost all farm and horticultural crops are grown as monocultures and the community of a field of oil-seed rape, wheat or Brussels sprouts is probably as far removed from any natural community as is possible (Fig. 55). Even so, these monocultures can teach gardeners certain ecological principles. The impact of pests and diseases will be very evident in almost any field where the farmer has neglected to take control measures, and the rapidity with which such problems can spread when no natural barriers are present is often self-evident. It is easy also to see the effect that competition with weeds can have when the weedkillers on which modern farming is so dependent have been applied too late, incorrectly or not at all. Oil-seed rape, the crop that has had an almost explosive impact on British farming since the 1980s, displays the ability of one particular plant to invade the existing environment. Roadside verges and hedgerows in many parts of the country are now coloured almost as yellow as the fields at flowering time. Notably, this is a crop not altogether alien, for its close relatives and some of its ancestors are either native or well-established members of our flora, and I consider the possible significance of this in the next chapter. It makes an interesting contrast, however, with most cereals, which rarely spread far beyond the immediate field boundaries and appear much less efficient competitors. Very few crop plants indeed have become so well established in Britain as to occur as integrated members of the flora. This may be partly, as with apples and other fruit trees, that they are hybrids and do not 'come true' from seed, but generally poor competitiveness with native vegetation is a major factor. For the gardener, this means that any crop plants that occur inexplicably in his garden are most unlikely to be relics from old cultivation; even fruit trees will be the old, planted individuals themselves rather than their progeny.

FIG 55. Most farm crops, no matter how ornamental, are grown as monocultures.

Woodland

Do not be misled by the extensive tracts of woodland that you will find in some parts of the country and possibly in or at least surrounding your garden. Although there are something over two million hectares of trees in Britain, most of them represent not the surviving parts of the ancient climax formation, but forest and wood artificially planted in recent times for either timber or game cover. To see woodland that is believed to be truly old, you will need to visit such areas as the Black Wood of Rannoch, as representative of the northern forest, or Wistman's Wood on Dartmoor, which is a depauperate form of old oak forest. The extensive areas of coniferous forest in Britain today are largely the results of planting by the Forestry Commission and by private landowners in the twentieth century. The species they contain are alien; Norway and Sitka spruces *Picea sitchensis*, western red cedar *Thuja plicata*, larches *Larix* spp. (Fig. 56), and various pines *Pinus* spp. – even the planted Scots pine bears little resemblance to the majestic native tree. These dark, often forbidding forests have been called ecologically sterile. This is a contradiction in terms, and, indeed, the bird life of some is surprisingly rich, but a monoculture of Sitka spruce certainly makes a formidable competitor for other plants and casts a year-round shade so dense that almost nothing else will grow beneath it. Only with the regular felling for timber every 30 years or so does the land burst forth again with lower-growing plants as long-dormant seeds germinate and others are blown in from neigh-bouring communities (Fig. 57). Even a tree as potentially massive as a Sitka spruce cannot compete on equal terms with bracken *Pteridium aquilinum*, native grasses and other herbaceous plants in its early growth, however, and it is the mark of the good forester to pay assiduous attention to weed control for the first few years after replanting a cleared site. It is often forgotten, by gardeners and foresters alike, that a young tree is no larger than many herbaceous species and, when it is an alien to boot, it will inevitably struggle for its life.

There has been much less planting of hardwood than of coniferous forest, because hardwood trees usually grow much more slowly and yield useful timber only after many more years. Their timber is uneconomic, moreover, for the paper pulp market that now devours so many of our conifers. In the past, extensive hardwood plantings were made on private estates and royal parks to provide house- and ship-building timber and firewood and to provide game cover. The two most notable survivors of the old plantings (although now greatly altered and containing many conifers too) are the New Forest in Hampshire and the Forest of Dean in Gloucestershire. All these forests were artificially managed, as some trees were removed, others planted, the shrub and field layers of vegetation were suppressed by cutting, and introduced deer were encouraged to browse. Even in

FIG 56. Most British forest today comprises plantations of alien species. This is European larch *Larix decidua* and Japanese larch *L. kaempferi* showing astonishing autumn foliage colour in Perthshire.

FIG 57. Modern British forestry works on a rotation of about 30 years. This is a Gloucestershire site cleared for replanting.

their early years, therefore, they were not dependent on the natural death and regeneration that is the hallmark of a natural climax community.

More recently, there has been a tendency for more planting of mixed hardwood and coniferous forest and woodland, largely for aesthetic and amenity reasons. This has been generally welcomed by ecologists as it gives an opportunity for a rather greater proportion of native species to survive than is the case in the purely coniferous stand, whilst providing a better financial return to the owner than the purely hardwood planting.

Several rather specially managed types of woodland must be mentioned as creating unusually interesting ecological communities. In the southern half of England, most especially, may be found deciduous woods of oak, hazel *Corylus avellana*, sweet chestnut *Castanea sativa*, hornbeam, birch, alder and ash in particular, in which the trunks arise in massed groups from a single base. These are the outgrown results of coppicing, a once widespread practice that was an attempt to obtain hardwood timber rather more quickly than waiting for trees to mature. A tree was felled and the cluster of small shoots that sprang up from the stump allowed to develop. Every 10 to 20 years, these were cut to provide poles for fencing or other uses. Sometimes, in the coppice-with-standards system, a proportion of the trees was allowed to grow to full height to provide larger timber. Pollarding, the regular cutting back of individual trees to the main trunk, is based similarly on the ability of some species to regenerate shoots in this way. It cannot be used with conifers which lack this ability. Both coppicing and pollarding are among the most functional and degrading uses to which a tree can be put and the resulting plants are unsightly; witness the pollarded limes of many of our urban streets which should teach gardeners a lesson in species selection. If you cannot accommodate a full-grown tree of any species in your available space, then choose a smaller species rather than hideously abbreviate a large one. Nonetheless, a functioning coppice (and there are still a few) does permit the observation, over a relatively short timescale, of the process of colonisation of a former woodland floor by herbaceous plants, but with the significant difference that the tree growth originates not with seedlings but with a mature stump and a mature root system, and can always therefore compete very effectively.

Finally, we come to perhaps the most interesting, although the most obviously artificial, subclimax woodland community: the hedgerow. A hedge, in very simple terms, can be thought of as a long, narrow wood subject to fairly rigorous management. The plant community comprising the hedgerow is normally dominated by the species planted to form the basis of the boundary; usually, hedges are planted with only one tree or shrub species, but others commonly colonise naturally as seeds are blown in or carried by birds or animals. The hedgerow equivalents of the field and ground layers are always the result of natural colonisation and, indeed, it is the field layer that is subject to periodic clearance in an intensively managed hedge. The total number of plant species recorded in British hedgerows is large – as many as 300 occur quite frequently – to the extent that the English names of some plants have hedge as a prefix: hedge garlic *Alliaria petiolata* and hedge mustard *Sisymbrium officinale*, for instance (Fig. 58). Whilst there are some marked regional variations in the species composition of hedgerows, reflecting climatic or historical factors (for example, fuchsia in the south-west of Britain or beech around Exmoor), there are also clear

FIG 58. Hedge garlic *Alliaria petiolata*, a favoured food plant of the orange tip butterfly *Anthocaris cardamines*.

national trends. The commonest tree species are oak, ash, beech and sycamore. Elm, which was formerly of major importance, has diminished dramatically as a result of Dutch elm disease. Sometimes, the trees of hedgerows are the result of individual specimens of the planted hedgerow species having been allowed to grow to maturity, sometimes they have been planted in addition to the main hedgerow species or, very frequently, they have colonised naturally and been allowed to grow to maturity. The plant used most commonly for farm hedgerow planting is hawthorn, although in gardens, the Japanese privet *Ligustrum ovalifolium* and some form of Lawson's cypress *Chamaecyparis lawsoniana* are easily the most frequent. Most other shrubs that now occur so commonly in hedgerows have colonised naturally; plants such as wild privet *Ligustrum vulgare*, dog rose *Rosa canina* or elderberry *Sambucus nigra* are most unlikely to have been planted as farm boundaries as, on their own, they are not robust enough to contain livestock.

As a result of extensive surveys of the species composition of hedgerows and careful study of old maps and recorded planting dates, it has been possible to devise a system for estimating the age of hedges (Pollard *et al.*, 1974). Given a number of qualifications, such as the need for several samples, the need to avoid lengths of hedge that adjoin woods or gardens (where, clearly, deliberate planting is a major influence), a rough rule of thumb is that the number of species of tree or shrub within a 30-metre run of hedgerow, counted from one side, indicates

FIG 59. Ancient beech hedges on Exmoor.

the age of the hedge in hundreds of years. I have found, moreover, that this system can be useful for old garden hedges. I have a length of boundary hedge containing hawthorn, yew *Taxus baccata*, ash, holly *Ilex aquifolium*, wild goose-berry *Ribes uva-crispa*, bramble and blackthorn. Whilst I do not pretend that this gives me a precise date for my hedgerow, I think the large number of wild species means it is safe to assume that it is probably the original boundary of the property (the house is about 350 years old), or even an earlier field hedge incorporated into the boundary. All hedges provide a 'pocket' example of a layered community, with dominant species and two or more understoreys, and display the effects on plants of shade, severely restricted water penetration and nutrient depletion.

Heath and moorland

A heath or moorland is a plant community largely shaped by an acidic soil and with extensive growth of small shrubs and bushy plants, in particular members of the family Ericaceae – heather *Calluna vulgaris* and heaths *Erica* spp. It may be the climax community of high, exposed areas such as some of the northern mountains, or a subclimax community, as in the south of England where, with the removal of such pressures as grazing by rabbits, deliberate cutting or fire, a mixed woodland of birch and pine would probably establish. Even so, there are lessons here for gardeners in their choice of ground-cover species (p. 43), because tree seedlings quite commonly fail to survive even on undisturbed heath due to the effectiveness of the ericaceous plants in limiting the penetration of light and water, and possibly because the mycorrhizal fungi needed for the establishment of some tree seedlings are inhibited by substances present in heather peat.

Heaths and heathers are not the only plants of heath and moorland communities, as anyone with a garden on or adjoining these areas will testify. Some sedges *Carex* spp. and other members of the family Cyperaceae, especially the misleadingly named deer grass *Scirpus caespitosus* and cotton grasses *Eriophorum* spp., are common and may be locally dominant. Bilberry *Vaccinium myrtillus* can dominate extensive areas of moor, usually at higher altitude than heather as it is more tolerant of exposure. Interestingly, it is more shade tolerant too, so also occurs at lower levels in the field layer of birch and other woods on acid soils. Moreover, in moorland, more than in almost any other British plant habitat, the lower plants, especially mosses and lichens, are of major importance and are often the most important plants in the ground layer. A garden on old heathland may be marvellous hunting ground for unusual lower plants and fungi.

For convenience, I shall stretch this account of moorlands to include mountain-top or 'arctic-alpine' habitats; not because they are especially similar, but because the former often grades into the latter with increasing altitude. Whilst I know of no garden situated on an exposed mountain top, the plants of this environment, or, at least, of comparable, although even higher, environments in other parts of the world, make up much of the flora of the alpine garden. That the growing of many alpine species is so often beset with problems is because of the great difficulty of emulating the conditions of a natural mountain. I appreciate that the mountain top itself is far from a uniform community, but it is one shaped by extreme paucity of soil and by extreme climatic conditions. Rainfall is high, but, because of the nature of the underlying soil and rock, any water drains away very rapidly. Temperatures fluctuate wildly, from long periods below freezing to almost unbearably hot. One of the most unusual environments within the mountain-top community, and one that is especially difficult to recreate in a garden, is scree, a collection of loose stones and boulders in a more or less unstable condition. Such a habitat has a minimal soil content, and very free drainage. Because of the drying effect of the wind, its sheer physical strength, the inadequacy of soil and the difficulties experienced by pollinating insects in flying more than a few centimetres above ground level, the climax community comprises cushion, rosette and creeping plants or very small shrubs, all with their survival buds well protected.

Water and marsh land

Although some gardeners, as they tell me constantly, have extremely wet gardens, relatively few – a lucky few – have plots that are on what are technically called wetlands. These are habitats where impeded drainage and/or a constantly replenished supply of water (either directly, as high rainfall, or indirectly, because of the proximity of a watercourse) ensures that the land hardly ever dries out. The most important of these communities in Britain are the various types of bog on highly acidic peat soils, fenland on less acid peats, and marshland on silty soils, together with the more local versions of them that occur on river- and lake-sides. The ecological community called blanket bog occurs in place of moorland where rainfall is high and drainage impeded. Mosses, especially species of *Sphagnum*, and occasionally even lichens, may be dominant in extensive areas of blanket bog. Where *Sphagnum* colonises the remains of fen vegetation, a bog can form over more alkaline soils and is then called a raised bog, a habitat that has become extremely scarce in Britain. Anyone whose garden includes one today is likely to be gardening on a Site of Special Scientific Interest (SSSI). Fenland is best seen in a few surviving areas in East Anglia, where it has formed on the upper parts of old river estuaries. The dominant plants, and those whose remains contribute to fen peat (which is much less acidic than the *Sphagnum* or moss peats), are the great fen sedge *Cladium mariscus*, common reed *Phragmites australis*, blunt-flowered rush *Juncus subnodulosus* and reed grass *Phalaris arundinacea*. The vegetation of marshes is essentially similar to that of bogs and fens, depending on the relative acidity of the underlying silt. A celebrated earlier New Naturalist author, Ted Ellis (*The Broads*), had one of the few gardens I know that was entirely fen.

Within the open water, in rivers and lakes, two main types of plant may be found. Floating plants, such as duckweed *Lemna* spp., have no anchoring roots, and obtain all their mineral nutrients from the water. The true water plants, such as water lilies *Nymphaea* spp. and milfoils *Myriophyllum* spp., are rooted in mud and have no aerial shoots, although the depth of water they can tolerate varies greatly from species to species; a fact to be borne in mind in the planting and management of pools in gardens. A few plants of this type, such as *Ranunculus fluitans*, thrive in and require fast-flowing water and are inappropriate inhabitants of a garden pond.

Coastal habitats

I shall mention the sea coast only in passing, for although many people do garden almost on the shoreline (Fig. 60), the communities are essentially the shrub, grassland or other types described already, with the difference that the

FIG 60. Some people do garden almost on the shoreline. Porlock Weir, Somerset.

species are those able to tolerate exposure, partly to wind, but more importantly to salt-laden air. I know of no-one, however, who gardens in the intertidal zone that represents one of the very few British plant communities dominated by algae.

A garden may once have been almost any of these communities, and at least part of that community may remain or may surround it still. Next, therefore, I shall consider how the native plant life of Britain that originated in these communities has responded to finding itself part of a garden.

CHAPTER 5

The Garden as a Habitat to which Native Plants have Adapted

A NATIVE PLANT growing in a garden is by definition almost – although not quite – bound to be considered a weed. It will compete with the garden vegetation and in a conventional garden (that is, not a wildlife garden) is generally unwelcome if it manages to do so successfully. In this chapter I consider what makes a successful weed and examine the ways in which different native species have assumed this role most effectively. I include here archaeophytes – those plants that may originally have been alien, but are believed to have been here since at least 1500. Alien weed species of more recent introduction – including some plants that, perversely, escaped originally from garden cultivation and then reinvaded it – are considered in the next chapter.

NATIVE OR ALIEN?

There have been remarkably few studies of the overall plant composition of British gardens, as opposed to gardeners' or garden designers' planting lists. Owen (1991) recorded the numbers of alien and British native species, including those that were planted and those that 'came in of their own accord', in her own Leicester garden. The annual average over the years 1975–86 was 214 alien and 146 (about 40 per cent, excluding grasses), native. Of the total of 360 species, 266 were cultivated deliberately and 94 were 'spontaneous introductions'.

The plants found by Gaston & Thompson in the 61 gardens of their Sheffield survey (p. 27) embraced 1,176 species, most of them, predictably enough, aliens. The native plants were mostly weed species because 'It's rather unlikely that rare native plants will arrive in gardens under their own steam' (Gaston & Thompson, 2002). However, when the same team sampled garden plant composition by means of 1 square metre quadrats, the pattern was rather different. They found only 438 taxa, of which 33 per cent were native, and of the 20 most frequent taxa (Table 9), 17 were native. It was fairly obvious that many were present as weeds, some were planted and some were probably self-sown from previous plantings.

Thompson *et al.* (2004) drew an interesting inference from their analysis of garden plant diversity. They pointed out that, together with other factors, the low population sizes of many garden plants may have consequences for their survival in that potential pathogens and herbivores may simply not find them. The plants may have what is called low apparency (Feeny, 1976). By contrast, species that are uncommon in the wild might be more susceptible to attack in gardens, and Thompson *et al.* cited shrubby cinquefoil *Potentilla fruticosa* as a plant on which no lepidopterous larvae have been found in the wild in Britain

TABLE 9. The 20 most frequent taxa of flowering plants found in 120 1m² quadrats in 60 private gardens in Sheffield (after Thompson *et al.*, 2004).

SPECIES	ORIGIN	NO. OF RECORDS
broad-leaved willowherb *Epilobium montanum*	native	34
dandelion *Taraxacum officinale* agg.	native	32
wood avens *Geum urbanum*	native	19
columbine *Aquilegia vulgaris*	native	18
red fescue *Festuca rubra*	native	18
creeping buttercup *Ranunculus repens*	native	18
hairy bitter-cress *Cardamine hirsuta*	native	16
common couch *Elytrigia repens*	native	16
primrose *Primula vulgaris*	native	16
Yorkshire fog *Holcus lanatus*	native	15
bramble *Rubus fruticosus*	native	15
lady's mantle *Alchemilla mollis*	alien	13
ash *Fraxinus excelsior*	native	13
rough meadow-grass *Poa trivialis*	native	13
foxglove *Digitalis purpurea*	native	12
herb Robert *Geranium robertianum*	native	12
montbretia *Crocosmia × crocosmiiflora*	alien	11
American willowherb *Epilobium ciliatum*	alien	11
ivy *Hedera helix*	native	11
Welsh poppy *Meconopsis cambrica*	native	11

(Leather, 1986) yet Owen (1991) found at least nine moth species using it in her garden in Leicestershire.

Analyses of the flora of specific areas within gardens are even more sparse and the lawn seems to be the only area examined properly. An interesting study of lawn plant composition was made as part of the study by Thompson *et al.* (2004). They used 1 square metre quadrats in 52 gardens in Sheffield, on lawns ranging in size from 9 square metres to 507 square metres, with a mean of 82 square metres (not wildly different therefore from Paskett's 'average lawn' of 100 square metres; p. 26). They found 159 species of vascular plants, albeit 60 of them only once. Fourteen species occurred in at least half of the lawns while one species, rough meadow-grass *Poa trivialis*, occurred in all. Although, unfortunately, the authors did not publish the full species list, other significant findings from their investigation were that native plants averaged 94 per cent of the species composition, were never less than 83 per cent, and that lawns:

> ... made a major contribution to the native vascular plant richness of gardens; species unique to lawns accounted for up to 69 per cent of the total native [plant] richness of our gardens, and 35 per cent on average.

Several of their other conclusions were fairly predictable. Many of the grass species present were invaders that were unlikely to have been present in the original seed mixture or turf. After common bent, red fescue and perennial rye-grass (those suggested as the main 'deliberate' components), five of the next six most abundant species were also grasses: creeping bent *Agrostis stolonifera*, Yorkshire fog *Holcus lanatus*, rough meadow-grass, smooth meadow-grass (which is present in some lawn seed mixtures – see p. 36) and annual meadow-grass *Poa annua*. No lawn, however, consisted entirely of grasses (bad news for the velvet sward fraternity) and the forb with the highest average cover was white clover *Trifolium repens* (Fig. 61), followed by daisy *Bellis perennis*, creeping buttercup *Ranunculus repens* and dandelion *Taraxacum* agg.

In passing I should add that a remarkable series of analytical studies into the structure of the lawn as an ecological community has been made by Stephen Roxburgh and his co-workers at the University of Dunedin, New Zealand, and for anyone interested in some serious lawn ecology, I commend this to them (see, for instance, Roxburgh & Wilson, 2000). It is also worth adding that the lawn is a splendid example of ecology in action and there is no better garden instance of the role of plant life forms (a classification based on their survival processes) in shaping their ability to thrive. The maintenance of a lawn, whether cut with scythe or mower, is simply a replication of the grazing action of animals and, as

FIG 61. White clover *Trifolium repens*, one of the commonest non-grass colonisers of garden lawns.

such, encourages the growth of grass with its protected basal meristem at the expense of taller plants. But it has also always encouraged the proliferation of rosette plants, their meristems sunk below cutting or grazing level, and also small, creeping species that similarly keep their vulnerable parts below the parapet. An examination of the life forms of the most important lawn weeds (to which I shall return later) reveals this perfectly (Table 10).

With such a paucity of data and little analysis of plant populations *in situ* in garden habitats, it seems appropriate to consider the most important native plants species by species, and attempt to place each in an historical and garden ecological context. I will begin with annuals, which make up a clearly defined weed type, generally dealt with by gardeners in the same way – hoeing, hand-pulling, digging or smothering by mulching are much the most important control methods, and annuals tend to be treated relatively little with chemical weedkillers.

TABLE 10. The most common lawn weeds (apart from weed grasses) and their means of survival.

SPECIES	COMMON NAME	ANNUAL/ PERENNIAL	SURVIVAL METHOD ON LAWNS
Achillea millefolium	yarrow	perennial	creeping underground stems and rosettes
Bellis perennis	daisy	perennial	central rosette
Cerastium fontanum	common mouse-ear	perennial	creeping stems
Convolvulus arvensis	field bindweed	perennial	creeping roots and stems
Medicago lupulina	black medick	annual/short-lived perennial	seeds and creeping stems
Plantago major	greater plantain	perennial	central rosette
Plantago media	hoary plantain	perennial	central rosette
Ranunculus repens	creeping buttercup	perennial	creeping stems rooting at nodes and forming rosettes
Soleirolia soleirolii	mind-your-own-business	perennial	creeping stems rooting at nodes
Sagina procumbens	procumbent pearlwort	perennial	central rosette and creeping stems, rooting at nodes
Taraxacum officinale agg.	dandelion	perennial	central rosette
Trifolium dubium	lesser trefoil	annual	seeds and creeping stems
Trifolium repens	white clover	perennial	creeping stems rooting at nodes
Veronica filiformis	slender speedwell	perennial	creeping stems

NATIVE ANNUAL WEEDS

The two annual sow-thistles, the prickly sow-thistle *Sonchus asper* and the smooth sow-thistle *S. oleraceus* (Fig. 62), commonly survive over winter in gardens and are most troublesome in vegetable plots and annual flowerbeds where they tend to

FIG 62. Smooth sow-thistle *Sonchus oleraceus* as a weed among a garden pea crop.

occur as isolated plants. The problem in gardens is their size – both can reach 150 centimetres – and the fact that they seem to develop unnoticed among cultivated vegetation. Both are prolific seed producers (up to 18,000 per plant for prickly sow-thistle and 6,000 for smooth sow-thistle), but the seeds are extremely light and are clearly widely dispersed by the wind, which explains why they seldom occur in groups or clusters. Outside gardens these species are common in disturbed habitats, trampled grassland and waste places generally, but are intolerant of grazing and hence are most readily controlled in gardens by hoeing when young. They occur throughout Britain, but the prickly sow-thistle is more frequent in upland and wetter areas. Both were presumably fairly sparse in ancient Britain, but adapted to farmland and cultivation; many early archaeological finds are associated with cereal stores.

Groundsel *Senecio vulgaris*, the depredations of *Puccinia lagenophorae* notwithstanding (p. 200f), is one of the commonest annual garden weeds and is one of the truly ubiquitous plants in modern Britain (Fig. 63). It grows in almost all types of habitat, in all soil types, and whilst not a large plant (although in well-fertilised garden soil it can reach a height of at least 45 centimetres) it is a troublesome and competitive weed occurring in swarms in garden beds and borders. It produces large amounts of wind-blown seed – up to 1,000 seeds per plant – and has the critical attribute of being able to germinate in every month

FIG 63. Groundsel *Senecio vulgaris* among garden lettuces.

of the year. Control of groundsel is not easy because the seeds continue to mature even if the plants are hoed down, so they must be raked up and carted away. It is hard to imagine groundsel ever being anything less than common in Britain, and it will never be truly dependent for its success simply on farming and gardening activities, although it may be significant that it has declined in the Scottish Highlands in recent years, a change that has been attributed to the abandonment there of marginal cultivations.

Several small annual brassicaceous species occur as weeds in beds and vegetable plots, but one has eclipsed all others in recent years. Hairy bitter-cress *Cardamine hirsuta* is the commonest annual weed in container-grown plants and must be the commonest weed in garden centres, from where it has been transported to almost every garden in the land. Its natural habitat is bare rocky places and it also commonly occurs in damp woods and by streams. Although there appears to be no British fossil record this may simply be because *Cardamine* species are difficult to identify from seeds or pollen. In recent times, it evidently found ideal conditions in soil-less, especially peat-based, potting composts. I have found swarms of it growing naturally at the margins of lowland peat bogs in Ireland, and I would not rule out some contamination of the peat itself with seeds before the composts are mixed. It is probably unrealistic to expect it to decline if and when peat usage really does drop as significantly as conservation bodies might hope (p. 255). I suspect the populations in gardens are now so high that it is a weed that is here to stay. It can be controlled fairly readily by hoeing or hand-pulling, but as a winter annual which in good years will produce three generations, the problem is that almost all specimens will bear mature fruits, except when very young, and although each plant produces only around 600 seeds, these are dispersed explosively for a distance of over a metre.

Common chickweed *Stellaria media* has long been one of the most important garden weeds, partly because of its spreading habit which tends to smother seedlings and partly because it grows preferentially in nutrient-rich soils (Fig. 64). It is a classic example of a native plant that has adopted the garden habitat because of its high nutrient status. Although it is now ubiquitous and occurs in almost every 10-kilometre grid square by virtue of its prevalence in gardens, it is also still found in what can only be presumed to be its original habitats: on naturally well-manured land, close to and on rotting vegetation and, apparently strangely but understandably, close to sea-bird colonies and on coastal strand-lines. The fossil record in the interglacials is considerable; further evidence of its significance in the absence of human habitation. It is an indicator weed – many an old gardener would recommend the purchase of land with a prolific chickweed growth because of its high fertility. It is most readily controlled by

FIG 64. Common chickweed *Stellaria media*, an indicator of a fertile soil.

hoeing the young seedlings; later, it roots along the procumbent stems and control by hoeing is effectively impossible. Hand-pulling is also impractical as the stems are too brittle. Like those of other successful annual weeds, its seeds will germinate in every month, seed production is prolific (up to 2,000 per plant), and seed longevity is considerable – up to 40 years.

Annual meadow-grass is the more significant of the two annual garden grass weeds and is one of the most common of all garden weeds. It is a small, slightly angular plant, extremely hardy and capable of flowering and seeding in every month, although most seeds are formed between April and September. It is not easy to control by hoeing because the roots are tough and any plants not collected up will re-root in damp conditions. Much the best method is hand-weeding with a small fork. Annual meadow-grass is almost ubiquitous in Britain and its tolerance of disturbance means it was probably originally associated with trampled areas, shifting shingle and similar habitats. Its less serious partner in crime is barren brome *Anisantha sterilis*, an archaeophyte which probably reached us from southern Europe with cereal seed. In this country it has long been an important weed of cereal fields, although it has become established in waste ground, grassland and gardens too. In gardens, control is best achieved by hoeing while it is still small as it eventually becomes a large plant (up to 90 centimetres tall) and the elongated rough seeds from its pendulous flowerheads are readily spread on animal fur and clothing.

Black medick *Medicago lupulina* and the very similar lesser trefoil *Trifolium dubium* are the most important annual or short-lived weeds in the Fabaceae, and in some gardens they can be extremely troublesome. They are both small, yellow-flowered plants with stems that lie flat on the soil surface and are most easily distinguished from each other by the small point at the end of the central leaflet vein on black medick. Both are commonest in lawns, although they are also frequent on paths and drives and between paving slabs. Mowing the lawn while the plants are seeding, even with a grass collector, serves to spread them further, and control is extremely difficult. They are tolerant of some lawn weedkillers and the only effective method is physically to sever them from the single taproot whilst they are young. Outside gardens and cultivated land generally, both are common in a range of bare and waste places as well as dry grassland where they probably existed historically, aided by their tolerance of trampling.

Black nightshade *Solanum nigrum* is a bushy annual with broad leaves and striking black fruits that reaches about 60 centimetres in height. Although it produces abundant seed – up to 10,000 per plant – most germination is late and seedlings do not usually appear before May. It is also frost tender. Whilst it can occur in considerable numbers on rich soils, it is seldom a serious problem in gardens and is readily controlled by hoeing – its broad leaves shrivel quickly. Its natural habitat is not obvious, but as it prefers rich soils, it presumably occurred in the past on well-manured open sites.

Nipplewort *Lapsana communis* is one of the tallest annual weeds and, oddly enough, one that few gardeners can name, despite its extremely common occurrence (Fig. 65). It tends to be dismissed as yet another yellow-flowered intruder. It has most of the attributes of a successful weed in its prolific seed production (up to 1,000 per plant), considerable seed longevity, rapid growth and the possession of seeds that can germinate in either spring or autumn. One feature that works against it, however, is that the seeds are not shed until a long time after they have ripened, unless the plants are disturbed. It is, moreover, easily pulled up by hand or controlled by hoeing. It was probably originally a plant of shaded woodlands and rocky places.

Procumbent pearlwort *Sagina procumbens* is the commonest weed species in a genus of remarkably similar little flowering plants that are often believed to be mosses, so insignificant are their flowers (Fig. 66). The confusion is aided by them occupying similar habitats – in the cracks in paving, on lawns and trampled areas generally, and also on the compost of plant pots. Procumbent pearlwort has a very similar annual relative in annual pearlwort *S. apetala*, but despite the plants being so low growing, the seeds are wind-dispersed, a feature facilitated by their extreme lightness. Germination is swift as there appears to be almost no dormancy; control, other than by chemicals, is all but impossible. Pearlworts occur widely in bare and rocky places and were probably always common where animals trampled.

Cleavers *Galium aparine* is the only one among several native *Galium* species to have become a successful garden weed; understandably so because of its

FIG 65. Nipplewort *Lapsana communis* among garden nasturtiums.

scrambling, climbing habit and hooked bristly hairs which enable it to cling to other vegetation, its rapid growth, and its highly efficient seed dispersal – the bristly seeds attach themselves to animals and clothing (Fig. 67). The seeds germinate in autumn and winter and part of its success has been attributed to this taking place whilst gardeners are hibernating, so that by the time spring arrives, it is already well established. It occurs in almost every 10-kilometre grid square in Britain and its habitats, if not ubiquitous, are at least highly varied and include shingle banks and scree slopes. It is most readily controlled by hand-weeding, and is as good an example as I know of the old adage about 'one year's seeding' leading to 'seven years' weeding'. When I acquired my own garden, it was almost overrun with cleavers, but rigorous pulling out of every plant seen (my young sons were paid a bounty for each bucketful), meant it had all but gone after seven seasons.

FIG 66. Procumbent pearlwort *Sagina procumbens*.

FIG 67. Cleavers *Galium aparine* at the base of a garden hedge.

Fat hen *Chenopodium album* is among the commonest garden weeds, readily identifiable by its rigidly erect habit, reddish stem and rather variable but usually more or less hastate leaves. It has good weed attributes in its abundant seed production, the potential for these to survive around 30 years, and its preference for highly organic sites such as compost heaps. Unless the composting process is well managed and consistently high temperatures are attained, the seeds may survive to be distributed with the compost itself. It should be possible to control fat hen by hand-pulling. Historically, it was probably an associate of animals and manure.

Fool's parsley *Aethusa cynapium* is the only annual garden weed in the Apiaceae, and although bearing a slight resemblance to parsley, I always think of it as more a 'fool's dill'. Although occurring on most soil types and common in gardens throughout much of England and Wales, it seldom achieves its weed promise. Despite a seed production of up to 6,000 per plant and potential survival of them for up to ten years, it is limited by its late summer flowering and late spring germination. It is commonest within gardens in vegetable plots and annual flowerbeds, and is fairly readily controlled by hoeing or hand-pulling. There is a suggestion that it may not be native, and the commonest weed form, the subspecies *agrestis*, might be an archaeophyte. It does not occur in significant numbers away from cultivation and in Britain may never have done so.

Turning now to the archaeophytes, hairy bitter-cress (above) has, in some respects, taken the place in gardens of shepherd's purse *Capsella bursa-pastoris*, another brassicaceous annual/biennial which has been one of the commonest weeds for generations of vegetable gardeners and arable farmers. Shepherd's purse is an extraordinarily variable plant, in size and in the form of the leaves and fruits. Like groundsel, it has seeds that will germinate in every month, and each plant produces up to 4,000 of them, capable of surviving in the soil for 30 years. In summer, it can complete its life cycle in six weeks, and three generations a year are commonplace, the later-produced plants forming rosettes which will survive even severe frost. Shepherd's purse can only effectively be controlled by hoeing before the seeds are set. It is difficult to hand-pull, having a long, strong taproot.

Two annual spurges, petty spurge *Euphorbia peplus* and sun spurge *E. helioscopia* (Fig. 68), are the most important weed species in a genus that has become incredibly popular as garden ornamentals. Both are European or Eurasian southern temperate species that are now widely naturalised outside their native range. Both are commonest in warm, sunny gardens on light, nutrient-rich soils, and are most generally found in vegetable plots, but rarely cause major problems unless they occur in large numbers. The seeds are

FIG 68. Sun spurge
Euphorbia helioscopia
in a vegetable plot.

explosively discharged and seed dispersal in sun spurge is believed to be aided
by ants. Both species can usually be controlled adequately by hoeing.

Common fumitory *Fumaria officinalis* is another of the common annual
weeds that rather few gardeners can name. It is a scrambling, bushy, rather
pretty purple-flowered plant and, whilst a successful farm weed, tends only to be
important in gardens in newly broken land on light, poor, alkaline soils. It was
probably introduced to Britain as a weed of ancient cultivation and is never
really common away from farmland.

Only two of the many introduced blue-flowered annual *Veronica* species have
become significant as garden weeds, although rather more occur on agricultural

land. Common field speedwell *V. persica* and wall speedwell *V. arvensis* are closely related and most simply distinguished by the erect habit of wall speedwell and spreading growth of field speedwell. Being shallowly rooted, both are readily controlled by hoeing.

So familiar is field poppy as an agricultural weed – and one making a significant comeback with recent changes in farm practices – that it is especially hard to imagine it having any other existence (Fig. 69). It is less common in gardens than on farms, although the considerable longevity of the seeds – up to 80 years – means that once present, it is likely to reappear, even if only in small numbers, for many years, a situation that can only be enhanced because of its almost ubiquitous inclusion today in annual wild flower seed mixtures. It is easily controlled by hoeing as its tissues are soft and shrivel quickly.

Although technically not an archaeophyte as it was not recorded in Britain

FIG 69. Field poppy *Papaver rhoeas*. Its seeds can germinate after many years of dormancy.

until around 1690, Canadian fleabane *Conyza canadensis* was almost certainly accidentally introduced with other North American plants and has probably always been predominantly a weed of cultivation in Britain, although it is also found on light, sandy soils and sand dunes. It is an unattractive, stiffly erect plant about 1 metre tall with tiny yellow-white flowers which mature to form typically asteraceous parachute seeds. It occurs in gardens in the southern half of England, and is fairly easily controlled by hoeing in the rather long period before the seeds develop or, later, by hand-pulling.

There are several archaeophyte annual weeds that have related perennial equivalents, notably annual dog's mercury *Mercurialis annua*, small nettle *Urtica urens* and red dead-nettle *Lamium purpureum*. Annual dog's mercury was probably introduced to Britain as a weed with cultivated plants – it has been found in Viking deposits in York. Although it is mainly a species of light soils in central southern England and is insignificant in gardens outside that area, it can be extremely troublesome where it does occur because it is a tall plant – up to 60 centimetres – and produces abundant, explosively discharged seeds which germinate rapidly. It is controlled by hoeing or hand-pulling, but this must be performed before the seeds have set. Small nettle is another plant that probably arrived as a weed of cultivation, and has essentially remained so. Like its more familiar perennial relative, it has stinging hairs and occurs throughout much of the eastern half of the British Isles. It can be a serious problem in gardens with light soils as it frequently arises in large numbers and must be hoed or hand-pulled (with gloves) before the seed is dispersed. Red dead-nettle is now almost ubiquitous and is one of the commonest of annual garden weeds, distinguished by its red flowers and often rich purple foliage, especially evident when it is stressed (Fig. 70). It is most readily controlled by hoeing, as the stems are rather brittle for hand-pulling, but seed production is fairly small for an annual weed and so it rarely occurs in large numbers. Its natural habitat in Britain is not obvious, although it is found in rough grassland and pasture. It has a close relative in another archaeophyte, henbit dead-nettle *Lamium amplexicaule*, which has smaller, rose-purple flowers and causes similar problems as a weed. It too is best controlled by hoeing, although as the stem fragments appear to be able to root, they should be collected up rather than left on the soil surface. The seeds have a dormancy period and seedlings will therefore continue to appear over a long period.

Two annual plants that were garden escapes have made fairly swift returns to home gardens as weeds: pineapple weed *Matricaria discoidea* and the South American gallant soldier *Galinsoga parviflora*. I describe these with other aliens in Chapter 7.

FIG 70. Red dead-nettle *Lamium purpureum,* an extremely common annual weed but not native.

NATIVE PERENNIAL WEEDS

Perennial weeds offer gardeners quite different problems from those presented by annuals, and in some measure tend to occupy dissimilar situations within gardens, reflecting their different biology and ecology. Whilst the success of annual weeds largely depends on their seed production and seed longevity, possession of a dormancy mechanism, rapidity of growth and general competitiveness, perennials rely much more on the efficiency of their vegetative growth and spread. Some of the most serious perennial garden weeds produce few if any seeds, but have deep, far-reaching and almost ineradicable roots or rhizomes. It is no coincidence that around one-eighth of the species I consider the most serious have the adjective 'creeping' as part of their common names.

Whilst digging or even repeated and persistent hoeing can keep some perennial weeds in check, chemical control, especially using the translocated total weedkiller glyphosate (N-(phosphonomethyl)glycine), is still much the most effective and reliable method – except on lawns where a selective product must be used. Even gardeners who otherwise eschew the use of chemical controls for garden problems recognise that glyphosate is often essential to ensure a fairly 'clean sheet' in a new garden or plot. It is a chemical of relatively short persistence – its half-life is from 3 to 130 days and it is degraded by soil micro-organisms, mainly to aminomethylphosphonic acid, which is then broken down further. The main breakdown product of the surfactant used in the commonest commercial product is carbon dioxide.

The species of perennial weed with the epithet 'creeping' are creeping bellflower *Campanula rapunculoides*, creeping (slender) speedwell *Veronica filiformis*, creeping thistle *Cirsium arvense*, creeping yellow cress *Rorippa sylvestris* and creeping buttercup. The first two were originally introduced as garden plants and I return to them in Chapter 7. Creeping thistle is the only thistle normally troublesome in gardens, although the biennial spear thistle *Cirsium vulgare* does occur as a garden weed, but can fairly readily be controlled by hoeing. Creeping thistle is a different matter as its creeping roots are extremely brittle and are easily damaged by digging and will regrow. Seed production is not usually important because the plant can be cut down before it flowers. It is principally a plant of grazed pastures, disturbed ground and cultivated sites generally throughout Britain, and its natural habitat is not obvious. Creeping yellow cress is in some respects a perennial yellow-flowered equivalent of hairy bitter-cress, and a plant that has become a serious weed in nurseries, garden centres and gardens throughout much of the southern part of Britain. It grows naturally in wet places – by streams and ponds and in damp grassland – but tends to favour drier situations on cultivated sites. Although it produces few seeds, it has extremely brittle roots that regrow effectively and swiftly. The only other important perennial garden weed in the Brassicaceae is hoary cress *Lepidium draba*, a tall, white-flowered southern European plant of dry, light soils. Introduced accidentally through Swansea and a number of other ports in the early nineteenth century it has since spread rapidly and become a problem in many gardens in the south-east of Britain because of its brittle, readily regenerating roots. Creeping buttercup is a remarkably successful plant and is one of only two serious garden weeds in a genus of around 30 yellow- and white-flowered terrestrial and aquatic buttercups. It occurs in almost every 10-kilometre grid square in Britain and in a huge range of habitats including wet grasslands, lake- and stream-sides, woodland clearings and dune slacks, all of which were probably its main habitats in prehistoric times. It only produces around 150 seeds per plant and they can persist for many years, but it is the rapidly growing creeping stems that constitute the main problems. They root at the nodes and enable a single plant to cover 4 square metres in a year. Creeping buttercup can be controlled by hoeing when young, but once mature it is a major problem. It can be difficult to eradicate from lawns as it seems to be tolerant of some of the principal components of most lawn weedkillers.

A close relative of the buttercups is lesser celandine *Ranunculus ficaria*, a plant that seems to give unjustifiable concern as a weed (Fig. 71). In the spring, gardens can be carpeted with its glossy foliage and bright yellow flowers, but by early summer it has all but vanished. Although for a few weeks it will smother other plants, I never consider it worthy of serious control. It is an interesting plant nonetheless, in seeming to possess all the necessary attributes for a successful perennial weed – it reproduces effectively by seed, and possesses brittle root tubers, with an additional form (subsp. *bulbilifer*) that seems normally to produce bulbils instead of seeds. If control is needed, digging is all but useless because

FIG 71. Lesser celandine *Ranunculus ficaria*, not a serious weed as it dies down in early summer.

the small tuber fragments will regenerate, but it is highly susceptible to contact weedkillers. The two forms of *Ranunculus ficaria*, subsp. *bulbilifer* and subsp. *ficaria*, differ in their natural distribution; one may be the ancient native type, but both are frequent in damp, slightly shaded places more or less throughout Britain. There are several most attractive cultivated variants including some slightly bizarre double-flowered sterile forms.

Although several species of willowherb, both annual and perennial, occur in gardens, only two are problem weeds. Rosebay willowherb, a plant that has experienced a number of recent name changes and is currently *Chamerion angustifolium*, is almost ubiquitous throughout Britain on wasteland and will rapidly colonise neglected gardens by means of its massive production of wind-blown seeds, and then use its creeping roots to build up dense clumps of vegetation (Fig. 72). Its British history is curious. It was what the *New Atlas* describes as 'a rare upland species' in the nineteenth century, but then began a major spread into gardens and cultivated habitats as well as woodland clearings and disturbed areas generally – it was a rapid and effective coloniser of Second World War bomb sites. One possible explanation seems to be that a more vigorous form was introduced from elsewhere. Broad-leaved willowherb *Epilobium montanum* is a typical *Epilobium* willowherb in its tall, slender form and tiny pink flowers. It is common in rocky places (hence, presumably, the name *montanum*) and is often to be seen on the top of dry-stone walls, although it is also frequent in woodland. Although it produces considerable quantities of

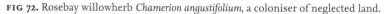

FIG 72. Rosebay willowherb *Chamerion angustifolium*, a coloniser of neglected land.

seed, its most important feature as a garden weed lies in its production of small leafy rosettes at the end of creeping stems which survive over winter and give rise to new flowering stems in the following spring.

An interesting clutch of six perennial species in the Asteraceae are significant as garden weeds, and among them is perhaps the best known if not the most important lawn weed, the dandelion. It is too well known to require description, and apart from forming the familiar rosettes on lawns, also occurs in beds and borders, on paths and drives and in many other places. It combines massive seed production (over 5,000 per plant) and efficient dispersal by the familiar parachute method with the ability to regenerate from any part of the taproot – a feature that makes hoeing useless and digging chancy. Dandelions are aggregate species: there are 229 apomictic microspecies in Britain, of which it is estimated around 40 are endemic and 100 alien. Although they occur in a huge range of natural and artificial habitats, individual microspecies do seem limited in their preferences and it is logical to suppose that some of those now common in gardens may have been much rarer in the past.

Superficially similar to dandelion in its flowerheads is coltsfoot *Tussilago farfara*, although it is otherwise distinctive, and its large, rather furry leaves do not appear until after the scaly-stemmed flowers. It is an unusual weed in producing seeds that, although widely wind dispersed, lack any dormancy and can survive for only three or four months. The problem it presents lies with its deeply penetrating rhizomes that are extremely difficult to eradicate. Once established, its broad, spreading leaves make it an aggressive competitor. It is also an effective pioneer coloniser of disturbed ground, and although it has adopted such artificial sites as railway embankments, its natural habitat is on rough grassland, scree slopes, shingle and sand dunes.

Perennial sow-thistle *Sonchus arvensis* is comparably problematic to its annual relatives, especially in heavy soils from which it is almost impossible to dig out, its extensive root system breaking readily and plants regenerating from the fragments. It is a typical sow-thistle in its slender stems, up to 120 centimetres tall, bearing narrow, toothed blue-green leaves and yellow dandelion-like flowers.

Yarrow *Achillea millefolium* is generally only a problem weed in lawns, and there mainly because it appears to be tolerant of many weedkillers. Its soft, finely divided leaves and flat heads of small white or slightly pink flowers are borne on stems 60 centimetres or more in height. Spread by seed seems fairly unimportant in gardens where the persistent, slowly creeping rhizomes create the problems. It occurs throughout the British Isles in grasslands of all kinds, as well as sand dunes, shingle and other habitats. Feverfew *Tanacetum parthenium*, with tall stems bearing heads of white and pale yellow, daisy-like flowers, is an archaeophyte,

FIG 73. Feverfew *Tanacetum parthenium*, an archaeophyte long grown for its medicinal use.

long grown as a medicinal herb and still widely cultivated, especially in the golden-foliaged form 'Aureum' (Fig. 73). It has become extensively naturalised on waste ground and path sides and is also found as a garden weed, although it can generally be controlled by hoeing.

Daisy is perhaps the most familiar of all weeds and is the lawn weed *par excellence*, although paradoxically, it is the one that gardeners in general are most content to tolerate because it is an undeniably pretty little thing. It is found in quantity nowhere else in gardens, and although grazed grassland is its most familiar natural habitat, it also occurs on lake- and stream-sides and other damp habitats throughout the British Isles. Its success derives from its tight rosette habit and short, creeping shoots which slowly enlarge the colony. It is readily controlled by digging (the daisy-grubber is one of the oldest and most familiar of garden tools) or with selective lawn weedkillers.

Two species of plantain, greater plantain *Plantago major* and hoary plantain *P. media*, are also problematic on lawns by virtue of their rosette habit, similar to that of daisies, which evades the lawnmower's blades, although, unlike daisies, they occur elsewhere in gardens too. Greater plantain is much the more widespread species, occurring commonly wherever land is trampled, and presumably was much less common in the past when only native hoofed animals obliged. Hoary plantain is typical of alkaline grasslands. Both species are most readily controlled on lawns by selective weedkillers or in beds and borders by digging. A third plantain, ribwort *P. lanceolata*, also occurs in gardens, but it is seldom troublesome as it is much more a plant of tall, undisturbed grass than close-cut lawns and it is an important component of many wild flower meadow seed mixtures.

Two species of dock, broad-leaved dock *Rumex obtusifolius* and curled dock *R. crispus*, are widespread throughout Britain and can be significant weeds in rough, neglected and damp areas in gardens as well as in rough grass such as orchards. Outside gardens, they are found typically in neglected grassland, but broad-leaved dock is also a plant of damp places – streamsides and river banks – while curled dock still occurs in what was probably its original habitat in coastal areas – sand dunes, shingle beaches, the upper parts of salt marshes and tidal river banks. Although curled dock commonly dies after flowering, this may be little compensation as seed production can be as much as 30,000 per plant, and the seeds can survive in the soil for around 80 years. Both plants are fairly tolerant of selective weedkillers, but digging, although hard work, can be profitable: unlike dandelions, docks will not regenerate from parts of the taproot deeper than about 15 centimetres.

There is only one significant perennial weed grass and it is, as gardeners will tell you, a 'real thug': common couch. Like several other garden weeds, it probably started life as a plant of sand dunes, salt-marsh margins and other coastal sites, to which its relative sand couch *Elytrigia juncea* and other species are still restricted. It is now found, however, in a wide range of relatively fertile disturbed habitats, and is one of the five most important garden weeds. Common couch rather rarely sets seed in gardens, and its persistence and effects are due to the white, creeping rhizomes. New aerial shoots arise in autumn or early spring from the rhizome tips or from the many small lateral buds. Even tiny rhizome fragments will regenerate, and when the plant is growing in heavy soil or among established shrubs or herbaceous perennials, it is almost impossible to dig up intact. At one time, a specific translocated weedkiller alloxydim-sodium was available to gardeners for control of common couch, but this was later withdrawn, although glyphosate-containing products remain effective.

Stinging nettle *Urtica dioica* always features on lists of important perennial garden weeds, although in reality it is rarely a major problem in established gardens (Fig. 74). The notorious stinging hairs seem to have given it an unjustifiably enhanced reputation. It is especially common on highly rich, fertile soils, and one common habitat is on and around neglected manure heaps. It is relatively easy to control as it is not deeply rooted, and although it produces creeping stems, clumps spread fairly slowly. The seeds survive in the soil for several years so seedlings may emerge over many seasons in vegetable and ornamental beds, but are readily controlled by hoeing. Its natural habitat seems to be damp, rich soils on sites such as river banks and places frequented by animals.

White clover is one of the commonest and most ineradicable lawn weeds. It is a plant that has become increasingly obvious during dry summers for it is clearly drought tolerant and remains conspicuously green when the grass around has turned brown. It is almost ubiquitous throughout Britain on grazed

FIG 74. Stinging nettle *Urtica dioica*, common on soils of high fertility.

grassland, but less frequent in longer grass, and it may therefore have been considerably less common in prehistoric times. Although it does produce seed, vegetative spread is much more common and important in gardens, the creeping stems rooting at the nodes. In time, extremely large patches may develop. It is difficult to control, remaining below the lawnmower blades and being relatively unaffected by many selective weedkillers.

White dead-nettle *Lamium album* is a somewhat unexpected problem weed. It looks as if it is easier to control than it is; perhaps by analogy with its annual relative, red dead-nettle (p. 122). It is also unexpected in that, like red dead-nettle, it is not native but an archaeophyte with a natural Eurasian distribution. Its British origin is not clear, but it tends to occur either close to habitation on cultivated ground or in semi-natural situations such as hedgerows and rough ground. It creates problems in gardens by virtue of its creeping rhizomes which are especially troublesome in established herbaceous borders from which it must be carefully dug out.

Enchanter's nightshade *Circaea lutetiana* is one of the less well-known garden weeds, although it can be extremely troublesome in herbaceous borders and seems particularly common in strawberry beds. It is an undistinguished-looking plant, reaching about 45 centimetres in height, with dull green leaves and tiny white flowers. I have long thought it one of the most boring British plants. It can only be dug out with difficulty as the creeping rhizomes are highly brittle. Its natural habitat is in fairly moist alkaline woodlands and it is not clear why it has adopted gardens.

Common mouse-ear *Cerastium fontanum* s.l. is a slender, trailing, densely hairy, little white-flowered plant that can form large patches on lawns. Its main means of spread is not vegetative, however, but through prolific seed production. It is susceptible to most lawn weedkillers. Although it is common in grassland almost everywhere, it also occurs in mountain habitats such as ledges and between rocks as well as on sand dunes and shingle.

The two bindweeds, field bindweed *Convolvulus arvensis* and its larger-flowered relative hedge bindweed *Calystegia sepium* (Fig. 75), still probably top most gardeners' lists of problem weeds. Field bindweed is more of a problem in herbaceous beds and shrub borders, hedge bindweed on fences, buildings and other vertical structures; it can be extremely troublesome on wire netting. Both are native throughout Britain, but are commoner in the south. While field bindweed produces large quantities of seed, especially in warm seasons, that can persist in the soil for around 30 years, hedge bindweed seeds much more sparsely and is more or less entirely dependent on vegetative spread – the aerial stems can grow back into the soil to form new rhizomes. Field bindweed is unexpectedly

FIG 75. Hedge bindweed *Calystegia sepium*, a native species largely dependent on vegetative spread.

vulnerable to frequent hoeing as the disturbance prevents it from forming creeping roots which are its most important means of spread. An old gardening maxim was to control bindweed by hoeing every weekend and so 'never let it see a Monday'. The natural habitat of field bindweed appears to be grazed grassland, that of hedge bindweed perhaps woodland edges, although it is also rather common in willow and alder carr. Both have almost certainly become commoner since the advent of gardens.

Field horsetail *Equisetum arvense* is, after Japanese knotweed *Fallopia japonica*, perhaps the weed that gardeners dread most. It is certainly in the top five of problem species by virtue of its extremely tough, creeping rhizomes from which the fertile shoots arise in spring, followed soon afterwards by the more familiar green, bristly sterile shoots which persist until well into the autumn. It is extremely difficult to dig out because the rhizomes easily fragment, and it is largely unaffected by weedkillers. Persistent use of glyphosate-containing products may weaken it, but its protective covering of silica particles renders uptake of the chemical rather poor. The name field horsetail is something of a misnomer, for whilst it is now closely associated with cultivation, both in gardens and on farms, its natural habitat is river banks, montane flushes and the coastal habitats such as fixed dune grassland and sea cliffs from which several other garden weeds have migrated.

It should be added in conclusion that a large number of spreading, invasive native plants – ramsons *Allium ursinum*, bracken, bluebells *Hyacinthoides non-scripta* and so forth – can be locally important as weeds where gardens abut or are created on their natural habitats, but they cannot be considered generally important.

CHAPTER 6

The Garden as a Habitat to which Vertebrates have Adapted

I MENTIONED IN Chapter 2 how misleading it is to equate the national garden area with a continuous expanse of land of equivalent size – the folly of reading anything into the 'area the size of Somerset' analogy. Gardens are topographically, climatically, geologically and ecologically quite different, but there is another factor too. Some important large animals, most notably deer and many raptors, are rare in gardens, while others – cats and dogs – are exceedingly common. There are about one million feral cats and a few feral dogs in Britain, but a recent survey by the Mammal Society indicated that the non-feral British domestic cat population comprises the main predators of British wildlife (Woods *et al.*, 2003). The survey estimated that 57 million mammals, 27 million birds, 5 million reptiles and amphibians and 3 million other creatures were killed by cats annually. This should not surprise anyone – the garden-inhabiting domestic cat population of around nine million is six times greater than that of all wild terrestrial predators combined. And the garden itself is the most important killing ground, paralleling its overall importance as a habitat for what are in some cases, really rather big animals. The fact that the birds, by and large, are diurnal while most of the mammals are nocturnal, gives a distorted general picture. Most garden owners do not have a clue about what goes in their gardens at night.

The adjectival phrase 'common or garden' is widely used to mean ordinary, everyday, unremarkable, of widespread occurrence, nothing unusual. It is curious therefore that only one British bird, the garden warbler *Sylvia borin*, has 'garden' as part of its recognised common name. There are no corresponding mammals, amphibians or reptiles, and few invertebrates. The Oxford English Dictionary offers garden-white for the large white butterfly *Pieris brassicae*, but this is not a name I have ever heard in use; cabbage white is the usual alternative, although even that is not generally recognised (Asher *et al.*, 2001). Garden carpet moth *Xanthorhoe fluctuata*, garden pebble moth *Evergestis forficalis* and garden tiger moth *Arctia caja* are fairly widely accepted and widely used names, along with garden chafer *Phyllopertha horticola*, garden slug *Arion hortensis*, garden snail *Helix aspersa*, garden spider *Araneus diadematus* (Fig. 76) and possibly garden centipede *Lithobius forficatus*, but that is about as far as it goes. A few native plants that are *cultivated* in gardens are colloquially called common or garden – the salad burnet *Poterium sanguisorba*, for instance, is sometimes referred to as common or garden burnet and *Atriplex hortensis* as the garden orache – but no official English names of native plants have acquired a 'garden' prefix by virtue of their natural occurrence in this habitat (Stace, 1997).

The explanation is that most colloquial animal and plant names were adopted in the seventeenth and eighteenth centuries, long before 'ordinary' folk had gardens. Garden warbler dates from as recently as 1832; before then it was called the pettychaps. The lack of 'garden' names is misleading therefore in giving no hint of the significance of gardens as habitats, breeding places or food sources to which wild animals and birds have adapted. Sometimes, as with mice and voles – and just as with native plants – the adaptation to gardens has been entirely of the creatures' own volition and gardeners have sought neither to foster nor to hinder

FIG 76. Garden spider *Araneus diadematus*, one of the few creatures with 'garden' as an epithet.

FIG 77. Birds have long found gardens useful nesting places, although the huge importance of the garden in aiding bird breeding overall has only recently been studied.

their presence. But sometimes, as with many birds, it has been with active human encouragement, and sometimes, as with rabbits, squirrels, moles and deer, in spite of active human *discouragement.*

BIRDS

It is appropriate therefore to begin with human encouragement of native vertebrates. There appears to be no historical record of when people first began deliberately to attract birds to their gardens for pleasure (as opposed to wanting to trap them for food), but it has certainly been a post-nineteenth-century phenomenon. Even 30 years ago, the only wildlife 'apparatus' likely to be found in domestic gardens were simple bird tables and bird nesting boxes, often home-made – and the latter generally with a single small hole to appeal to tits and not much else. By contrast, the commercial brand leader in Britain in 2004 offered over 50 different feeders and numerous nesting boxes. Much of the change in bird feeding came from advances in ornithological study and a recognition that different types of garden bird feed in different ways. At its simplest, there are two distinct groups – clinging feeders including titmice and many finches, and ground feeders including thrushes, robins *Erithacus rubecula* and collared doves *Streptopelia decaocto*, although some birds, like starlings, feed in both ways. A combination of table feeders (either hanging or, more usually, raised on a post to provide some protection against cats) and hanging, tubular feeders therefore appeals to a wide number of species. Table feeders range from the traditional wooden table to modern plastic or metal contraptions, some probably highly functional, but also hideous to behold. The tubular feeders are of two main kinds. Wire mesh tubes with a mesh diameter of approximately 5–6 millimetres are used to hold peanuts – the holes are too small for birds to pull the nuts out whole – while transparent plastic tubes with perches and holes at strategic intervals are used for seeds and mixed foods. Both are available in a range of sizes. I recently asked one manufacturer whether many people really bought his largest plastic tubes which are 120 centimetres long with 12 feeding holes or ports and hold 3.5 kilograms of food. I was told that many do, largely in the belief that they will have to fill them less frequently. The reality seems to be, however, that the larger the feeder and the greater the volume of available food, the larger the number of birds attracted, and so the required frequency of filling does not alter, although the cost of buying the food does. The manufacturer smiled!

Modern bird feeders often have optional protection against squirrels – surrounding wire cages for example – and one company gives a Squirrel Defence Rating (SDR) to its feeders, ranging from 'offers the very best protection' (a 5-squirrel SDR rating) to the unclassified 'will only defeat squirrel "wimps"' (Fig. 78). More recently manufacturers have suggested that squirrels tend to take the easiest option when feeding and this had led to the superficially bizarre notion of the squirrel feeder. Baited with peanuts or other food, the theory is that the squirrels will preferentially feed from there and leave the bird feeders alone. My own experience is so far equivocal.

Coincident with the increase in variety of bird feeders has come increased awareness of the importance of positioning them. The RSPB has produced a comprehensive summary of the main requirements (Anon, 2002a):

> Quiet – if possible, your bird table should be placed where the birds will not be disturbed regularly by human traffic – that is, the back garden rather than the front, and by a 'quiet' window if you have the choice. Don't, however, place it so far from the house that you can't see it – the fun of feeding birds is being able to watch them!
>
> In the open and safe – with a good all round view so that the birds can see they are safe from predators while they feed. The table should be safely away from cat ambush

FIG 78. Garden bird peanut feeder with surrounding wire cage to protect against squirrels.

sites. These include fences and trees from which cats can leap and dense bushes in which they can hide.

Sheltered – in a position where it gets neither too much sun nor too much cold wind.

With a lookout point – a small bush about two metres from the table gives the birds somewhere safe to perch while they look to see if it is safe to feed, to 'queue up' for a place on the table, and to dash to if disturbed. Bramble clippings placed around the bush will prevent cats lurking.

Mounted – a raised bird table has the advantage of being visible from the comfort of a chair. It can be placed on top of a post, hung from a branch or a bracket or even from the washing line. Some birds, however, such as blackbirds, other thrushes and chaffinches, prefer to feed on the ground, so consider providing more than one type of feeding station.

The seasonality and nature of garden bird feeding has changed too. As recently as 1989, it was being said by reputable and authoritative authors: 'The range of suitable kitchen scraps which can be fed ... is almost limitless ... Experiment with different kitchen foods ... Any type of nut will do the job ...' (Soper & Lovegrove, 1989).

Conventional wisdom and advice until recently was to feed birds principally in the winter and certainly not to do so when they were feeding their young, largely because the food offered, generally bread and kitchen scraps or peanuts, were (rightly) considered unsuitable and potentially harmful to fledglings. Again in 1989, Soper & Lovegrove said:

> Opinion is divided but in general the view is that there is no need to continue through the breeding season and the time of summer plenty: better to let the birds seek out the right natural foods especially for feeding to the young.

But it was not just young birds that were at risk from the types of foods used. The ingredients were often inappropriate for the species they were intended to benefit, and some were positively toxic. Peanuts with high concentrations of aflatoxin produced by contaminating *Aspergillus* mould were commonplace (one industry source believes most peanuts used in the mid-1980s were toxic); and some gardeners even used salted nuts. When they were available, cheap, unsophisticated mixes of cereals (wheat, barley, oats and millets) and other seeds were also put on garden bird tables and incidentally provided a common route for the introduction into gardens of some alien plant species (p. 192).

Unformulated foods relying on low quality ingredients are still sold and still used, but spurred by the overall decline in the numbers of birds, especially on farmland, research led by the RSPB and BTO has resulted in reasoned advice and the careful formulation of feeds appropriate for use all year round. The RSPB still endorses the use of 'kitchen scraps – breadcrumbs, cooked rice or potatoes, fat and fruit' and says 'It is safe to feed birds throughout the year, but don't give them peanuts in the summer unless they're in a mesh containers (big pieces of nut could choke the young)'. There has, however, been a significant move away from home-produced scraps to purpose-formulated foods. Leading manufacturers, endorsed by the research organisations, now offer a wide range of safe and beneficial products. One of the biggest changes has been the decline in the importance of peanuts from 70 per cent of the total in 1987 to around only 15 per cent in 2004, and the coincident introduction of black sunflower seeds with around 40 per cent oleic acid rich oil content. In older mixtures, any sunflower seeds used were generally larger, striped varieties which have only

30 per cent oil content and also a thicker husk that many birds cannot crack.

Sunflower kernels or 'hearts' are also now available, which have the additional benefit that there are no piles of the husk litter that can be unsightly, especially in small urban gardens. They cost around twice as much as sunflower seeds, however, because of the 50 per cent loss that occurs in hulling. A modern food mixture 'suitable for all year-round feeding' with a high oil content and high energy value might typically contain black sunflower seeds, sunflower hearts, peanut granules, kibbled maize, millet, nyjer seed (an Ethiopian member of the Asteraceae, *Guizotia abyssinica*), rapeseed, safflower seed *Carthamus tinctorius*, pinhead oatmeal, canary seed *Phalaris canariensis* and hemp. Other ingredients used in mixes intended for ground-feeding birds such as dunnocks *Prunella modularis*, finches and robins are naked rolled oats, raisins, sultanas, peanut granules, mixed corn and flaked maize. Live foods including mealworms (larvae of the grain-feeding mealworm beetle *Tenebrio molitor*), earthworms and waxworms (larvae of the greater wax moth *Galleria mellonella*) are now also available for gardeners to buy for insectivorous species such as wrens. Apart from loose seeds and other feeds, bird food 'cakes' have also been used for many years, although home-made cakes with a fat base have largely given way to various proprietary cake formulations with additions to attract specific types of bird – tallow and peanut flour for instance to appeal to tits, greenfinches *Carduelis chloris*, chaffinches *Fringilla coelebs*, woodpeckers and nuthatches *Sitta europaea*; even a 'blackcap special' containing peanut flour, tallow and dried insects to be specially attractive to insect eaters such as blackcaps *Sylvia atricapilla*, which are now overwintering in Britain in ever-increasing numbers. The importance of cleaning out bird feeders and generally being hygienic in their use has recently been recognised too. It is known that goldfinches *Carduelis carduelis*, for example, are particularly susceptible to *Salmonella* infection, while the fact that some bird diseases can be passed to humans is a further justification for caution.

The wild-bird food industry has seen enormous growth over the past quarter of a century, both in Britain and globally, and although precise data are curiously elusive, an indication of its importance can be gained from a report produced by the University of North Dakota which estimated that over the period 1991–3, around 250,000 tonnes of sunflower seed was consumed annually for bird feeding in the United States. In Britain it is estimated that in 1987, the retail value of wild bird food was about £30 million, with 10,000 tonnes of peanuts and 20,000 tonnes of seeds sold. In 2003, the retail market was believed to be worth between £150 and £180 million with a projected rise to £600–£700 million over the succeeding ten years. The potential must be partly explained by the intriguing statistic that 80 per cent of garden bird feeders are thought to be empty at any one time (Fig. 79) (Writtles, pers. comm. and Toms, 2003).

The overall result, however, is that whereas in the mid-1980s, perhaps ten species of bird were significantly attracted by garden bird foods, many more are now being fed; and gardeners are playing an invaluable role in helping to maintain the vitality of many bird species populations at a time when their traditional food sources on farmland have declined or disappeared (Chamberlain *et al.*, 2003). As I mention in relation to other forms of wildlife, however, especially butterflies (p. 235), attraction and providing a food resource is one thing, albeit important. Aiding species survival by encouraging breeding is another, and the importance of gardens for bird breeding was for long a more neglected area of study. I would guess that most people who provide bird feeding sites in their gardens do so for the almost equally important motives of

FIG 79. At any one time, 80 per cent of garden bird feeders are thought to be empty.

enjoyment and to help the bird population. I would similarly guess that most people who place bird nesting boxes in their gardens do so almost entirely for the pleasure of seeing young birds and their parents, with rather little consideration given to the impact it might have on populations at large.

Cannon (1999), representing the British Trust for Ornithology, was one of the first authors critically to consider the importance of gardens for bird conservation. And he certainly was critical. It was a compelling and thought-provoking contribution. He began on a cynical platform and it is worth quoting his opening remarks:

> What is the real global conservation value of a British suburban garden, with its neat little lawns, nut feeders and nest boxes? In my garden, fledgling blue tits Parus caeruleus, a species of no conservation concern, are busy devouring expensive imported peanuts whose production occupied prime agricultural land in a poor country. Pure entertainment, a sentimental luxury. On my patio is a table made from Vietnamese hardwood which could have been logged from precious imperial pheasant Lophura imperialis habitat (it was a gift!) and many of the plants and trees are exotic species, hosting few of the invertebrates needed to support a sustainable bird community. Historically the typical British garden, prioritizing recreation and the decorative display of botanical curiosities, exploitative and ecologically depauperate, has been a simulacrum, a hyper-reality imposed upon and substantially divorced from surrounding natural ecosystems.

Not much ambiguity there! But perhaps the most important word in Cannon's pontification was 'global', and he proceeds systematically to dismantle his own thesis and concedes that:

> ... gardens can be our training ground, not just for ornithologists ... They are a springboard from which concepts of sustainable use and respect for biodiversity are launched into the wider community ...

Moreover, the possibility that gardens might be playing a rather unexpectedly significant role was highlighted recently in a widely publicised paper from the same organisation (Bland et al., 2004). Bland and his colleagues used a questionnaire survey of 12,687 British households who were members of the Garden BirdWatch scheme (p. 146). Around half responded. Participants were asked to record the number of birds' nests in their gardens or on their house during the year 2000, and the findings were compared with those estimated in *The New Atlas of Breeding Birds* (Gibbons et al., 1993). Only nests containing at least one egg

FIG 80. Sometimes providing more feeding ports does result in more birds.

were counted, and account was taken of the type of house and the size of house and garden. The authors recognised several shortcomings in their approach – for instance, that properties belonging to members of the Garden BirdWatch scheme are not typical of the nation's gardens, that all nests in each garden were not found, that some nests are much easier to spot than others and so on, and accepted that their results were biased, but they were nonetheless able convincingly to extrapolate their findings to obtain a picture of the significance for bird nesting of British gardens as a whole (Table 11). The conclusion was that the importance of gardens for bird breeding had been seriously underestimated for some species, and the study as a whole raised some fascinating questions and options for further research. The relationship between bird feeding by householders and bird nesting populations is an obviously tempting topic.

Notwithstanding the many statistical caveats that the authors attached to their study, and the evident need for further research, it is clear that the national importance of gardens as nesting sites for some species is enormous.

TABLE 11. Estimates of numbers of pairs of birds nesting in gardens in Great Britain – with indications of the extent to which Bland *et al.* (2004) considered their estimates biased.

SPECIES	NUMBERS OF BIRD PAIRS (THOUSANDS)		
	BLAND *ET AL.* (2004)	GIBBONS *ET AL.* (1993)	
	Gardens	*All habitats other than farmland*	*Whole country*
Somewhat underestimated			
wood pigeon	492	586	2,100
collared dove	447	43	200
wren	981	1,641	7,100
dunnock	907	295	2,000
greenfinch	579	114	530
goldfinch	97	35	220
Approximately unbiased			
swift	395	–	80
robin	1,343	755	4,200
spotted flycatcher	148	11	120
jackdaw	472	108	390
chaffinch	709	1,153	5,400
Overestimated			
swallow	772	146	570
blackbird	3,259	1,040	4,400
song thrush	527	176	990
coal tit	256	64	610
starling	2,231	327	1,100
house sparrow	5,098	200	3,600
tree sparrow	286	3	110
Clearly overestimated			
house martin	1,165	–	375
blue tit	6,748	629	3,300
great tit	2,388	204	1,600

I referred earlier to the traditional nesting box of a few decades ago with its single small hole that primarily attracted tits – popularly called a tit box. Today, although there is a much wider variety of boxes available, with holes or openings of different sizes, they will inevitably, by their nature, appeal to birds that are natural cavity nesters, using hollow trees, wall or similar sites. Birds that build open nests in trees, hedges or on the ground will not be interested. The BTO suggest the following guidelines for nest boxes for different species (Table 12, Toms, 2003).

TABLE 12. Recommended nest-box type for bird species commonly using boxes.

SPECIES	BOX TYPE	SIZE	HOLE SIZE
blue tit	tit	small	25 mm
great tit	tit	medium	28 mm
coal tit	tit	small	25 mm
house sparrow	tit	medium	32 mm
tree sparrow	tit	medium	28 mm
nuthatch	tit	medium	32 mm
starling	tit	large	45 mm
jackdaw	tit	very large	150 mm
robin	open-fronted	small/medium	–
wren	tit/open-fronted	small	30 mm
pied wagtail	open-fronted	small	–
spotted flycatcher	open-fronted	small	–

But even these have now been joined by larger boxes still for owls and kestrels *Falco tinnunculus* (Fig. 81); resin and cement boxes for fixing beneath the eaves of a house to attract house martins *Delichon urbica*; tree-creeper *Certhia familiaris* boxes that lie flat along the trunk of a tree (Fig. 82) and others. The general advice over the siting of nest boxes is fairly vague and varies from facing north-east to facing south-west, but provided the box is protected from the prevailing rain and wind, it probably does not matter much. However, the presence of water in the garden is certainly an asset to attracting birds to potential nesting sites.

Television programmes, a positive plethora of bird guide books and an increasing number of wildlife magazines have all encouraged a fascination not simply in bird feeding and nesting, but also in the nature of the bird population of gardens; and there has been some, although much less significant, comparable increase in interest in other garden vertebrates. But nothing has given as great an impetus to both active and passive interest in garden birds as the officially

FIG 81. Nesting box for owls. These are usually taken over by squirrels.

organised national and local surveys. The two biggest of these, specifically targeting gardens, both have irritatingly similar and syntactically perverse names. The RSPB Big Garden Birdwatch, 'the UK's biggest garden bird survey', commenced in 1979 and is fairly limited in scope but high in popular appeal with impressive attendant publicity and sponsorship by a major house-building company. The much more extensive Garden Bird Feeding Survey of the British Trust for Ornithology was launched in 1970–1, and its successor, the on-line Garden BirdWatch scheme, 'the largest year-round citizen science project on garden birds anywhere in the world', began in 1995.

The Garden Bird Feeding Survey worked on the basis of recorders making weekly counts of those bird species using supplementary foods between October and March each year in 277 gardens. In its final year of 2001–2, the numbers of seven species (great tit *Parus major*, coal tit *P. ater*, goldfinch, wood pigeon *Columba palumbus*, great spotted woodpecker *Dendrocopus major*, nuthatch and pheasant *Phasianus colchicus*) were higher than ever before, a situation attributed to a lack of vital wild fruits in hedgerows and woodlands, an increasing reliance by birds on gardens, and improved seed-mixes and food provision. By contrast, house sparrow *Passer domesticus* and starling were the two common species at an all-time low. During the same period, a red kite *Milvus milvus* became the 162nd species to be seen at volunteers' garden feeding stations in the 32-year history of the survey.

Big Garden Birdwatch, which takes place over the last weekend in January, asks participants to spend one hour counting the birds in their garden, school grounds or local park, and to record the highest number of each species seen at any one time. In 2003, 303,000 people including 44,000 children took part. This was claimed to be the world's largest ever 'bird event'. Over 187,000 gardens were surveyed and 5,773,000 birds representing over 80 species were reported (Table 13).

FIG 82. Tree-creeper nest boxes lie flat against the trunk.

TABLE 13. National results for the 'top 10' birds in the 2003 Big Garden Birdwatch survey.

RANK	SPECIES	MEAN NUMBER PER GARDEN	TOTAL SEEN
1	starling	4.9	918,362
2	house sparrow	4.8	910,868
3	blue tit	3.1	585,052
4	blackbird	2.7	511,849
5	chaffinch	2.2	411,272
6	greenfinch	1.9	351,471
7	collared dove	1.7	317,182
8	great tit	1.5	275,444
9	robin	1.4	256,611
10	woodpigeon	1.3	248,899

For a joining donation of £12, subscribers to the BTO's Garden BirdWatch receive 'The chance to participate in an important national project – The opportunity to contribute valuable scientific information that can be used by conservationists – An 80-page Handbook on Garden Birds – A quarterly, colour magazine, *Bird Table* ... – Useful discounts off quality bird food and equipment ... – Expert advice to help you identify and look after the birds in your garden.' The scheme accepts records by paper, using forms that cover a 13-week period, or on-line, and its attraction to participants is its versatility. All it asks is that a 'simple note' is kept of the birds seen in the garden during the course of a week. How much time is spent recording is up to each participant – all that is asked is that there is consistency from one week to the next. The observations are added to a national database, building up a pattern to show 'how bird species change their use of gardens throughout the year and from one year to the next'. The continually updated results are presented on-line in a variety of ways with both national and regional summaries. The results for the 41 core species (plus marsh tit *Parus palustris* and willow tit *P. montanus*) for the first quarter of 2003 (Table 14) make an interesting comparison with those of the RSPB Big Garden Birdwatch (Table 13) which took place during the same period.

Abundance as indicated by Big Garden Birdwatch did not mirror distribution – the most widespread species in both surveys were not starling and house sparrow but blackbird, blue tit *Parus caeruleus* and robin. The importance

TABLE 14. BTO Garden BirdWatch Quarter 1 2003 compared with average Quarter 1 1995–2002.

POSITION IN 2003	SPECIES	AVERAGE PER CENT OF GARDENS REPORTING THE SPECIES 2003	AVERAGE PER CENT OF GARDENS REPORTING THE SPECIES 1995–2002	AVERAGE POSITION 1995–2002
1	blackbird	97.9	97	1.00
2	blue tit	95.7	96	2.00
3	robin	95.0	92	3.00
4	dunnock	85.0	81	5.25
5	chaffinch	83.5	83	4.50
6	great tit	82.0	81	6.00
7	greenfinch	83.0	77	8.50
8	collared dove	75.8	76	8.50
9	starling	73.6	75	9.00
10	house sparrow	73.0	78	7.25
11	woodpigeon	64.5	55	11.50
12	coal tit	51.1	48	13.13
13	magpie	50.0	53	11.88
14	wren	48.2	42	14.00
15	goldfinch	41.0	20	23.80
16	song thrush	34.7	34	15.00
17	long-tailed tit	34.6	26	17.00
18	carrion crow	25.1	27	16.88
19	siskin	24.3	17	22.38
20	jackdaw	22.7	22	18.38
21	great spotted woodpecker	22.7	19	20.00
22	pied wagtail	13.7	13	23.63
23	blackcap	13.2	11	25.00
24	nuthatch	13.2	12	24.38
25	jay	18.0	11	24.75
26	sparrowhawk	15.0	11	26.00
27	feral pigeon	13.0	11	25.38
28	bullfinch	9.6	7	31.63
29	rook	8.4	10	26.88
30	mistle thrush	8.3	10	27.00
31	goldcrest	7.0	6	32.75
32	tree sparrow	5.9	5	34.00

TABLE 14. *cont.*

POSITION IN 2003	SPECIES	AVERAGE PER CENT OF GARDENS REPORTING THE SPECIES 2003	AVERAGE PER CENT OF GARDENS REPORTING THE SPECIES 1995–2002	AVERAGE POSITION 1995–2002
33	redwing	5.4	6	33.75
34	marsh tit	4.1		
35	black-headed gull	4.0	7	31.25
36	fieldfare	3.9	4	36.25
37	tawny owl	2.9	3	38.25
38	treecreeper	2.9	3	39.00
39	brambling	2.6	4	36.50
40	yellowhammer	2.2	3	37.25
41	reed bunting	1.8	2	40.00
42	willow tit	1.6		
43	marsh/willow tit		7	31.88

© BTO 2003.

of continued monitoring is, moreover, amply demonstrated. The starling and house sparrow were consistently the most abundant garden birds throughout the 15 years of the Big Garden Birdwatch recording, yet there has been a well-publicised dramatic decline in their absolute numbers and to a lesser extent in their distribution (Tables 15 & 16).

Clearly, the significance of gardens as bird habitats has many facets and, despite the mass of data now being collected, much remains to be done. Flegg (2002), in his fine survey of what is known of the migration routes of common British birds, summarised the situation admirably:

> In the comparatively affluent latter part of the twentieth century and the beginnings of the twenty first, never have householders lavished such attention not only on their gardens but on providing nest boxes, water and foodstuffs for visiting birds. True, there are negative aspects; though modern gardens provide ample semi-natural nest sites, modern buildings (in comparison with those in the past) certainly do not, and much remains to be done to compensate for this, for example with Swifts. Natural predators like the Sparrowhawk and Magpie readily capitalise on the greater food resource available to them, the Magpie as a nest predator, the Sparrowhawk taking birds in

flight ... Dead ringed birds are far more likely to be found in towns and gardens than in the surrounding countryside, particularly if the unfortunate victim is brought in by the cat. Perhaps the best measure of the impact of these urban-related mortality factors is that most garden birds continue to flourish, a tribute to the ability of their population dynamics to soak up punishment.

TABLE 15. Starling and house sparrow – Big Garden Birdwatch national results (average number of birds per garden) for 1979, 1989, 1999 and 2003.

	1979	1989	1999	2003	CHANGE (PER CENT) 1979–2003
starling	15.0	7.9	6.0	4.9	−67
house sparrow	10	5.0	5.0	4.8	−52

TABLE 16. Starling and house sparrow – Garden BirdWatch national results (average per cent of gardens with the species) Quarter 1 1995–2003.

	1995	1996	1997	1998	1999	2000	2001	2002	2003
starling	79.0	82.1	79.9	75.8	72.5	71.3	70.5	67.3	73.6
house sparrow	82.6	83.9	82.3	79.5	76.6	73.9	72.7	71.1	73.0

MAMMALS

If the importance of gardens as habitats for birds has been neglected in the past, how much more true is this for other forms of animal life? Little serious study has been done other than on a small-scale local basis. A survey of the mammals that are seen in gardens, with over 3,500 participants, was conducted relatively recently by The Mammal Society and the People's Trust For Endangered Species, but apart from a few distribution maps, the results have not been published.

The principal group of mammals that gardeners are being encouraged to attract is the bats, paradoxically a collection of animals that most people have never seen at close quarters and would tend to shy away from if given the opportunity, and which are all but impossible to identify by the lay observer when on the wing. Nonetheless, bat conservation has had a good press, and with powerful lobbyists in the shape of the Bat Conservation Trust, local bat groups and County Naturalists' Trusts and the well-publicised legal protection all bats now enjoy, the message seems to have been understood. However, frustratingly, no sources I approached in 2003 were able to give me even an approximation of the percentage of British gardens that contain at least one bat box, let alone if these were having any effect.

Insectivores occur frequently in gardens, the common shrew *Sorex araneus* (and occasionally also the pygmy shrew *S. minutus*) along with the hedgehog being welcome, the mole emphatically not. Unlike many animals called 'the common', the species known as the common shrew really is. It is not only the most frequently found British shrew, but is also, after the field vole *Microtus agrestis*, the second commonest British mammal with a national population estimated at over 40 million. Its natural habitat is among dense grass and other vegetation in woods and at woodland edges, although it has adapted well to roadside verges, often burrowing below ground, feeding on earthworms, beetles, spiders, slugs, snails and other invertebrates. Areas of rough grass in gardens – and wildlife gardens in particular – will always attract it. Pygmy shrews are much less numerous and less likely to be seen in gardens, as much as anything because they do not burrow, prefer more open habitats and are more easily disturbed and found by cats – which kill but generally do not eat them, presumably finding the liquid produced by certain skin glands to be distasteful.

Hedgehogs are very common garden mammals (Fig. 83) – even if they are seen infrequently, their tell-tale droppings will often be found on the lawn, and on damp spring and autumn mornings, you will find trails where the dew has been disturbed as they search for food. They are especially welcome because slugs and

FIG 83. Hedgehog *Erinaceus europaeus*, attracted to gardens by the slug population.

snails are among their preferred food. Many gardeners put out food to attract them, but the often-recommended saucer of milk should be avoided as they are unable to digest it properly. Although gardens are attractive to hedgehogs, many come to grief from strimmers used to cut down long grass in which they may be sleeping, and from their custom of hibernating in bonfire heaps or compost bins. Although they are good swimmers, they can drown in straight-sided garden ponds from which there is no escape.

Moles are a different matter, however, and although they are infrequent in urban gardens, those plots adjoining open fields are always vulnerable. Although moles do not preferentially head for lawns, it certainly seems that way when their hills of discarded soil form such obvious disfigurements. Moles have been thought of as pests as long as men have tilled the land. In 1697, John Worlidge in his work *Systema Agriculturae: The Mystery of Husbandry Discovered* wrote:

> Moles are a most pernicious Enemy to Husbandry, by loosening the Earth, and destroying the Roots of Corn, Grass, Herbs, Flowers, etc, and also by casting uphills to the great hinderance of Corn, Pastures etc.

Over the centuries, they have been trapped, gassed and threatened with foul smells and electronic vibrators, and supposedly unappealing plants have been grown to deter them. The caper spurge *Euphorbia lathyris* is often suggested today as a garden deterrent, but it is as useless as anything else. Trapping has consistently proved the only really effective control measure, and mole-catching was one of the skilled and essential country crafts of the past.

Little serious study appears to have been made of the importance of gardens as a habitat for rodents, although any gardener who has ever sowed peas and beans or stored crocus corms in the garden shed will give ample testimony that there are plenty of them. Voles seem almost hypnotically attracted to crocuses, and both mice and voles remove pea and bean seeds from the ground. A common but now outlawed practice among an older gardening generation was to dress the seeds with a form of lead oxide (red lead) as a deterrent. The combined total of British voles (almost entirely bank voles *Clethrionomys glareolus* and field voles) is reckoned to be around 100 million (Yalden, 1999) and they must easily be the commonest garden mammals. Although nationally, bank voles are outnumbered by field voles by about 3 to 1, they appear to be the commoner species in gardens as they seem less timid, and are the only voles I have known to enter the house.

The commonest garden mouse by far is the phenomenally abundant wood mouse *Apodemus sylvaticus* (formerly known as the long-tailed field mouse), although locally the yellow-necked mouse *A. flavicollis* and the harvest mouse

Micromys minutus occur too (see p. 275 for the most celebrated garden appearance of harvest mice). There is also an 'indoor' mouse, the house mouse *Mus musculus*, which sometimes ventures outside, and the brown rat *Rattus norvegicus* which often does. Both are introduced rodents and both serious pests worldwide. Contrary to common belief, house mouse populations in Britain are not confined to houses and can be divided conveniently into three groups. There is a large urban group found in houses, factories and warehouses, a second rural one associated with farms, and a smaller population found in the fields. The survey reported by Langton *et al.* (2001) showed that gardens played some part in influencing the likelihood of properties to be infested with mice and rats in that the presence of domestic rabbits, chickens and caged birds markedly increased the numbers of rodents, while houses with larger and older, more mature gardens were also more likely to be seriously affected. And it was reassuring if hardly surprising to see the results of the study by Baker *et al.* (2003) that the abundance of wood mice in residential gardens was 'negatively related to the abundance of cats'. It was also negatively related to the distance from the 'nearest patch of natural or semi natural vegetation'. The dormouse *Muscardinus avellanarius* occasionally appears in gardens close to woodland and can sometimes cause problems by entering garden crop stores. Dormice may also use bird nest boxes – the Mammal Society suggests erecting boxes with the hole facing a tree trunk specifically to attract them.

Most mustelids, and more specifically the commonest species, stoats *Mustela erminea* and weasels *M. nivalis*, are not common garden visitors, much less residents, because although they are likely to find food there, they appear too susceptible to disturbance. Badgers, however, are common and potentially problematic in gardens (Fig. 84). Great Britain supports some of the highest densities of badgers in Europe, and they have taken advantage of the opportunities offered by gardens in both rural and urban areas as sources of food. Both badgers and their setts are protected under the Protection of Badgers Act 1992, although provision exists for action to be taken under a Defra licence for the purpose of preventing serious damage to property. In gardens, the most frequent damage arises to lawns when badgers dig shallow foraging pits as they seek invertebrates, including earthworms and insect larvae such as cockchafer grubs and leatherjackets. They also disrupt ornamental and vegetable beds when seeking rhizomes, corms, bulbs and tubers, and will sometimes damage low-hanging branches of fruit trees when obtaining fruit. In larger gardens, latrine pits and even setts may also be excavated and can cause serious disruption. Defra has produced guidelines on preventative measures including low-voltage electric fencing (also recommended by the RSPCA).

FIG 84. Badgers *Meles meles* are common but generally unwelcome visitors to gardens.

Deer have long been a problem in larger, rural gardens close to parkland when native roe deer or introduced and escaped fallow deer have wandered in to browse on almost any vegetation they encounter. The problem has been greatly magnified, however, with the arrival in Britain of Reeves' muntjac *Muntiacus reevesi* from Southeast Asia. Although they were first found living wild in Britain in the 1920s, it is only in the past 25 years or so that these small, dog-sized animals have spread to become what one zoologist has described as the 'ungulate equivalent of the brown rat'. They are now present across a wide swathe of the English Midlands, East Anglia and the south of England, with isolated pockets elsewhere, and although rather seldom seen, their raucous barking call is commonly heard at night, even in inner city gardens. The fact that they tend to live in pairs or as isolated individuals rather than in herds is little compensation. One muntjac in one night can do a fearful amount of damage to a garden.

Perhaps the greatest habitat change by any British mammal in recent times has been the adaptation of the fox *Vulpes vulpes* to urban living, and foxes are now common visitors to gardens almost everywhere. Although occasionally seen, their calling cards of a characteristic rank odour and holes dug where they have scavenged are familiar. The change has been well documented: a questionnaire sent to 139 local councils and 44 local mammal groups in England and Wales requesting data on changes in urban fox densities between 1987 and 1997 produced 152 responses, of which 41 per cent believed numbers had increased, 42 per cent believed numbers were unchanged and 7 per cent believed fox numbers had decreased (Wilkinson & Smith, 2001). Most of the increases were perceived to be due to increased food availability, and much of this is found in gardens – dustbins, bird tables and compost heaps as well as growing plants. Interestingly, it has separately been shown that unlike rural foxes, those living in some urban areas eat many small birds and feral pigeons. As I know to my costs, hedges and 2-metre high fences are no barrier to foxes entering gardens, and one caller recently came to within a few metres of the house one night and carefully buried a large rabbit in the centre of my knot garden, uprooting some new lavender plants as it did so.

Two other mammals are common and important garden visitors; the grey squirrel and the rabbit *Oryctolagus cuniculus*. Both are introduced species that have proved exceptionally successful, the rabbit over the course of about 900 years and the grey squirrel over not much more than 90. As recently as 1921, Edward Step was writing:

> *In some places in the London district a light grey Squirrel may be seen, and thought to be a colour variation of our native species. It is really an American visitor, distinct in colour and without tufts to the ears ... British naturalists of a not-distant future will probably have to include two species of Squirrels in their lists.* (Step, 1921)

In less than a century, the grey squirrel has become the bane of gardeners almost everywhere, presenting them with the special problems of controlling a creature that operates in three dimensions. Whilst corms and bulbs can be covered with chicken wire to prevent them from being dug up, it is almost impossible to protect anything else, and the most frustrating if not literally most serious damage often arises from squirrels digging up seeds and nuts they have buried in lawns.

Rabbits seldom have an opportunity to take up residence in other than the largest gardens, but they are highly adept at entering through or under garden boundaries to feed on plant life. Some years ago, I drew up a list of plants that rabbits were reputed not to eat, but correspondence with countless gardeners since then has resulted in most names being crossed off as one after another reported their own sorry experiences. Short of another virus disease equivalent to myxomatosis (and rabbit viral haemorrhagic disease (VHD) is a possibility), it seems nothing will stop their inexorable progress – although the huge increase in the national population of buzzards *Buteo buteo* might help. It is a salutary thought, moreover, that whilst myxomatosis reduced the rabbit population by around 95 per cent in the 1950s, it really did not take many years to recover. At least rabbits, unlike squirrels, do not swing from trees, and a wire netting boundary, turned outwards for about 30 centimetres by 90 degrees at the base and pegged down over the soil surface, will generally deter them.

REPTILES AND AMPHIBIANS

Reptiles as a group are not common garden inhabitants. Of our three native snakes, the smooth snake *Coronella austriaca* is much too rare and local, while the adder *Vipera berus*, although occurring in a wider variety of habitat than any other British snake, is generally far too intolerant of human interference and is much more likely to be found in coastal sand dunes, on chalk hills, moorland and woodlands; almost anywhere that is relatively sunny and undisturbed. The grass snake *Natrix natrix* does, however, occur in gardens relatively frequently – I expect to find at least one in my own Warwickshire garden each year, usually in or close to one of the ponds (Fig. 85). Garden compost bins are attractive places for them to hibernate, and gardeners should always take especial care when turning compost or emptying the bins in winter that no snakes (or indeed hedgehogs) are disturbed.

FIG 85. Grass snake *Natrix natrix* among exotic garden ferns.

FIG 86. Common frog *Rana temporaria* in garden lily pond.

Our two native lacertid lizards, the common lizard *Lacerta viridis* and the sand lizard *L. agilis*, are also uncommon garden animals, the latter especially so because, like the smooth snake, it is too local. The slow worm *Anguis fragilis* is found fairly regularly, however; I expect to see one perhaps every two years. They are especially welcome because they dine on slugs and they are also the most tolerant of all British reptiles of the presence of people.

The importance of gardens for amphibians is considerable and, impelled by the decline in the number of farm ponds, their role has been studied in considerable detail, not least by Trevor Beebee, co-author of the New Naturalist volume *Amphibians and Reptiles* (Beebee & Griffiths, 2000). An early study of the presence of the three commonest British amphibians, common frog *Rana temporaria* (Fig. 86), common toad *Bufo bufo* and smooth newt *Triturus vulgaris*, embraced around 200 ponds in Sussex (Beebee, 1979). Beebee found that at least half of the garden ponds included were used as breeding sites by the amphibians, in the frequency order frogs, newts and toads. They were generally scarcer near the most intensively developed areas of town centres, but neither pond volume nor local geology had a significant effect on species distribution. Presence of aquatic vegetation was also unimportant, but toads tended to be absent from ponds without fish while newts seemed to prefer such ponds – not surprising in view of the well-known fondness of fish for newt tadpoles. Beebee concluded that these three species of amphibian at least have benefited enormously from the popularity of garden ponds, and calculated that the population density of frogs in his study area was about seven animals per hectare – similar to the densities estimated for the British countryside generally in the mid-twentieth century before the well-publicised declines began. In a more recent report of a 20-year study of three ponds in his own Brighton garden Beebee speculated that there may be a natural succession in colonisation, with frogs as very effective pioneer colonisers, expanding quickly to high numbers, followed by a decline as tadpole predators such as newts become established (Beebee, 1996). He remarked that it is 'very unusual to find any type of newt doing well in goldfish ponds', although my own small water lily pond belied this for many years. There was always a thriving population of smooth newts and some frogs, although both have now declined.

FIG 87. Overgrown farm pond, Somerset, largely the result of stagnation.

CHAPTER 7

The Garden as the Route by which Alien Species have been Introduced

ORTICULTURE IN THE wide sense and gardening in the restricted sense have a great deal to answer for. Depending on your point of view and on the species concerned, they have either enriched or corrupted our natural flora and fauna. A large number of plants and a handful of animals now occur in a more or less naturalised state in Britain that would not be here without the activities of horticulturists. Sometimes their introduction into the wild has been deliberate; more commonly it has been accidental. Sometimes it has arisen through (generally unwitting) carelessness or stupidity. Standard British Floras (Clapham *et al.*, 1962; Stace, 1997) are littered with the expression 'garden escape', and the *New Atlas of the British Flora* uses two categories which embrace these and other alien plant species. Plants are divided into archaeophytes: 'a plant which became naturalised before AD 1500'; and neophytes, which became naturalised after 1500 AD.

Almost half of our current vascular plants have been introduced, the greater proportion by man and the greater proportion since 1500. I have taken a fairly subjective view of what to include here, although in most cases my selection has been relatively straightforward and I will concentrate on those that almost certainly originated in gardens where they were being grown deliberately for food or ornament, are especially interesting, have had the greatest impact on native vegetation, have been conspicuously important for whatever other reason and/or are presently increasing in the wild at a particularly rapid rate. A fairly lengthy list of 'garden plants as weeds' was given by Salisbury (1961) and even more comprehensive information may be obtained from the *New Atlas*. There are also a few plants and animals that have been introduced to Britain deliberately or accidentally for some other reason, but which have had an impact on gardens. Particularly important examples in recent years have been the southern hemisphere flatworms (p. 217f).

Clement & Foster (1994) showed that the overall alien flora of Britain is dominated by plants from Europe, many introduced accidentally, while Thompson *et al.* (2004) pointed out that garden aliens are more likely to have been introduced deliberately and to have come from more distant places, especially Japan and New Zealand (Fig. 88). In an analysis of garden plants as native or alien, they placed quadrats at random in separate cultivated borders in 60 gardens in Sheffield in July 2001 and identified all the species present. Some gardens had been carefully tended; others were 'completely overgrown and neglected'. Of the 20 most frequently recorded taxa, only three (lady's mantle *Alchemilla mollis*, montbretia *Crocosmia × crocosmiiflora* and American willowherb *Epilobium ciliatum*) were alien and I discuss these findings further in Chapter 5.

FIG 88. The origins of the 289 alien taxa of flowering plants recorded in 120 1m² quadrats in 60 private gardens in Sheffield (after Thompson *et al.*, 2004), compared with the origins of all UK alien taxa.

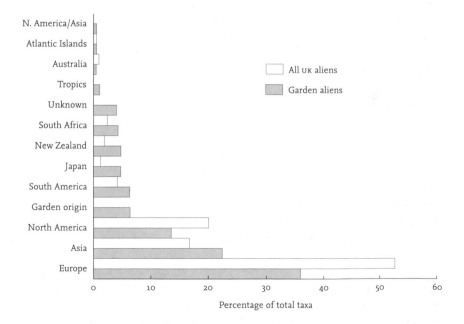

PTERIDOPHYTES

Among the lower pteridophytes (the quillworts, clubmosses and horsetails), the only garden escape is a pretty Central and South African species, Krauss's clubmoss *Selaginella kraussiana*, which was introduced in 1878 to British greenhouses where it often forms an all-embracing, lush and most attractive if invasive ground-covering carpet. Over the past century it has crept outdoors, initially in the south and west, but has since spread rather widely and with climate change bringing warmer, wetter conditions, this may be expected to continue. It might just become a problem lawn weed in milder areas in years to come.

Most of the numerous garden fern cultivars are forms of native species and relatively few of the rather commonly cultivated aliens have become naturalised, perhaps because they lack an appropriately effective dispersal mechanism. One exception, probably aided by its stoloniferous habit, is the ostrich fern *Matteuccia struthiopteris*, or, as it is sometimes called because of its distinctive shape, the shuttlecock fern. It is typically a plant of wet, cool woodland and has become especially popular for bog gardens. It was introduced to British gardens in 1760, has been established in the wild since at least 1834 and is probably increasing. It is for sale in almost every garden centre and is clearly still being widely planted by gardeners.

The one fern that has certainly become widely established to considerable effect, however, is one of the most unusual. The tiny floating water fern *Azolla filiculoides* was a British plant during interglacial periods – it is particularly common at Hoxnian sites (Godwin, 1975) – but as a native is now confined to the western Americas, although it is widely naturalised elsewhere in Europe (Fig. 89). It was first recorded in Britain in 1883 and is now widespread in ponds and waterways throughout England and Wales. Its sale and planting are now actively discouraged by all leading authorities because it multiplies vegetatively at an astonishing rate and multitudes of its extremely pretty little fronds, each barely 2 millimetres in diameter and turning bright red in autumn, quickly build up to form a porridge-like mass which can block channels as well as causing serious detriment to other aquatic life through shading and competition. It also presents an insidious danger by appearing like an inviting carpet on the surface of ponds over which children might be tempted to walk. It has been introduced to many water gardens in the form of a few contaminating fronds adhering to other water plants, although my experience has been that birds probably play a significant part in its dispersal too: a visiting pair of mallard left it as a legacy in one of my

FIG 89. *Azolla filiculoides* in a garden pond, introduced by birds.

own ponds. In an attempt to limit its further spread, responsible nurseries have deleted it from their stock lists. It has not been listed in the RHS *Plant Finder* since 2002, although it can still be found at some smaller retail outlets, and as recently as 2004, the gardening columnist of the *Sunday Times* was advising people to introduce it to their gardens as a floating ornamental. Ironically, this irresponsible advice appeared at the same time as an exhibit on the danger of invasive alien plants was winning a Silver-Gilt medal at the Chelsea Flower Show; *Azolla filiculoides* itself could not be displayed because the Royal Horticultural Society (RHS) had by then a policy prohibiting it from being sold or exhibited at any of its shows. There is some prospect of biological control of *Azolla* by a species of weevil.

WATER PLANTS

Arguably the most notorious garden escapes, and a group that collectively has probably had the greatest impact on the wider environment, are water plants. I have referred already to the water fern *Azolla filiculoides*, but there are several others, and the problems they have caused underline the vulnerability of the aquatic environment to invasive aliens of all kinds. A series of interconnecting rivers or drainage channels offers scope for them to spread quickly and widely.

It is a phenomenon that has been seen in Britain with alien frogs and fish, and the danger from introduced water plants was realised as long ago as the mid-nineteenth century.

All these species rely largely or exclusively on vegetative reproduction, and this seems to be a feature of many invasive aquatic plants throughout the world. The first warning of the trouble to come arose with the submerged North American oxygenating plant Canadian waterweed (commonly still called Canadian pondweed) *Elodea canadensis*, which has rather attractive masses of whorled leaves on highly brittle stems. It was almost certainly introduced as an ornamental (there seems to be no other reason) and was first found growing wild in Ireland in 1836 and in Britain six years later (Preston & Croft, 1997). It spread rapidly (see also p. 194), causing particularly serious problems in slow-moving waters such as canals. Subsequently, its vigour declined, and the explanation is believed to be that the original introduction was of a vigorous male clone which has slowly died out. Canadian waterweed is still widely sold, but the form now available for garden and aquarium use is a much more quietly growing female clone.

Nuttall's waterweed *E. nuttallii*, a related pond plant introduced from North America, was first found naturalised in Britain in 1966. It is also now widespread and spreading rapidly, replacing *E. canadensis* in some areas. It too is a female clone, but no longer appears to be sold to gardeners. Yet another related plant, and another female, is still being sold, and is also spreading rapidly, almost certainly as a result of material being discarded from clearing operations in garden ponds. The southern African curly waterweed *Lagarosiphon major*, formerly called *Elodea crispa*, was first found to be naturalised in Britain in 1944, and is particularly successful in base-rich waters. It does not, however, appear to be causing problems at present, although it has become extensively naturalised in New Zealand where it is known as oxygen weed and is listed as a Class B noxious weed. It would appear to be a plant that needs careful monitoring.

New Zealand pygmyweed *Crassula helmsii*, also called Australian swamp stonecrop and formerly known as *C. recurva* or *Tillaea recurva*, was until recently widely available at aquatic plant nurseries and garden centres, although its sale is now actively discouraged. It is thought to have been introduced to Britain from Tasmania in 1911 but was not available commercially until 1927 when it was sold as an oxygenating plant at Amos Perry's Hardy Plant Farm at Enfield, Middlesex, a particularly well-known establishment. *Crassula helmsii* was first found growing naturally in 1956 some distance away at Greensted Pond near Ongar, Essex, and in recent years it has spread quickly and aggressively. It forms small, pale green tussocks on sediments at a depth of up to 3 metres. These merge rapidly to form a dense vegetation mat that is a highly effective competitor, depleting oxygen and severely limiting the growth of other aquatic flora and fauna.

Parrot's feather *Myriophyllum aquaticum* is an extremely pretty, feathery, submerged plant from Brazil that has been widely planted in British water gardens since its introduction in 1878. It too is thought to have been spread into the wild when garden ponds were cleared out, and it was first recorded as a naturalised species in Surrey in 1960. It has since spread extensively in the southern half of Britain and causes huge problems in lakes, reservoirs and canals, depleting oxygen, causing shade and generally choking other aquatic life. It too seems fortunately to have been withdrawn from sale in most major retail outlets, and its planting is in any event unnecessary because the native spiked water-milfoil *M. spicatum* performs a comparable oxygenating role much less aggressively. In reality, my own experience and view is that all submerged plants are quite superfluous for oxygenating purposes in any domestic garden pond if a fountain or comparable means of oxygenating the water is provided. They do, however, supply invaluable spawning and breeding areas for fish and other pond creatures.

Floating pennywort *Hydrocotyle ranunculoides* is a North American species easily confused with the native marsh pennywort *H. vulgaris*, but it has thinner, larger leaves. It is a particular cause for concern as it seems to be spreading extremely rapidly by a range of efficient means: rooted plants flower and set seed while floating plants reproduce vegetatively. It was first found naturalised in Essex in 1990, and although no longer listed by major water garden suppliers, it is almost certainly still being sold by some smaller outlets. It is highly competitive when established and in 2004 eradication measures in non-garden water habitats were estimated to be approaching £300,000 in herbicide costs.

CONIFERS

Most of the numerous naturalised species of coniferous trees almost certainly escaped from forest plantings rather than gardens; in most cases, even those planted as ornamentals tend to be, or have been, grown for timber too. Certainly most are much too large to have reached maturity and seed production in any small home gardens, although for up to 400 years some have been planted extensively on larger estates and landscaped parks. Several were recorded growing wild within a relatively short time after their introduction. Austrian pine *Pinus nigra* was introduced in 1814 and was recorded growing wild within 100 years. Others took much longer; one of the first introductions, European silver fir *Abies alba*, for instance, took some 300 years after its arrival in 1603 before it was recorded in the wild, although the delay in finding it may simply be because no-one looked. The extreme example, however, must be Norway spruce, still the species most widely used as a Christmas tree. It was a British interglacial native and although Harvey (1981) claimed it was among the plants being grown in Anglo-Saxon gardens in 995, it was not recorded growing wild until 1927.

There are six important large naturalised conifers that have seldom if ever been grown here as timber trees and that owe their existence in Britain solely to their ornamental appeal in big gardens. Three of them are cedars, now all usually considered distinct species: cedar-of-Lebanon *Cedrus libani*, the North African atlas cedar *C. atlantica* and the Himalayan deodar *C. deodara*. Interestingly, all three cedars occur in the wild in Britain with comparable frequency and distribution even though *C. atlantica* and *C. deodara* are Victorian introductions, while *C. libani* is much older, having been introduced in 1638–9, and was always much more widely planted. For over 300 years, scarcely a grand English garden worthy of the name was without its cedar-of-Lebanon. Now all three species are widely naturalised throughout England and Wales, and a detailed survey of their occurrence in relation to the proximity of stately homes would be interesting.

The three other conifers are two massive western North American trees, the coastal redwood *Sequoia sempervirens* and the wellingtonia *Sequoiadendron giganteum*; and the South American monkey-puzzle *Araucaria araucana* (Fig. 90). The coastal redwood was introduced to Britain in 1844 and is fast growing and very big; examples in its native California are currently probably the tallest trees in the world. The comparably sized wellingtonia arrived here seven years later and both species are now naturalised widely throughout England, Wales and Scotland. The curiously ungainly monkey-puzzle, which needs to be very big to look remotely attractive, was introduced in 1795. It became a favourite of Victorian gardeners and was almost obligatory in nineteenth-century gardens – not necessarily large ones, as the many examples of big trees in rather small urban front gardens still testify. Although large monkey-puzzle trees produce cones and abundant seed, regeneration seems relatively infrequent, which partly explains why it has such a sparse and scattered naturalised distribution. Clearly, the fact that is so distinctly different from anything else and so profoundly ugly must also draw attention to it and militate against seedlings being allowed to survive.

One of the most curious neophyte records in the *New Atlas* is of a plant that is not only a garden escape, but is also undoubtedly of garden origin. Currently the fastest growing tree in Britain, Leyland cypress × *Cupressocyparis leylandii* (*Chamaecyparis nootkatensis* × *Cupressus macrocarpa*) is a hybrid that has arisen here

FIG 90. The South American monkey-puzzle *Araucaria araucana* is not necessarily a wise garden choice.

several times, first at Leighton Hall garden in Montgomeryshire in 1888. There are several cultivars of it, some of which flower, but all are sterile, so the rather extensive naturalised distribution recorded in the *New Atlas* must be solely the result of trees having been deliberately planted in the wild. The late Alan Mitchell, the renowned tree expert, writing in 1985, predicted that 'unless wholesale topping and clipping starts very soon, all these areas [in town and suburban gardens] will in 40 years be under dense forest 30 m tall'. This has not quite happened, but the plant has on various occasions been the subject of threatened Government legislation to restrict its planting, especially in the form of hedging. The Control of Residential Hedgerows Bill 1998/1999 did not reach a second reading; The Statutory Nuisances (Hedgerows in Residential Areas) Bill (1999/2000) did reach report stage in the House of Lords, but then failed to progress further, while the Private Member's High Hedges Bill 2000/2001, despite Government support, failed to complete all its stages of scrutiny before the 2001 general election, and so also did not become law. Eventually, so-called 'nuisance hedges', which are not by any means restricted to Leyland cypress, fell under a more general piece of legislation, The Anti-social Behaviour Act 2003, the relevant part of which, Section 8, became law in June 2005.

Leyland cypress notwithstanding, the most successful ornamental coniferous tree species in Britain is the western North American Lawson's cypress. It was not introduced until 1854, but now exists in more cultivars than any other tree, a consequence of it being highly variable, hybridising freely and regenerating extremely readily from seed. The current edition of the RHS *Plant Finder* lists 200 cultivars presently available. Although it is used as a shelter-belt, most plantings are undoubtedly in gardens and it is from there that it has become so extensively naturalised.

Although grown primarily as a timber tree, one naturalised conifer, albeit a deciduous one, cannot be ignored, simply because it is so stunningly beautiful and is found in many gardens, sometimes fairly small ones. The European larch *Larix decidua* was in cultivation here by 1629 as it is mentioned by Parkinson (1629), although he considered it rare, but by the time John Evelyn published the first edition of his *Sylva* (Evelyn, 1664) trees of considerable stature were established. Seventy years later Miller (1731) said they were 'now pretty common in English Gardens'. Although European larch sets seed freely and germination and seedling growth are good in exposed localities with poor soil, seedlings are rarely found beneath lowland garden trees. Nonetheless, it is well established throughout Britain and was considered naturalised by 1886. Among the early Scottish sites where European larches were grown was Dunkeld, and following the subsequent planting on the Duke of Atholl's estates there of a later

FIG 91. Lawson's cypress *Chamaecyparis lawsoniana* exists in more varieties than any other tree.

introduction, the Japanese larch *Larix kaempferi*, a novel and vigorous fertile hybrid now called *Larix* × *marschlinsii* first appeared at the beginning of the twentieth century. It too is now naturalised.

NON-CONIFEROUS TREES AND SHRUBS

Although there are many introduced non-coniferous trees among the British flora, few have arrived via gardens, and almost certainly none via small domestic gardens for the same reason as conifers – the gardens are simply not big enough for the trees to reach maturity and reproduce. Large country house gardens and historical estates have again, however, played their part. Two of the longest-established and most imposing of the introduced trees are close relatives and close European contemporaries: sycamore (Fig. 92) and Norway maple *Acer platanoides*. Sycamore was introduced to Britain in the sixteenth century and was recorded in the wild as long ago as 1632. It was extensively planted from the eighteenth century onwards, notably in the large landscaped parks that were so much in favour at the time (p. 17f). It was also planted as an effective coastal shelter belt tree, and to some extent still is, as it is highly tolerant of salt spray. It has also proved extremely valuable in colonising and stabilising sand dunes.

FIG 92. Self-sown sycamore *Acer pseudoplatanus* colonising a railway embankment, Derbyshire.

Sycamore is a highly effective and aggressive competitor, spreading far and quickly into a wide range of habitats by producing a huge number of fertile seeds, as any gardener with one nearby will testify. It is probably the most successful alien tree in Britain, certainly as far as its distribution goes: it is now present in almost every 10-kilometre grid square in Britain and Ireland. Ironically, its former horticultural popularity obscures the fact that it is a poor garden plant, growing too large too quickly and, quite apart from its production of vast numbers of offspring, it is a 'dirty' tree, attracting large numbers of aphids which excrete honeydew that in turn attracts sooty moulds. But aphids aside, it appeals to little wildlife and its contribution to biodiversity is dismal.

Norway maple has much more quietly gone about the same business, although it is less successful at altitude than sycamore. It was introduced to Britain some time before 1683 and was naturalised by 1905. Unlike sycamore, it has much to commend it as a garden tree, albeit a big one (it has an Award of Garden Merit from the RHS), although it is one of the most variable large deciduous trees and the purple-leaved forms such as 'Crimson King' are more usually seen. Because of its continuing popularity, it is still being extensively planted in gardens and in consequence, is continuing to spread by seed into the wild.

Where would the English village be without its 'spreading chestnut tree' and conker matches? Yet this most archetypal of spring flowering trees, equally at home on village greens and cricket grounds, is an alien. The horse chestnut *Aesculus hippocastanum* was introduced from the Balkans around 1612 and, like other large deciduous trees, contributed to the flora of the landscaped park. It has always been too big and wide spreading for domestic gardens, and its present distribution is probably due as much to it being planted in public places as in genuinely private gardens, of whatever size. It seeds abundantly, but seedling growth is not good and, according to the *New Flora*, it is rarely fully naturalised.

Two alien oaks are well naturalised in Britain and both were almost certainly introduced as garden plants. The Turkey oak *Quercus cerris*, from southern Europe and south-western Asia, was being cultivated in Britain by 1735 and it was recorded as naturalised by 1905. It is an efficient coloniser with prolific seed production and has extended widely onto waste ground and from there into grassland and heaths. *Quercus cerris* is one parent of an interesting and most handsome semi-evergreen hybrid tree, the Lucombe oak *Quercus × crenata* (*Q. cerris* × cork oak *Q. suber*), which arose in the Exeter nursery of William Lucombe (now the municipal Pinces Gardens) around 1762, only 30 years after Turkey oak's first introduction. It is a variable plant but, fairly unusually for a hybrid, is fertile and it too has now begun to spread throughout England and was naturalised by 1964. Probably the most obvious and familiar naturalised exotic oak, however, is the Mediterranean evergreen oak *Q. ilex*, the familiarity stemming from the very fact that it is the only common evergreen oak and is almost the only very large, fully hardy evergreen tree of any kind. It has been cultivated in gardens since the sixteenth century and was an important tree (because of its large, evergreen habit) in landscaped parks. It is also commonly seen in churchyards and cemeteries. It was reported to be fully naturalised by 1862 and is an aggressive and vigorous competitor that is still actively spreading.

Many species, varieties and cultivars of *Prunus* have escaped locally from gardens and a few have become established more widely. The most notable ornamental is Japanese cherry *P. serrulata* with its white, pink-tinged flowers, a Chinese garden plant introduced to Britain from Canton in 1822. It produces seed and is naturalised in scattered localities and may still be spreading actively. This is unlikely to be as a result of fresh garden escapes, as the species itself has fallen from favour as a garden plant having been replaced by various cultivars, most conspicuously the sterile double-flowered form 'Kanzan'. Because of (or more appropriately, despite) its almost luminous masses of bright pink flowers, 'Kanzan' became one of the most widely planted flowering trees after the Second World War, in streets as well as gardens. Curiously it too is now recorded as naturalised, presumably as a result of deliberate plantings, but, thankfully, it is now in decline as a result of a debilitating dieback disease of unknown etiology (Buczacki & Harris, 2005).

Cherry plum *Prunus cerasifera* has been cultivated since the sixteenth century and is now extensively naturalised, although it infrequently sets seed. By contrast, wild plum *P. domestica*, one of the plants that Harvey (1981) considered an Anglo-Saxon garden tree, is extensively naturalised on waste ground and in hedgerows. The origin of wild populations of plum is generally obscure. Whilst many must be relics of cultivation, plum stones discarded by travellers must also be the source of many apparently wild trees. Another species of *Prunus* that has made its presence felt in the British countryside is the Balkan cherry laurel *P. laurocerasus*. This is a quick-growing, large-leaved and hardy evergreen shrub or small tree (up to about 7 metres tall) that became especially popular in Victorian gardens as a shrub and hedging plant. It was the species most responsible for the epithet 'gloomy' being so often attached to descriptions of nineteenth-century garden shrubberies. It sets seed fairly freely, was naturalised by 1886 and seems to be spreading actively, aided no doubt by its continuing popularity for amenity planting on roadsides and other places as ground cover, although the low spreading cultivar 'Otto Luyken' is now generally preferred to the species.

Among other fruit trees, cultivated pears *Pyrus communis* s.l., which have long been cultivated here (Murphy & Scaife, 1991), are often found naturalised, but they probably result from humans throwing cores away in the countryside rather than genuine spread from gardens by fruit-collecting birds and mammals. Apples also occur naturalised, but it is difficult to distinguish plants of garden origin (*Malus domestica*) which also commonly originate from cores, from native crab apples (*M. sylvestris* s.s.). Most bush fruits also have a comparably long and uncertain history, although blackcurrant *Ribes nigrum* was not grown in British gardens until the seventeenth century, and so the now widespread wild populations must be either escapes or relics. Gooseberry *R. uva-crispa* has a much longer history as a garden plant and was being grown in Britain in the thirteenth century. It too is now widespread.

Although several types of poplar are naturalised in Britain, almost all originated from trees grown for timber or as windbreaks or screening. Two that have, however, been planted extensively in landscaped parks and gardens and from where some spread may have occurred are forms of the Italian Lombardy poplar *Populus nigra* and the hybrid black poplar *Populus* × *canadensis* (*P. deltoides* × *P. nigra*), which is of garden origin and probably arose in France around the middle of the eighteenth century.

Walnut *Juglans regia* is probably of south-west Asian origin, but it was growing in Roman gardens in Britain (p. 5) (Murphy & Scaife, 1991) and is now widely naturalised, its spread almost certainly enhanced since the nineteenth-century arrival of grey squirrels, which are especially fond of collecting and burying its nuts.

Although two British lime species, the large-leaved lime *Tilia platyphyllos* and the small-leaved lime *T. cordata*, are native for at least part of their range, the more common and familiar tree is the hybrid between them *Tilia* × *europaea*, which is almost exclusively planted. It is not and should not be a tree for small gardens as it not only grows large, but is notoriously aphid-prone and drips honeydew onto any seats, cars and people who happen to be parked beneath. It has, however, been a popular parkland tree since the late seventeenth century and was especially favoured for lining grand entrance drives because it is almost always propagated vegetatively, a procedure that guarantees uniformity. In reality, hybrid limes set seed rather sparsely, and the extensive and widespread distribution suggests that most spread has been by suckering from numerous plantings.

Laburnum *Laburnum anagyroides* is native to the mountains of central Europe and as it was mentioned by Gerarde (Gerarde, 1597), it was clearly in cultivation here before the end of the sixteenth century. It was naturalised by 1879. It became a popular garden tree for its mass of early yellow flowers, relatively small size (rarely more than 10 metres) and hardiness: 'No foreign tree is better adapted to our climate' (Bean, 1973). It is also a prolific seed producer and has spread widely, especially onto waste ground; it is commonly found in much the same places as *Buddleja davidii* (see below). It is still spreading rapidly, although there is likely to be little further augmentation from gardens because old trees are gradually disappearing (laburnums tend to be fairly short-lived, often succumbing to decay) and modern garden plantings are of more floriferous forms, especially the beautiful *Laburnum* × *watereri* 'Vossii', which does not produce any of the notoriously poisonous seed.

The butterfly bush *Buddleja davidii* was a late but astonishingly successful arrival in British gardens, introduced from China at the very end of the nineteenth century (Fig. 93). The many earlier references to garden buddleias were to the South American orange-ball tree *B. globosa*, which is only a rare escape from cultivation. The butterfly bush by contrast soon began to appear everywhere, especially on waste ground and in urban situations, colonising walls, old buildings and railway embankments. It is the floral welcome to Euston and

FIG 93. Buddleia *Buddleja davidii* has colonised waste ground everywhere.

FIG 94. *Fuchsia magellanica* from South America is a familiar sight in planted and naturalised habitats especially in the west of Britain.

many other railway stations. It continues to spread rapidly although now, as with laburnums and numerous other flowering shrubs, with little addition from gardens where its place has largely been taken by more attractive cultivars, many of them of hybrid origin and many of them sterile.

Two evergreen South American shrubs that are accepted as everyday plants in milder and especially in coastal areas where they have escaped from gardens are escallonia *Escallonia macrantha* and fuchsia *Fuchsia magellanica* (Fig. 94). Escallonia was introduced around 1847, fuchsia in 1788, and both were and still are used as attractive hedging in many seaside gardens, particularly in the west. Escallonias set viable seed while fuchsias spread by suckering, but both have been similarly successful, and the landscape of many parts of western Britain would be the poorer without them. Both species are still widely planted in gardens because although there are now many cultivars and hybrids, especially of *Fuchsia*, most are derived from different species and have different attributes and appeal.

Cotoneasters are among the most popular of garden shrubs and are grown principally for their prolific production of ornamental fruits, most of which contain viable seeds, so it is hardly surprising that many of them should have become naturalised. Probably well over 100 species, hybrids and cultivars are established as garden escapes in one or more parts of Britain, but I will mention only two of the most familiar, both deciduous. In general the deciduous species seem to have become naturalised as garden escapes more successfully than the evergreen forms. The wall or herringbone cotoneaster *Cotoneaster horizontalis* is now so common and so well known that it is hard to believe it was not introduced to Britain from China until 1879, reaching us via France where seed had been sent by the missionary plant collector Père Armand David. It must be one of the most widely planted of all shrubs, its fruits are highly attractive to birds and its flowers to bees, and seedlings are common in gardens wherever it is grown. The mystery, therefore, is why it was not recorded in the wild until 1940, although it is now spreading rapidly, especially onto waste ground and fairly bare, rocky places. The Himalayan *C. simonsii* is almost equally familiar and has been grown almost as extensively since its introduction to gardens in 1865, but it has naturalised more quickly and perhaps more extensively. Whilst *C. horizontalis* is now planted rather less than it used to be, *C. simonsii* remains highly popular, as much in amenity planting schemes as in domestic gardens, so its spread is being further encouraged.

Probably because flowering shrubs tolerant of dry shade are at a premium, that most robust but workaday species the Oregon grape *Mahonia aquifolium* remains popular. Despite its familiarity in North America, it was not brought to Britain until 1823. It rapidly gained favour, not only for ornamental garden use, but also as game cover – after the breech-loading shotgun was effectively married with the centre fire cartridge in the 1860s, such things took on a huge importance. Not only does Oregon grape produce plenty of bird-dispersed seeds, it also spreads readily by suckering, so was always admirably equipped to break out of gardens. It is now well established in woodland, hedgerows and other dry shady places throughout much of England. It has been joined in such habitats by two low-growing, evergreen, ground-smothering plants, the European periwinkles: the lesser *Vinca minor* and the greater *V. major*. Harvey (1981) believed the archaeophyte lesser periwinkle featured in Anglo-Saxon gardens, and the greater periwinkle too has been here a long time; it was recorded by Gerarde in 1597, and is considered to be a neophyte. Their success has been attributed to a means of dispersal that is becoming rather frequent. Because they are both fairly vigorous, growth in gardens often has to be thinned and large quantities of material are commonly dumped, a procedure that has become known as green fly-tipping.

In some areas, woodlands have all but been subsumed by one of the few shrubs to be so vigorous and to have been so successful a competitor as commonly to be called a 'woody weed'. *Rhododendron ponticum* from the Pontic Alps on the Black Sea coast of Turkey and also from the Iberian Peninsula was introduced to Britain as a garden plant in the late eighteenth century. Like that other invasive 'alien' *Azolla filiculoides*, it was present here during the interglacials. The year 1763 is often cited as the date for its artificial reintroduction, although Bean (1973) believed that whilst seeds may have been acquired by Kew in that year, it did not become commercially available until it appeared a few years later in the stock of the nurseryman Conrad Loddiges, whose career at the celebrated nursery in Mare Street, Hackney did not start until 1770. Recent research (Milne & Abbott, 2000) suggests our stock originated mainly from Spain.

It has been said that *Rhododendron ponticum* was not an immediate garden success because the beautiful purple-mauve flowers were of a shade not popular at the time; and it was expensive. It has also been claimed that the inhospitable winter of 1878–9 (one of the only two winters on record when the mean temperature in England and Wales was below freezing for two consecutive months) was its making because it survived the extreme cold when many other plants failed. It soon escaped from gardens, began to be planted as game cover and was first recorded growing wild in 1894. On British acidic soils, it found conditions greatly to its liking and, aided by its copious production of wind-dispersed seeds, high fertility, laterally spreading growth habit and overall vigour, it has had a most serious impact since the first half of the twentieth century on many native habitats. The markedly lateral spreading habit has been a particularly advantageous feature, meaning it can create dense shade over relatively wet areas while its roots remain in drier soil nearby. It has had a major impact in overwhelming small woodland streams, and is believed to have had an adverse effect on fish such as trout that depend on other types of streamside vegetation for a supply of insects. By altering habitats through its aggressive competitiveness, it has been blamed (probably correctly although not always with the fullest evidence) for the demise of some woodland butterflies, birds and other creatures – dormice are often mentioned. It prevents the successful growth of tree seedlings and woodland regeneration, interferes with the ease of logging and forest management and also has foliage that is tough, unpalatable and possibly poisonous to livestock. Even the fact that the large flowers are immensely attractive to many pollinating insects, especially bumblebees, is held against it because there is evidence that they are preferentially attracted to rhododendron flowers to the detriment of other, less showy native species. And, needless to say, it is difficult to control by either chemical or physical means. Arguably no other plant, introduced with the best of intentions to British gardens, has had such a major, long-term impact on the wider environment.

A shrub with a somewhat comparable British history is the North American snowberry *Symphoricarpos albus* which was introduced in 1817 as a garden plant and used later as game cover. The flowers are small and pink, not objects of great beauty, but the masses of spherical white fruits that inspired the common name are rather striking. It is a plant with which gardeners soon become bored, however, and they often dig it up and throw it away. This action, combined with its planting for game, means it is now naturalised widely throughout almost all of the British Isles except the Highlands and west of Scotland. Most of the spread, however, is by suckering, as regeneration from seed is infrequent, partly no doubt because despite their appetising appearance, the fruits are effectively ignored by birds.

There are many native rose species in Britain and many thousands of cultivars in British gardens. Most garden roses are sterile, perpetuated by the grafting or budding skill of nurserymen, and only one alien has become seriously naturalised as a garden escape. The atypical, coarse-foliaged and remarkably tough *Rosa rugosa* was introduced from Japan and neighbouring parts of eastern Asia in 1796, and is not in reality among everyone's favourite garden roses, although cultivars such as 'Fru Dagmar Hartopp' and 'Roseraie de l'Häy' are undeniably beautiful (Fig. 95). It has, however, become popular because of its value for rose hedging and for its toughness as an amenity plant in such unlikely locations as the central reservations on dual carriageways. That it has become so

FIG 95. *Rosa rugosa* has the merit of single flowers that attract insects, unlike most cultivated roses.

FIG 96. Duke of Argyll's tea plant *Lycium barbarum.*

widely naturalised over the past century or so is in part from these origins, but also because it has been used extensively as a rootstock:

> It is these which appear almost from nowhere, in derelict gardens as the result of having reproduced themselves from the original root of a standard rose, having long ago cast off its enforced, more delicate charge ... (Beales, 1977)

When I began reclaiming my own Warwickshire garden after its years of dereliction, I discovered that a once fine old boundary hedge of native species had been effectively taken over by a botanical conundrum. I called the interloper *Lycium barbarum*, the Duke of Argyll's tea plant (Fig. 96) because, until recently, there has been some doubt over the correct identity of the two *Lycium* species, which has now been resolved. There seems to be some confusion over the Duke of Argyll too, and the plants are sometimes called Chinese box thorns instead. They are willowy, prickly deciduous shrubs, the very devil to remove, and produce masses of viable bird-transmitted seed, and it is small wonder they have adapted so well to the British countryside. They came to Britain before the end of the seventeenth century and were particularly favoured as screening in coastal gardens due to their relative tolerance of salt spray. I have seen other hedges too that were quite simply unable to compete.

Another group of naturalised flowering shrubs that are considered botanically difficult are the spiraeas, called brideworts by botanists although hardly ever by gardeners. They originate from a wide range of temperate localities across the northern hemisphere and have been grown in British gardens since at least the mid-seventeenth century; the assertively rich-red flowered 'Anthony Waterer', a clone of *Spiraea japonica* dating from around 1880, has long been among the most popular garden shrubs. In one form or another, these spiraeas are now widely established in hedges, fairly fertile waste ground and on river banks, many from garden discards.

Gardeners either love lilacs or loathe them. Their flowers are beautiful and fragrant for a few weeks, but after this they die disgracefully and all that remains is month after month of dismal foliage. So familiar is *Syringa vulgaris*, however, that most gardeners would probably hazard a guess at it being native rather than introduced from south-eastern Europe. In reality it is a 'pre-Gerarde' plant, described by him in his herbal (1597) but probably not here for long before then. Its heyday was the nineteenth century, and most of the numerous single- and double-flowered cultivars date from then or from the early years of the twentieth. It became a widespread practice to graft them onto wild lilac rootstock which suckers copiously, and it is largely by this vegetative spread that lilac has now left gardens and become so familiar a feature of the wider environment into which it continues to spread with ever greater enthusiasm.

Shrubs with classically daisy-shaped flowers are always popular with gardeners and one of the longest in cultivation is the yellow-flowered evergreen Mediterranean silver ragwort *Senecio cineraria*, which was being grown in gardens here by the first quarter of the seventeenth century. It was naturalised by the early nineteenth century and is now especially common on waste ground and on coastal sites. There has for years been confusion about the real identity of the yellow-flowered shrubby 'senecios' and one of the commonest, a plant of garden origin long called *Senecio greyi* but now known as *Brachyglottis* 'Sunshine', is also becoming increasingly established in the wild, especially in coastal sites such as sand dunes.

Among the many species of *Hypericum* are shrubs that gardeners call 'thugs';
coarse, relatively unattractive, aggressive, invasive plants that turn on other
inhabitants of the garden. It is surprising that more have not become naturalised,
but one of the most important is of south-east European origin: rose-of-Sharon
H. calycinum. Its spread within gardens is by vigorous suckering and the situation
in the wild where it has become established on railway sides and waste places
is evidently similar. It was introduced in 1676 and, as the *New Atlas* points out:

*All naturalised plants appear to have been derived from the original introduction, as
fertile seed is sparsely and erratically produced owing to self-incompatibility. Damp
autumns also reduce seed-set, and seed and the rare seedlings suffer predation by
sparrows.*

The western North American tree lupin *Lupinus arboreus* is a curious plant in
that it is not especially widely grown, popular or familiar in gardens, although it
does have an RHS Award of Garden Merit. It was introduced in 1793 and was long
treated as half-hardy. In recent years, however, it has spread rapidly through its
copious production of fertile seeds, and is now threatening native sand-dune
vegetation in some coastal localities; it is used in New Zealand and other areas
for sand-dune stabilising.

Three important foliage shrubs, two in particular used widely as hedging
plants, have escaped from gardens. One, box, is native but is generally believed
to be so only in a few restricted localities, such as Box Hill, Surrey, and its
present extensive distribution, especially in England, is believed to be due to
its enormous popularity in formal hedging for which it has been used since
the Roman occupation (p. 5). In recent years, dieback caused by the fungus
Cylindrocladium buxicola has been an increasing and serious problem in gardens
on box and its cultivars, including the popular 'Suffruticosa' often used for dwarf
hedging. However, it seems unlikely that this will be important on naturalised
plants because the fungus is favoured by the dense, tight foliage produced as
result of continual close clipping.

The archetypal English garden hedge for many years was privet. Sometimes
the native *Ligustrum vulgare* was used, but the broader-leaved Japanese species
L. ovalifolium, now called garden privet, has largely replaced it. Following its
introduction in 1842, it achieved widespread popularity, as much as anything
because it would tolerate atmospheric pollution in towns and would grow in dry,
impoverished soil where little else could survive. It has been called boring, but
compared with Lawson's cypress and other conifers that gradually took its place
in the years following the Second World War, this seems a hollow criticism. It is

FIG 97. Bay *Laurus nobilis*, an important naturalised evergreen shrub.

now widely distributed throughout lowland Britain, largely as a result of green fly tipping as gardeners oust it in favour of something else.

The third of the important naturalised foliage shrubs is bay *Laurus nobilis*, a Mediterranean native that has been grown here since Roman times, but has only recently begun to spread extensively in the south of England (Fig. 97). I can see two possible reasons for this: with warmer summers, bay increasingly sets viable seed which is bird carried, while warm and moist conditions may mean more ready rooting of clippings, tipped out from gardens.

HERBACEOUS PLANTS

The number of naturalised herbaceous plant species to have arrived in the countryside through gardens is legion. One of the most widespread and certainly one of the most striking and obvious, because of its vivid orange flowers, is monbretia *Crocosmia × crocosmiiflora*. It is a relative newcomer, however, a hybrid raised in France in 1880 from two South African species, *Crocosmia aurea* and *C. pottsii*. Within 20 years, it was established in the wild in Britain and is still spreading rapidly. I suspect this is yet another example of gardeners having tired of it, dug it up and thrown it out, as although it does set some viable seed, most spread is vegetative.

Crane's-bills or geraniums (sometimes called hardy geraniums to distinguish them from their less hardy relatives in *Pelargonium*) are increasingly popular as garden perennials, and it is perhaps unexpected that so few of the many forms grown have become naturalised. One problem may be the difficulty of certain identification by plant recorders as there are many cultivars, confusingly similar to each other and to their parent species. The beautiful deep-purple-flowered central European dusky crane's-bill *Geranium phaeum* (sometimes called the mourning widow by gardeners) has, however, been known in the wild since 1724 and is extensively established in shaded, relatively undisturbed places (it is rather common in churchyards). In gardens, one of the most vigorous geraniums and one that self-seeds with abandon is Druce's crane's-bill *Geranium × oxonianum* (*G. endressii × G. versicolor*) (Fig. 98) and it is no surprise that both it and its parent French crane's-bill *G. endressii* now occur in the wild.

Two garden perennials on the list of plants officially called invasive aliens are considered so damaging to the wider environment that under the provisions of the Wildlife and Countryside Act 1981 they may not legally be introduced into the wild. As always with such legislation, this is closely akin to bolting the stable

FIG 98. Druce's crane's-bill *Geranium × oxonianum*, a widespread self-seeding hybrid.

door far too late. The most monstrous, in every way, is giant hogweed *Heracleum mantegazzianum* from south-west Asia. I suspect it is the tallest herbaceous perennial in Britain, reaching almost 6 metres in height. It was introduced early in the nineteenth century for its statuesque appearance, but soon gained an evil reputation. It is a prolific seeder that has spread rapidly, subjugating all in its path, and more recently it has been found to be a cause of dermatitis. The general ignorance of such matters displayed by many so-called gardening 'experts' was exemplified when, within the past few years, the presenter on a major national television programme displayed *H. mantegazzianum* as an interesting architectural plant.

The second prohibited perennial is perhaps the most dangerous plant in Britain, Japanese knotweed *Fallopia japonica* (Fig. 99). It too was introduced to gardens early in the nineteenth century and was recommended and sold widely by the great and the good of horticulture, including some of the most celebrated gardening names of the period. The utterly fascinating story of the introduction, sale and dissemination of *F. japonica* and its two close relatives (below) has recently been unravelled (Bailey & Conolly, 2000), but it is a salutary reminder of the legacy of our innocent gardening forebears that William Robinson could write in his classic and seminal work *The English Flower Garden* (1883): 'The great Japan Knotworts (*Polygonum*) are handsome in rough places in the wild garden', while Gertrude Jekyll included it in at least two of her garden plans and

FIG 99. Japanese knotweed *Fallopia japonica* var. *compacta* established along a garden stream in Wiltshire.

described a woodland with a wide paved way where '… we have in widespread groups plants of rather large stature; Bamboos and the great Knotweeds of Japan, and Tritomas and the Giant Reeds …' (Jekyll, 1932). It is now established in Britain almost everywhere except the Highland regions and is spreading aggressively. It grows extremely rapidly, regenerates from tiny rhizome fragments, is a most vigorous competitor and is extremely difficult to control with weedkillers. It is the subject of active research into a possible biological control method, perhaps using a fungal pathogen. It has close relatives that, whilst not legally restricted, are also spreading from gardens in a threatening and potentially damaging manner. Giant knotweed *Fallopia sachalinensis*, also from eastern Asia, is almost as invasive as *F. japonica* but bigger – up to 3 metres tall. It was introduced in 1869 but planted less extensively in gardens simply because it is so big, but it is now particularly well established on coastal sites and river banks. As if these two aggressive plants were not threat enough, there is a hybrid between them at large in Britain. *Fallopia × bohemica* is of European origin and has been cultivated in gardens here since 1872, but its serious nature has only recently been appreciated. Although some of the wild populations are garden escapes, the hybrid is known to arise in Britain spontaneously and the combination of hybrid vigour and the fact that male plants are at least partly fertile is rather worrying. Bailey & Conolly (2000) showed there are a number of clearly identifiable population clusters of *Fallopia × bohemica* in Britain, including one suspiciously centred on the 'Surrey Hills' and Gertrude Jekyll's home and source of gardening influence at Munstead Wood.

Thanks to recent taxonomic rearrangements, the most vigorous climbing plant in Britain is now also in the genus *Fallopia*. Russian vine *F. baldschuanica* was introduced from Central Asia at the end of the nineteenth century, and soon found favour for rapidly covering old buildings and other garden eyesores. It is certainly both rapidly growing and vast; plants with stems over 15 metres long are known. When covered with white blossom, it is also rather attractive and, whilst it is certainly naturalised, it is seldom found far from habitation and seems to pose little threat. It is so vigorous that it has even been thought that some plants recorded as growing in the wild may actually be rooted in gardens many metres away.

Among a big group of other garden escape herbaceous perennials now commonly seen in the wild (at least locally) and often assumed to be native are bear's breeches *Acanthus mollis* (Mediterranean, early sixteenth century), hollyhock *Alcea rosea* (unknown origin but in Britain before 1573), lady's mantle (southern Europe and western Asia, 1874), pearly everlasting *Anaphalis margaritacea* (North America and eastern Asia, before 1596), Michaelmas daisy *Aster* spp. (North

America, eighteenth century), peach-leaved bellflower *Campanula persicifolia* (Europe, before 1596), perennial cornflower *Centaurea montana* (central and southern Europe, before 1596), two very familiar wall plants, red valerian *Centranthus ruber* (Fig. 100: southern Europe, before 1596) and wallflower *Erysimum cheiri* (western Europe, at least medieval, an archaeophyte), caper spurge (southern Europe, another archaeophyte), red hot poker *Kniphofia uvaria* (South Africa, 1705), shasta daisy *Leucanthemum* × *superbum* (*Leucanthemum lacustre* × *L. maximum*) (garden origin, 1816), purple toadflax *Linaria purpurea* (southern Europe, before 1648), dotted loosestrife *Lysimachia punctata* (Europe and western Asia, before 1658), lungwort *Pulmonaria officinalis* (Europe, before 1596) and Canadian golden rod *Solidago canadensis* (North America, 1648). Two others merit special note.

The purple-flowered Indian balsam *Impatiens glandulifera* was introduced from the Himalayas in 1839 and, aided by its highly efficient explosive seed discharge mechanism, it has enveloped many damp waterside sites throughout Britain where it suppresses almost all native vegetation (Fig. 101). My own observations in Derbyshire suggested that only butterbur *Petasites hybridus* stood up to it. Interestingly, on one Derbyshire site that I studied for many years, it cohabited amicably with three other garden escape balsams, touch-me-not *Impatiens noli-tangere*, small balsam *I. parviflora* and orange balsam *I. capensis*. Indian balsam continues to spread along river banks at an alarming rate, as does a relative of butterbur and another plant fondly planted in many a Victorian

FIG 100. Red valerian *Centranthus ruber* colonising old buildings in Gloucestershire.

FIG 101A. Indian balsam *Impatiens glandulifera* dominant on the banks of the River Severn, Herefordshire.

FIG 101B. Red hot poker *Kniphofia uvaria* established on the Hampshire coast.

garden, winter heliotrope *Petasites fragrans*. A male clone was introduced from the Mediterranean in 1806 and was naturalised by 1835. It is a large, robust plant with a deep, penetrating rhizome that can be a serious problem in gardens, especially when it invades rock gardens, lawns and paths.

ALPINES

Size is no indication of efficiency as a competitor and some of the most aggressive perennial garden escapes are low-growing plants, often falling into that loose group that gardeners call alpines, irrespective of whether their origin is anywhere near any sort of mountain. Several species of *Sedum* are widely naturalised, including white stonecrop *S. album* (north temperate, archaeophyte), reflexed stonecrop *S. rupestre* (Europe, seventeenth century) and Caucasian stonecrop *S. spurium* (Caucasus, 1816), as is the closely related houseleek *Sempervivum tectorum* (Europe, at least since the twelfth century), a characteristic feature of old cottage roofs where it was deliberately planted as protection against lightning and other evils. One of the commonest and loveliest small, trailing plants of old walls throughout Britain is ivy-leaved toadflax *Cymbalaria muralis*, introduced to gardens from central and southern Europe at the end of the sixteenth century. It clearly spreads readily in the wild by seed, although curiously it is extremely difficult to germinate. In an attempt to establish it in a wall in my own garden, I obtained some from a seed company who refused to take any money for it, so unlikely did they consider it that I would succeed. They were right. Much more successful at germinating in gardens and in old walls and stonework is a small perennial central American daisy, the Mexican fleabane *Erigeron karvinskianus*, introduced in 1836 and much loved by Gertrude Jekyll who planted it in the garden at Hestercombe in Somerset where it established readily among Edwin Lutyens' stonework to the extent that one flight of garden steps is now known as the daisy steps.

Two creeping campanulas, Adria bellflower *Campanula portenschlagiana* (Balkans, 1835) and trailing bellflower *C. poscharskyana* (Europe and western Asia, 1931), are well established in southern Britain. They have the reputation of being extremely invasive in gardens and will soon subjugate rock garden plantings, but it appears that native vegetation is rather better at holding its own against them. Snow-in-summer *Cerastium tomentosum* was introduced from the Mediterranean in 1648 and gained favour for smothering walls with its woolly foliage and white flowers. It is an unsatisfactory garden plant, however, as it fades miserably after flowering to become an unappealing dry brown mass. It has spread rapidly throughout Britain, onto not only walls but also waste ground, dunes and shingle banks where it poses a particularly aggressive threat. The tiny Corsican mint *Mentha requienii*, which has among the smallest leaves and flowers of any European plant, must be a strong candidate for increased spread into the wider environment (Fig. 102). It was introduced in 1829 and is a splendid little peppermint-scented carpeting species for damp paving and similar areas in gardens. From one small plant introduced about 15 years ago, I now have patches in almost all parts of my 0.5 hectare garden, and I suspect it is only its relative unfamiliarity to gardeners and the fact that it is not cultivated more extensively that has prevented it from being more widely known in the countryside. Aubretia *Aubrieta deltoidea* (the best-known gardening example of a 'flying vowel') was introduced from southern Europe and western Asia in the early eighteenth century and is increasing, although it is typically found close to human habitation; village waste sites are often coloured purple by its flowers in spring.

Two plants that have become a nuisance in gardens as perhaps the most familiar of lawn weeds, as well as in the wider environment, are slender speedwell *Veronica filiformis* and mind-your-own-business *Soleirolia soleirolii*. Many small British *Veronica* species are introduced, but most of them came here long ago as agricultural weeds. Slender speedwell is probably the only one to have been introduced deliberately as a garden plant. It arrived around the

FIG 102. Corsican mint *Mentha requienii* established between garden paving.

end of the eighteenth century from Turkey and the Caucasus and began to be planted widely as an ornamental in about 1920. Its extension into the wild is an interesting phenomenon. It rarely sets seed in Britain because most of the British population seems to have originated with a single strain that is extremely self-incompatible, and so virtually all spread in Britain is vegetative. Its establishment in gardens is easily understood, however, because it is spread by lawn mowings – the recent abandonment by many gardeners of grass collectors on their lawnmowers and the wider use of rotary mowing (p. 35) have been significant factors. Although a similar process would explain the spread of *V. filiformis* along roadsides and verges, it is harder to understand its success in colonising streamsides and other areas not subject to human interference. Mind-your-own-business was introduced from the Mediterranean in 1905, initially as an indoor and greenhouse plant before its hardiness was recognised. It has spread extensively within and without gardens and this will surely continue as it is still sold extensively as a house plant and the fly-tipping of lawn mowings continues apace.

Although less popular now than formerly in gardens, sweet Alison *Lobularia maritima*, introduced as a bedding plant around the beginning of the eighteenth century, continues to spread in the wild, especially in coastal habitats. It is not fully hardy and in gardens is invariably grown as an annual. Other garden annuals too have become established as escapes, but as the majority of modern British garden annuals are only half-hardy, there are fewer than might be expected. With an increasingly warm climate, this could change, although it is significant that an increasing proportion of garden annuals, like modern vegetables, are F1 hybrids that set seed erratically, if at all, and/or produce feeble, uncompetitive offspring. Among the more important annual escapes are snap-dragon *Antirrhinum majus* (southern Europe, probably sixteenth century) which is well established on old walls and waste places and continues to spread despite its susceptibility to the North American antirrhinum rust *Puccinia antirrhini*, another garden escape which was first recorded in Britain in 1933; and opium poppy *Papaver somniferum*, in reality an archaeophyte, perhaps originally from the eastern Mediterranean, but widely cultivated since the Bronze Age for its medicinal, culinary and ornamental appeal. It is still extensively grown in gardens and is common on waste ground and in other disturbed places. Larkspur *Consolida ajacis*, introduced from southern Europe/western Asia in the sixteenth century, is one of the easiest of all garden annuals to grow; it is often recommended for children's gardens because of its rapidity and reliability, and it has reliably spread onto waste ground and also now occurs rather commonly in eastern England as an agricultural weed. Honesty *Lunaria annua*, which

FIG 103. *Lobelia erinus*, a South African plant, is becoming increasingly common in urban streets where it self-seeds from containers.

despite its name is a biennial, is of unknown origin, but was certainly here in the sixteenth century. It is now extremely common in many areas of Britain on waste ground and has become particularly familiar as a hedgerow plant.

Two of the less expected garden escapes are common, half-hardy annuals that survive as seeds and, in mild urban locations, as plants. Lobelia *Lobelia erinus*, a South African plant cultivated here since the mid-eighteenth century, is becoming increasingly common in urban streets where it grows among paving cracks, the seed having fallen from hanging baskets, and I know sheltered localities where it remains in flower all year round (Fig. 103). Similarly, tagetes *Tagetes patula*, which reached Britain from Mexico as long ago as the mid-sixteenth century, is beginning to be seen more frequently on waste sites.

A small group of plants occur both as conventional garden escapes and also as 'bird-seed aliens', having become established from seed falling from bird tables and seed feeders (p. 137). Pot marigold *Calendula officinalis* is not generally used in modern bird-seed mixtures, although it is grown extensively as an ornamental and pot herb. It is of garden origin and is among the plants mentioned by Harvey (1981) as Anglo-Saxon. It is especially common on and around waste tips, its detection aided by its conspicuous bright orange flowers (Fig. 104). The North American sunflower *Helianthus annuus* was another pre-Gerarde plant, arriving here sometime between 1492 and 1596. A much wider range of cultivars (many of them disappointingly dwarf) has become available for gardens in recent years, but it seems likely that much of its increasingly frequent (and very obvious) occurrence in the wild is the result of garden bird feeding. Canary grass *Phalaris canariensis* (the 'Canary' refers to the Canary Islands, not the birds) is still a most important constituent of bird seed mixtures (p. 139f) and is becoming common, although it rarely persists as a sustaining population and technically is more a casual.

FIG 104. Pot marigold *Calendula officinalis* growing with field poppy *Papaver rhoeas* and other native species on a waste tip in Herefordshire, in May.

VEGETABLES

Relatively few vegetables have become established as garden escapes, although it is not easy to distinguish between modern or historical escapes from agricultural activity and relics or escapes from gardening. The abundant populations of *Brassica napus* now to be seen along roadsides, for instance, are almost invariably of subsp. *oleifera*, oil-seed rape, rather than old garden swedes subsp. *rapifera*. Most wild *Vicia faba* is likely to be field rather than garden broad beans while the widespread populations of horse-radish *Armoracia rusticana*, spearmint *Mentha spicata* and American winter-cress *Barbarea verna* (which, despite the name, is actually a long-cultivated European plant) have probably been here for many centuries. One plant that certainly came here from Europe as a medicinal herb long ago (possibly with the Romans), but which has certainly made its presence known in gardens and in the wild, is ground elder *Aegopodium podagraria*. It now occurs throughout the British Isles, from the Scillies to Orkney, spreading locally by invasive rhizomes and over greater distances by seed.

'BULBOUS' PLANTS

A number of bulbous plants (I use the term here in the broad horticultural sense) have become notoriously invasive in gardens and they are among a group of bulbous species that have also escaped to the wider environment. Several species of *Oxalis* have been especially successful. The origin of procumbent yellow sorrel *O. corniculata* is unknown, and whilst it is almost certainly no longer cultivated it was being grown in British gardens as an ornamental by the mid-seventeenth century. Today it is a widespread annual or short-lived perennial weed, not only in gardens, but also in cultivated areas generally as well as on waste ground. Two rather similar South American species that probably arrived here as ornamentals in the nineteenth century are extremely troublesome. Pink sorrel *O. articulata* and garden pink sorrel *O. corniculata* are almost impossible to eradicate once well established as they are tolerant of many weedkillers and spread most efficiently by bulbils or tiny rhizome fragments.

It seems hard to credit that three-cornered garlic *Allium triquetrum* and few-flowered garlic *A. paradoxum* were among a group of *Allium* species originally brought here from southern Europe for garden cultivation in the eighteenth and nineteenth centuries. They have now spread extensively by seed or bulbils to many hedgerow, roadside and damp shady sites. Garden grape hyacinth

Muscari armeniacum (Balkans and Caucasus, 1878) and the white-flowered star of Bethlehem *Ornithogalum angustifolium* (brought from southern Europe before 1548) are the two other truly troublesome and invasive bulbous plants in gardens, and it will come as no surprise that they are also increasing in the wild.

Less obvious harm to native biodiversity has been caused by other garden ornamentals such as spring crocus *Crocus vernus* (introduced in the sixteenth century from central Europe), sowbread *Cyclamen hederifolium* (before 1596, central Europe) and winter aconite *Eranthis hyemalis* (also pre-1596 from southern Europe), all of which appear to be increasing in the wild. And few would deny that snowdrop *Galanthus nivalis* has enhanced many areas of native woodland since its first recorded escape from gardens in the eighteenth century, although it had been in cultivation here long before then and has at times been thought to be native. There must be mixed feelings, however, about daffodils *Narcissus* spp., grown here for centuries as cultivars representing a wide range of parental species. Modern daffodils with their bright, showy flowers are aesthetically intrusive when they turn up as garden rejects on waste sites and roadsides, but of greater concern is their impact on the genetic purity of populations of our only native daffodil *N. pseudonarcissus* subsp. *pseudonarcissus*. It is, moreover, another garden bulb that offers perhaps the greatest and most serious instance of genetic pollution by a garden escape. The large-flowered Spanish bluebell *Hyacinthoides hispanica* was being grown in British gardens before 1683 and is still planted extensively. It is only recently, however, that the significance of its hybridisation with the native bluebell *H. non-scripta* has been appreciated. The hybrid is fertile and although it was first recorded in the wild as recently as 1963, it has spread dramatically in the past 20 years.

ESCAPES FROM BOTANIC GARDENS

Finally, if only to demonstrate that unthinking, uncaring or sometimes simply innocent home gardeners are not always to blame for creating a situation that allows so many alien genes to escape into the environment, it is worth mentioning some particularly dramatic breakouts from professional garden care. Cambridge University Botanic Garden played a significant and deliberate part in the spread of Canadian waterweed (p. 164) by placing some plants in a nearby stream in 1848 from whence they spread throughout Fenland (Preston & Croft, 1997). Oxford ragwort *Senecio squalidus*, now known to be a hybrid between two Mediterranean species *S. aethnensis* and *S. chrysanthemifolius*, was being grown in the Oxford Botanic Garden in the early years of the eighteenth century. By 1794 it had been recorded in the wild and then gradually turned up at an increasing number of localities in the area. Around 1879, it reached the railway and with a speed and efficiency that would be the envy of many a modern rail traveller, it spread to all parts of England and beyond at an ever-increasing rate. It is now common on waste ground, roadsides and paradoxically, home gardens too; and, like most ragworts, it is toxic to livestock. Another member of the same family with an even more widespread distribution – it occurs in almost every 10-kilometre grid square in the British Isles – is pineapple weed, a North American and East Asian species that must now be a weed in most British gardens. Yet it was not recorded in the wild until 1871, when it turned up after escaping from the Royal Botanic Gardens, Kew. Like Oxford ragwort, it has since reclaimed gardens in its capacity as a highly successful weed (p. 122), and has been described as one of the fastest-spreading British plants of the twentieth century.

The South American annual gallant soldier was introduced to Kew shortly before 1796, but was on the loose by 1860 and no attempt was made to disguise its origin – it was called Kew weed. It has extended its range steadily ever since, and occurs as a weed of cultivation throughout much of England, helped by further escapes from nurseries and domestic gardens and by further introductions as a wool alien. Curiously, its culinary value does not seem to have been recognised here; it is highly prized as a herb in parts of South America under its Colombian Spanish name *guasca*.

ANIMALS

The data for animals, fungi and other groups are more obscure than for plants, but again, in most cases, not too difficult to assess. I will hazard a guess that no species of animal has been deliberately introduced to Britain solely through the medium of gardens or the activities of gardeners. Gardeners certainly have not been responsible for introducing any birds, mammals or fish, although possibilities might just lie with a few reptiles and amphibians that have been deliberately or accidentally liberated from garden ponds; at least if it is assumed that keepers of exotic pets are also gardeners. Two of the strongest candidates might be the huge American bullfrog *Rana catesbeiana* about which English Nature has voiced serious concern ('it will eat anything that will fit into its mouth') and the red-eared terrapin *Trachemys scripta elegans* which is certainly present in many large ponds and which may or may not breed here (Beebee & Griffiths, 2000).

Even taking the wider arena (commercial growing as well as home gardens), creatures employed for biological control are, apart from pollinators, arguably the only animals deliberately introduced through any sort of horticultural activity. Most biological control organisms are used in greenhouses, simply because they are required to control greenhouse pests and it is only in such a confined interior space that the populations of control agents vis-à-vis pests are large enough to be effective. Even those that escape will generally survive only for a short period and generally not over a British winter. At least one exception is the small hymenopteran whitefly parasite, *Encarsia formosa*. Its origin is unknown – it was first found in a glasshouse in Idaho (Gahan, 1924) and it is now almost cosmopolitan – but its taxonomic affinities suggest it came originally from 'the tropical and subtropical Western Hemisphere' (Polaszek *et al.*, 1992). This seems, not surprisingly, to have been the origin of the glasshouse whitefly itself (Russel, 1949: see below). *Encarsia formosa* is certainly established in some places in the southern half of England, and with climate change may be expected to move northwards. Gardeners have found it appearing in new greenhouses where there was no possibility of it having overwintered from the previous season; in consequence they are saved the expense of buying fresh cultures annually to protect their tomatoes.

The only biological control organisms currently being used by gardeners outdoors in Britain and which are reliably capable of surviving over winter seem to be nematodes. *Phasmarhabditis hermaphroditica*, which is used to control slugs by introducing pathogenic bacteria into their bodies, is active at a soil temperature as low as 5°C and has been employed for several years. The more important entomopathogenic nematode *Steinernema kraussei*, which is used to control vine weevil larvae and is active at a similarly low temperature, was first made available to home gardeners in 2004. It appears, however, to have a very widespread distribution, and like other species of nematode used as biological control agents, is almost certainly native or long established here (Willmott *et al.*, 2002).

The potential risks inherent in biological control have been amply demonstrated by the case of the harlequin ladybird *Harmonia axyridis*. This Asian species was introduced first to North America as a control for aphids and then sold extensively for the same purpose throughout Europe, but turned its attention to other ladybird species, lacewings, butterflies and other insects and in 2004 was found in Britain for the first time.

A large number of horticultural pests and pathogens have arrived in Britain on imported plant material and are now well naturalised. In many instances, especially with vegetable and fruit pests and pathogens, commercial cropping rather than gardening must be held responsible, but in view of the fact that the home gardener is the biggest client of the commercial trade in ornamental plants, it is equally arguable that without gardens, many of the organisms would never have arrived. Fortunately, relatively few have transferred from gardens and exotic hosts to native or naturalised species in the wider environment.

Perhaps the most important insect pests that have arrived here via gardens are whiteflies. They are sap-sucking insects of worldwide distribution, but tend to be more significant as crop pests in warm temperate and tropical regions where they are important virus vectors. Whilst there are many native species, the most significant interloper is the familiar glasshouse whitefly *Trialeurodes vaporariorum* which, as I have mentioned (p. 15f), arrived here at some unknown date and is now a most serious glasshouse pest that is increasingly surviving outdoors over winter. Two related species are also now well established in southern England after having arrived on imported garden plants. The rhododendron whitefly *Dialeurodes chittendeni* is Himalayan and came in the early part of the twentieth century, being first recorded at Chiddingfold in Surrey in 1926, while the viburnum whitefly *Aleurotrachelus jelinekii* was first found around 1936 (Mound, 1962). Two other sap-sucking insects now familiar in Britain also arrived with garden plants. The bay sucker *Trioza alacris* is widely distributed in Europe and North America, although its origin is unknown. It was introduced to Britain in the 1920s and is now the most important pest of bay, causing distortion, curling and yellowing of the leaves. The woolly aphid *Eriosoma lanigerum* has the double distinction of having been one of the earliest accurately recorded garden pest introductions, and of being found for the first time by Sir Joseph Banks, who discovered it in London in 1787. It is now one of the more important pests of apples and also occurs on some related plants including cotoneasters and pyracanthas, although it remains most significant in gardens (Fig. 105). The extent to which it occurs on naturalised rosaceous shrubs does not seem to have been documented. Azalea leaf miner *Caloptilia azaleella* is another insect that has essentially remained predominantly a garden pest rather than moving into the wider environment, mainly because its principal hosts are glasshouse azaleas, although it does occur on outdoor plants in sheltered localities.

Among the more important exotic, warm climate pests established in British garden greenhouses are several species of root-knot eelworms *Meloidogyne* spp., the glasshouse symphylid *Scutigerella immaculata*, the house cricket *Acheta domesticus*, an African and Asian species, and the glasshouse leafhopper *Hauptidia maroccana* (= *Zygina pallidifrons*). The latter was introduced to Britain in about 1918 and is now well established, causing coarse white mottling of the upper leaf surfaces on glasshouse and house plants, the leaves becoming completely

FIG 105. Woolly aphid *Eriosoma lanigerum*, imported from North America in the eighteenth century, seen here on apple.

blanched in severe attacks. One or other species of cockroach, the common cockroach *Blatta orientalis* and American cockroach *Periplaneta americana*, both probably North African in origin, the Australian cockroach *P. australasiae* and the Surinam cockroach *Pycnoscelus surinamensis*, occur occasionally in heated garden greenhouses, and in a few areas, even species of stick insect (Phasmida) have become established, although they have not achieved pest status. Species of alien thrips are also now spreading in greenhouses, and some also outdoors.

Many species of scale insects are common in British greenhouses, having been introduced on plants from warmer climates. The female insects usually lay hundreds of eggs under wax scales, under coverings of woolly wax or under their bodies. Young nymphs, known as crawlers, hatch some weeks or months later and disperse over plants before settling to feed on plant sap. As with other sap-sucking pests, the consequent development of sooty moulds on the excreted honeydew is often at least as significant as the debilitating effects of the insects themselves. At least four species of sap-sucking mealybugs – *Planococcus citri*, *Pseudococcus obscurus*, *P. longispinus* and *P. calceolariae* – have become established in garden greenhouses after having been introduced on plants from the tropics and subtropics. They are particularly problematic on indoor plants, especially cacti and other succulents, not least because they tend to accumulate in the inaccessible crevices that are prevalent on these plants. The wingless females have soft, rounded bodies covered by white powdery wax, and although winged males develop from delicate white cocoons and may appear in large numbers at times, the females can reproduce parthenogenetically when males are not present and some species are almost entirely parthenogenetic.

A considerable number of invertebrates must have arrived here on plant material but, not being active pests, have remained unnoticed. Two groups that are only marginally damaging but striking enough not to have been overlooked are ants and woodlice. Although native ants, particularly the common little black ant *Lasius niger*, will invade greenhouses and can cause root disturbance through their burrowing activities, introduced ant species, especially Pharaoh's ant *Monomorium pharaonis* and the Argentine ant *Linepithema humile* (= *Iridomyrmex humilis*), have also become established in greenhouses. Exotic woodlice too have been found in heated greenhouses. Among those reported by Harding & Sutton (1985) were *Miktoniscus linearis* from North America, *Cordioniscus stebbingi* from Europe and Asia, the pantropical *Nagurus cristatus*, and *Agabiformius lentus*, widely distributed in warm areas. Admittedly these have mainly been in botanic gardens, but it is interesting that Harding & Sutton suggested in their species list: 'the current [sic] practice of using insecticides on a regular basis may prevent any long term establishment of these [alien] species'. That practice has now changed dramatically (p. 63) and exotic woodlice may indeed become more frequently found.

FUNGI

Among fungus-induced plant diseases too there are many that have been introduced on garden plants but have more or less stayed there, among them antirrhinum rust *Puccinia antirrhini* (North America, introduced around 1933), carnation rust *Uromyces dianthi* (unknown origin, around 1890), chrysanthemum rust *Puccinia chrysanthemi* (Japan, 1895), chrysanthemum white rust *Puccinia horiana* (Fig. 106: China and Japan, 1963), erythronium rust *Uromyces erythronii* (unknown origin, 1936), hollyhock rust *Puccinia malvacearum* (South America, mid-nineteenth century), mahonia rust *Cumminsiella mirabilissima* (North America, 1922), pelargonium rust *Puccinia pelargonii* (South Africa, early twentieth century), rhododendron rust *Chrysomyxa ledi* var. *rhododendri* (Europe, 1913), dahlia smut *Entyloma calendulae* f. *dahliae* (South Africa, unknown date) and American gooseberry mildew *Sphaerotheca mors-uvae* (North America, around 1900). However, two notable introduced fungal diseases, both closely related rusts, stand out as having had a major impact beyond the garden. The disease generally called cineraria rust is caused by an Australian fungus *Puccinia lagenophorae*. Horticulturally, it is important on cineraria *Pericallis* × *hybrida* and it is believed to have been brought to Europe on this host plant in 1961. Its greatest impact in Britain, however, has been on groundsel, which it distorts and stunts and in

FIG 106. Chrysanthemum white rust *Puccinia horiana*, an introduction from Japan.

extreme cases, unusually for a rust disease, may kill. It is now difficult in many areas to find populations of groundsel that are free from the disease.

History all but repeated itself when the related Australian rust fungus *Puccinia distincta* was found in Britain for the first time at Dungeness in Kent in 1997, causing damage on cultivated *Bellis* daisies. It almost certainly reached us from France where it had been found the previous year, but its arrival in Europe was almost equally certainly on imported garden plants. It has since spread widely and rapidly on cultivated forms and also on wild *Bellis perennis*.

Just as plant pathogenic fungi can easily be brought from elsewhere unseen as mycelium buried within their host plant's tissues, so macro-fungi too may arrive concealed in soil, compost or plant products. Among the most celebrated because they are so strikingly different from anything else in Britain are three clathroid fungi. Devil's finger *Clathrus archeri*, which is sometimes known as the octopus fungus, originated in Tasmania and was first reported from Britain in a Cornish garden in the 1940s. It has since spread rather widely into parks and gardens across the south of England. The basket fungus *Ileodictyon cibarium* is common in New Zealand, but it has been established in a few gardens in the south-east of England since the 1950s. *Aseroë rubra*, another Australian species with a striking appearance, was found once in a greenhouse in Kew in the nineteenth century and then was not found again until it appeared in a Surrey woodland in the 1990s.

The most obvious introduced garden toadstool is the beautiful, bright yellow tropical species called the plantpot dapperling *Leucocoprinus birnbaumii*, which has been known for many years in greenhouses and in the compost of pot plants, although it has also recently been found growing outside for the first time in southern England (Fig. 107). Climate change may mean more gardeners and perhaps the wider public will be able to appreciate its stunning appearance. Two introduced species of the important, striking and generally poisonous genus *Amanita* are found mainly associated with conifers in gardens in southern England. *Amanita inopinata*, which occurs principally with yew and Lawson's cypress in gardens, cemeteries and parks scattered across the south-east, is from its structure and taxonomic affinities clearly extra-European, but its origin is unknown and it was described as new to science from English material. *Amanita singeri* from Argentina was found at Kew in the 1990s. I discuss elsewhere (p. 258f) the significance of bark chips and other garden mulches as substrates for native fungi, but some exotic species appear to have been introduced with imported mulching material too. Among them are *Melanoleuca verrucipes*, a distinctive white species first recorded in south-eastern England in 2000; the equally distinctive brown-capped *Gymnopilus dilepis* (rather like a small *Tricholomopsis*

FIG 107. Plantpot dapperling *Leucocoprinus birnbaumii*, an exotic toadstool becoming common in greenhouses.

rutilans), first recorded in England in 1995, sometimes occurring in greenhouses; and the pale brown agaric *Agrocybe putaminum*, first recorded in 1986. The white and probably alien species *Leucocoprinus cepistipes* is sometimes also found on compost heaps outside.

Two presumably introduced agaric toadstools stand out as having been first recorded in Britain within the past century, both at the Royal Botanic Gardens, Kew, but are now widespread. *Psilocybe cyanescens*, which occurs in England and North Wales, was first recorded in 1910, and *Stropharia aurantiaca*, which is already scattered across England and Northern Ireland (there are 200 records in the British Mycological Society Fungal Records Database), as recently as 1957 at Kew. One species with a particularly distinguished type locality is *Panaeolus atrobalteatus*, described originally from mulched flowerbeds in the gardens of Buckingham Palace (see also p. 234). Many introduced agarics must come, albeit not always noticed, attached to their mycorrhizal hosts. One that is particularly widely distributed in parks and gardens with *Eucalyptus* is *Laccaria fraterna*, which has been found at many sites, especially in south-west England.

Rather less frequently seen, for understandable reasons, are subterranean or hypogeous fungi, but two of these also are *Eucalyptus* associates and presumably arrived with it. The false truffle *Hydnangium carneum* was first found in 1875, while its relative *Hymenangium album* was initially recorded by Sir William Hooker in

Glasgow Botanic Garden in 1830, properly described from specimens collected in Edinburgh in 1880, and then, 120 years later, appeared in 2000 in association with *Eucalyptus* at Kew. The New Zealand ascotruffle *Paurocotylis pila* was first recorded in Nottinghamshire in 1973 and has since been found in garden soil and other sites from as far north as Orkney.

It is apparent that apart from the relatively obvious and well-documented introductions to gardens and subsequent spread outwards of many flowering plants, the garden has served as the route into the British countryside for many other organisms too. Even with well-studied and well-recorded groups in such a well-documented country as Britain, those among the micro-organisms and invertebrates that have been noticed must be but the tip of a large iceberg.

CHAPTER 8

The Slightly More Hidden Garden

As with most other habitats, the garden holds the bulk of its wildlife in concealment. The populations – of both species and individuals – of invertebrate animals, non-flowering plants, fungi, prokaryotes (bacteria and related unicellular organisms) and protoctists (relatively simple, generally microscopic, unicellular or multicellular organisms that do not fit into any other group) exceed by many times those of flowering plants and vertebrates. And they have their equivalent natural history, their own ecology, no less important and probably far more complex than any we can see. With few exceptions, however, microscopic organisms lie outside the scope of this book, but even in limiting myself in this chapter principally to a consideration of the place and role in gardens of 'lower' plants, invertebrate animals and fungi, I have laid before me a vast, largely unappreciated, largely unstudied and highly complex situation. It opens, in an almost literal sense, a whole can of worms.

I know of no single study devoted to the behaviour and distribution of the smaller living things of gardens, and they are almost absent from studies of a more general nature. I have therefore scraped together such nuggets of information as do exist and have supplemented them with my own observations. I will consider the main garden habitats in turn rather than review each taxonomic group, as the microflora and microfaunas of different habitats differ so widely. The lichens of lawns, for example, are widely different from those of walls. And as the lawn is the most unusual and individual of all garden habitats, it is here that I will start.

LAWNS

Bryophytes

Lawns are not only ecologically unusual (p. 109); potentially they also offer one of the richest of garden habitats for lower organisms, although it is a sad fact that many of the routine lawn treatments discussed in Chapter 3 are designed specifically to control or eradicate them. Where these treatments do not succeed, several moss species proliferate. 'Lawn moss' is a general term used by gardeners, and it comes as a surprise to most to realise that there is more than one type of moss – on lawns or anywhere else. Yet British gardeners have a concern and anxiety about mosses that borders on the phobic. It is a statistic both breathtaking and alarming that in the year 2001, the sale of ferrous sulphate for garden moss control (mainly as a component of lawn sand) in the United Kingdom was almost 3,500 tonnes, an increase of 26 per cent on the previous year (p. 65). Indeed ferrous sulphate accounted for 70 per cent of all active ingredient sales for garden pesticides, fungicides and weedkillers combined. Admittedly, most modern pesticide ingredients have a much more powerful effect per unit weight than compounds such as ferrous sulphate, and therefore simple weight comparisons may not be particularly meaningful. Nonetheless, the fact that 3,500 tonnes are being unloaded onto garden lawns still says a great deal about the British obsession with the lawn; and, in particular, of what constitutes a good one. It is true that much of Britain and certainly much of England experienced above average rainfall during both the spring and autumn of 2001, giving rise to conditions in which lawn mosses would be expected to flourish; but I still find the statistic remarkable.

Among the commonest moss species I find on well-fertilised lawns is the pale green rough-stalked feather-moss *Brachythecium rutabulum*, sometimes with the less conspicuous *Eurhynchium praelongum*. Thompson *et al.* (2004) found this frequency reversed in their study, although unfortunately they published no details of other bryophytes found. Impoverished lawns and those on more acidic soils may support copious growth of spring turf-moss *Rhytidiadelphus squarrosus* with its characteristic star-like shoot tips and recurved leaves, the silver-tinted heath plait-moss *Hypnum jutlandicum* and the silky shoots of whitish feather-moss *Brachythecium albicans*, which is usually so pale it looks almost bleached. Really dry lawns on acidic soils will attract the stiff, distinctive juniper haircap *Polytrichum juniperinum* and broom fork-moss *Dicranum scoparium* (Fig. 108). Wetter lawns often support extensive growth of the distinctive pointed spear-moss *Calliergonella cuspidata* with shoot tips that appear sharply pointed because

FIG 108. Lawn mosses, predominantly juniper haircap *Polytrichum juniperinum.*

of the tightly convoluted young leaves. This species can sometimes be extremely lush and prolific and in damp gardens is often the most troublesome lawn moss. Shaded, damp lawn sites may support the worm-like shoots of neat feather-moss *Scleropodium purum*, many-fruited thyme moss *Plagiomnium affine* and its relative, palm-tree moss *Plagiomnium undulatum*. Foliose (leafy) liverworts also sometimes occur in damp lawns, although they tend more usually to be present in the longer grass that discourages moss growth, and I have never seen a lawn where they created any horticultural problem. They are clearly incapable of adversely affecting grass growth. The most frequent species seem to be bifid crestwort *Lophocolea bidentata* and white earwort *Diplophyllum albicans*. I have never found more than a token presence of thallose liverworts, although dotted hornwort *Anthoceros punctatus* and other species can sometimes be found on severely neglected lawns.

Lichens
Foliose lichens can be present in quantity on lawns, although they tend to be symptomatic of general neglect, soil stagnation and shade rather than being intrinsically problematic. The commonest by far are the dog lichens *Pelitigera*, and their presence comes as a considerable surprise to those accustomed to thinking of lichens as invariably slow-growing organisms. Nonetheless, as Gilbert (2000) pointed out, growth rates of young thalli in the 'steady high rate growth phase' are significantly greater than those displayed by older thalli; foliose lichens (such as *Peltigera*) generally grow faster than placoid and crustose species, and *P. canina* had the fastest growth rate of all the species he cited. Given a

FIG 109. Dog lichen *Peltigera* on a lawn, a sign of neglect.

growth rate of 17 millimetres per annum in its early years as Gilbert quoted, it is evident that almost all the dog lichen I have seen on lawns has reached its size in less than two years; a common length of time for lawns, or at least parts of them, to be neglected (Fig. 109).

Fungi

If the questions raised by gardeners are any criteria by which to judge, lawns are certainly significant habitats for fungi. Queries about the implication for their lawns of fairy rings and of the numerous scattered patches of small brown toadstools are matched only by those seeking information on how to eradicate them. Most of the higher basidiomycete toadstools on lawns represent the limited number of those grassland species that can survive the disturbance brought about by the operations of garden lawn care. The classic garden lawn fairy ring, a circular pattern of toadstools, generally with darker grass to the outside and depauperate growth within, is caused by the appropriately named fairy ring mushroom *Marasmius oreades* (Fig. 110), although other fungi sometimes occur in the same ring, most notably white species of *Clitocybe*, including the deadly poisonous fool's funnel *C. rivulosa*. The possible presence of such species underlines the importance of not eating fungi from a fairy ring unless an experienced collector has checked the identification, although *Marasmius oreades* itself is both edible and good. In larger areas of grass such as grazed pastures and parkland, many other agarics occur. St George's mushroom *Calocybe gambosa*

FIG 110. Fairy ring mushroom *Marasmius oreades*.

and several species of *Lepista* and *Agaricus*, and also the puffballs (*Lycoperdon* species and even the giant puffball *Calvatia gigantea*), rather commonly form rings, but this is extremely rare in gardens, and such rings do not have the characteristic inner circle of dead grass which seems to be unique to *Marasmius oreades*. Fairy rings undoubtedly disfigure a velvet sward, mainly because of the dying grass in the inner concentric ring, which appears to be the result of a mat of fungal mycelium in the soil impeding the penetration of water to a zone of soil already depleted of nutrients. The outer ring of more lush grass is believed to be the result of enhanced nitrogen released by the action of the advancing fungal colony. Fairy rings, like other toadstool colonies, cannot be removed, simply because of the impossibility of eradicating the extensive mycelium growth that permeates the soil beneath. I have commonly had to resort to offering gardeners a rather glib piece of advice based on the knowledge that the radial growth rate seems to range between about 8 and 34 centimetres per year so, given sufficient patience, your fairy ring will therefore eventually migrate into the neighbour's garden.

Perhaps 25 other types of toadstool occur commonly on lawns – although, as I describe on p. 243, the potential number is significantly greater if it proves possible to encourage species of *Hygrocybe* to grow more freely in home gardens. The majority of common lawn fungi are small, often brown and relatively unimpressive species of *Panaeolus*, *Psathyrella*, *Mycena* and other common genera. To the mycologist many are known collectively as LBJs – little brown jobs – a term that reflects their insignificant nature and in some instances, the difficulty of identification. They cause no harm to the grass, and it is sad that their presence seems to offend so many gardeners. Nonetheless, they are far from the only fungi associated with lawns. A review of the British Mycological Society Fungal Records Database for fungi associated with the commonest genera of lawn grasses revealed the following records (records, not individual species): 1,874 for *Poa*, 131 for *Festuca*, 94 for *Lolium* and 91 for *Agrostis*. And in the rhizosphere beneath the lawn, innumerable other fungal species, both micro- and macro-scopic, occur and pass their lives unnoticed and unappreciated while playing a critical role in the recycling of organic nutrients. Where trees grow in or adjoining lawns, the large fruit-bodies of mycorrhizal species such as brown birch bolete *Leccinum scabrum* with birch and larch bolete *Suillus grevillei* with larch may occasionally appear and cause both interest and excitement, but generally, lawn mowing is once again responsible for keeping them below ground. Mycorrhizas are intimate associations of fungal mycelium and the roots of higher plants. Precisely how the mycorrhizal mycelium assists its host plant, and vice versa, is still imperfectly understood, but it seems that the fungus obtains much of its necessary supply of carbon from the host's roots (and so imposes a considerable drain on the plant) but, in return, acts as an intermediary in the uptake of such nutrients as nitrogen, phosphate and potash from the soil. The mycorrhizal fungus seems better able to achieve this uptake, especially from poor soils, than does the plant acting on its own. Although originally thought to be largely peculiar to trees, it is now known that most flowering plants as well as some pteridophytes and bryophytes also benefit from mycorrhizal associations – these are the rule rather than the exception – and gardeners may come across evidence of this without realising it. A species of toadstool hitherto unseen in their garden sprouting forth close to a new plant might be the only clue. Sometimes, plants bought from a nursery will have been artificially inoculated with mycorrhizal fungus in order to aid their establishment. Conversely, when obtaining plants from another garden, it may make sense to take some soil from around the roots too. I think that many if not most instances of a particular type of plant failing to establish in a garden with otherwise suitable conditions when taken from another in which it is growing prolifically must be due to the absence of mycorrhizal growth around the roots.

Fungus-induced diseases of lawn grasses occur in gardens, and snow mould *Monographella nivalis*, Ophiobolus patch *Gaeumannomyces graminis* and dollar spot *Sclerotinia homoeocarpa* all cause problems from time to time, resulting in patches of dead, dying or discoloured grass. Much the commonest, however, is red thread *Laetisaria fuciformis*, which is becoming increasingly frequent in seasons with wet springs both on newly laid turf and on established lawns, especially of fine grasses. Its presence is evidently encouraged by the leaching of nitrogen from the soil and presumably the consequent weakening of the grass (Fig. 111). It is characterised by the presence of striking patches of dying grass foliage enmeshed by pinkish fungal mycelium and bearing red, needle-like bodies called stromata in which spores develop and which can survive in the soil for up to two years before germinating, infection then taking place through the leaf stomata. Replenishment of the nitrogen by additional feeding will generally bring the fungus under control.

Myxomycetes (also known rather inappropriately as slime moulds), which are quite harmless to garden plants and biologically fascinating, are more likely to be seen on the lawn than anywhere else in the garden. The commonest species is *Physarum cinereum* with globose, stalkless, off-white, clustered spore-bearing bodies or sporocarps and off-white or yellow plasmodia – semi-liquid objects, like large, wandering amoebae. In damp weather on grass that has been unmown for a week or so, the masses of sporocarps can cause entire patches of lawn to appear as if they have been covered with a coarse grey-white dust. *Badhamia foliicola* is also fairly common on lawns with its globose, stalkless or short-stalked sporocarps in small clusters and yellow-orange plasmodia. On large lawns or on rough grass in orchards and shrubberies, especially on alkaline soil, *Mucilago crustacea* may occasionally be found; it has large, chalky, sponge-like sporocarps and cream-white to pale yellow plasmodia.

FIG 111. Red thread disease of turf grass, *Laetisaria fuciformis*.

Invertebrates
Common sense suggests that the invertebrate fauna of lawns, both above and
below the soil surface, is likely to be fairly large. It comes as no surprise, however,
that it has been studied relatively little, certainly in Britain, although some
compelling findings emerged from a study in California by Falk (1976) (see also
p. 37) which can reasonably be expected to be relevant to British lawns too; at
least as far as invertebrates are concerned. Falk showed that the dominant lawn
invertebrates fell into one of two categories: very small and mobile organisms
which live near the tops of the grass blades and avoid danger by rapid escape,
and organisms which live in the mulch layer of the soil where they avoid the
lawnmower, and where the cushioning effect of the thatch minimises mortality
due to trampling. He confirmed that lawns have developed a distinctive fauna
which includes many common grassland species, although because of the
unusual selective pressures, other grassland species are absent. The common
herbivorous invertebrates in California were aphids, chironomid midges, cicadas,
frit flies, thrips and isopods. The common scavengers were collembolans,
earwigs, snails, oribatid mites, sciarid flies, sand flies and dung flies. Omnivorous
ants and carnivorous staphylinid beetles, braconid and chalcidoid wasps and
mesostigmatid mites were also numerous. Other typical grassland invertebrates,
like spiders (which presumably were repelled by the constant disturbance), were
scarce, representing only 1 per cent by weight of the total invertebrate population.
Falk also made interesting observations on the relative seasonal fluctuations of
the different groups and it would be fascinating to see how these are reflected
in our climate.

Most British studies pale by comparison. For example, mysteriously and
most unfortunately, although Owen (1991) operated 11 pitfall traps in her
Leicester garden over many years, none was in the lawn. The most extensive
study specifically of lawn arthropods was probably that of the 15 sites chosen for
the survey of ground arthropods using pitfall traps in inner and outer London
gardens by Davis (1979), although it only lasted for one month, from mid-May
to mid-June 1977. Indeed, a lawn was the only habitat type surveyed at all of the
15 sites, and at all except two, they were mown in the usual way. But, as in so
many studies of British gardens, the published data appear as little more than
stamp collecting, with lists of species frequency at each site, but with no
indication of the habitats within each garden where each was found. Davis listed
33 beetles, 5 centipedes, 8 millipedes, 7 woodlice, 59 spiders, 2 harvestmen and
2 pseudoscorpions. Clearly he must have collected more information and I am
baffled as to why it was not presented. An earlier study, that of 'The Coleoptera
of a suburban garden' by Allen (1964), similarly appeared promising, but proved

hollow. Allen's study extended for ten years, but he trapped nothing and only noted what he saw by turning over stones and debris. No serious conclusions can be drawn from it. But even earlier, it appears that authors themselves were already recognising the fairly feeble nature of the contributions they were making. Henderson's pedestrian paper 'The beetles of a suburban London garden in Surrey' (Henderson, 1945) was followed the next year by the even more dispiritingly titled 'More beetles of a suburban London garden in Surrey' (Henderson, 1946). Some information can be gleaned from the few studies that have been made of parklands, but it is dangerous to draw too many analogies between these and lawns because, apart from the much longer grass that occurs even in heavily grazed parklands, grazed grass will of course be subject to the rather different influence of large and continuing quantities of dung.

It is a pity that more students of garden invertebrates have not taken the same approach as those who devised the British Isopod Survey (Harding & Sutton, 1985). This nationwide survey, carried out over many years, resulted in a provisional distribution map but, rather more importantly, included provision for recording not only first order habitats, which included domestic gardens, but also second order habitats (cold frame, rockery, lawn and so forth) and 'microsites' (soil, litter, stones and so on). Thus, the analysis of garden isopods not only told us that two species, common shiny woodlouse *Oniscus asellus* and common rough woodlouse *Porcellio scaber* (Fig. 112), were much the most numerous, but also showed that they had little habitat preference within gardens, while other species clearly did (Table 17).

FIG 112. Common rough woodlouse *Porcellio scaber*, a ubiquitous species.

TABLE 17. Frequency of woodlice species in garden habitats as revealed by the British Isopod Survey (Harding & Sutton, 1985) – adapted from Harding (pers. comm.).

Woodlice species in lawns.

SPECIES	NO. OF RECORDS
Oniscus asellus	35
Philoscia muscorum	32
Porcellio scaber	29
Trichoniscus pusillus	25
Armadillidium vulgare	16
Platyarthrus hoffmannseggi	10
Androniscus dentiger	9
Porcellionides cingendus	6
Armadillidium depressum	3
Porcellio spinicornis	3
Trichoniscus pygmaeus	3
Trachelipus rathkei	1

Woodlice species in cold frames.

SPECIES	NO. OF RECORDS
Oniscus asellus	7
Porcellio scaber	5
Androniscus dentiger	3
Trichoniscus pusillus	3
Philoscia muscorum	2
Armadillidium nasatum	1
Platyarthrus hoffmannseggi	1
Trichoniscus pygmaeus	1

Woodlice species in compost or refuse heaps.[1]

SPECIES	NO. OF RECORDS
Oniscus asellus	142
Porcellio scaber	116

TABLE 17. Woodlice species in compost or refuse heaps – *cont.*

SPECIES	NO. OF RECORDS
Philoscia muscorum	69
Armadillidium vulgare	68
Trichoniscus pusillus	62
Porcellionides pruinosus	34
Androniscus dentiger	21
Haplophthalmus danicus	10
Porcellio laevis	10
Platyarthrus hoffmannseggi	7
Trichoniscus pygmaeus	6
Armadillidium depressum	4
Armadillidium nasatum	4
Cylisticus convexus	3
Trachelipus rathkei	3
Eluma purpurascens	2
Ligia oceanica	2
Ligidium hypnorum	2
Porcellio dilatatus	2
Porcellionides cingendus	2
Trichoniscus pusillus f. *provisorius*	2
Trichoniscus pusillus f. *pusillus*	2
Haplophthalmus mengei agg.	1
Porcellio spinicornis	1
Trichoniscoides albidus	1

[1] may include some non-garden sites.

Woodlice species in 'flower beds' [sic].

SPECIES	NO. OF RECORDS
Porcellio scaber	66
Oniscus asellus	59
Philoscia muscorum	31
Armadillidium vulgare	27
Androniscus dentiger	19
Platyarthrus hoffmannseggi	16
Trichoniscus pusillus	16

TABLE 17. Woodlice species in 'flower beds' [sic]. – *cont.*

SPECIES	NO. OF RECORDS
Porcellionides pruinosus	9
Trichoniscus pygmaeus	8
Cylisticus convexus	6
Porcellionides cingendus	6
Trachelipus rathkei	6
Haplophthalmus mengei agg.	4
Porcellio spinicornis	4
Armadillidium depressum	2
Haplophthalmus danicus	2
Porcellio dilatatus	1

Woodlice species in rockeries.

SPECIES	NO. OF RECORDS
Oniscus asellus	70
Porcellio scaber	70
Philoscia muscorum	35
Trichoniscus pusillus	29
Androniscus dentiger	26
Armadillidium vulgare	22
Platyarthrus hoffmannseggi	11
Trichoniscus pygmaeus	7
Armadillidium depressum	6
Porcellio spinicornis	4
Armadillidium nasatum	3
Cylisticus convexus	3
Haplophthalmus danicus	3
Haplophthalmus mengei agg.	2
Porcellionides pruinosus	2
Ligia oceanica	1
Porcellio laevis	1
Porcellionides cingendus	1
Trichoniscoides albidus	1
Trichoniscoides sarsi agg.	1
Trichoniscus pusillus f. *provisorius*	1

The lawn insects of which gardeners are most aware are craneflies or daddy long-legs (tipulids), which emerge in considerable numbers in late summer, and their leatherjacket larvae, which are not always appreciated as a common cause of bare areas and dying patches of grass (Fig. 113). They did not feature in Falk's Californian study but, together with the cutworm caterpillars of noctuid months, they are among a group of creatures that typically live beneath grassland in Britain and are particularly obvious when gardens are established on newly broken land. The presence of such insects means that some birds – starlings and green woodpeckers most obviously – are generally seen more frequently on lawns than anywhere else in gardens. Starlings are valuable in consuming large numbers of pest larvae while green woodpeckers are additionally attracted by ants.

The archetypal lawn invertebrate is the earthworm, the curse or scourge of gardeners depending on the extent of their knowledge of earthworm biology and their devotion to a billiard-table surface. There are 25 British earthworm species, and the most significant family is the Lumbricidae. This contains the genus *Lumbricus*, familiar from school biology lessons and including the largest British species, *L. terrestris* which may, *in extensis*, reach 35 centimetres in length, and also *Allolobophora*. The latter is responsible for producing casts of expelled soil on lawns (other earthworms deposit the expelled matter in the upper parts of their burrows). The soil is ingested at depth, its digestible organic parts removed, and the remainder expelled. *Allolobophora longa* and *A. nocturna* are usually the

FIG 113. Leatherjacket larvae of tipulid flies.

commonest cast-formers and it is their casts that cause so much anguish. These two species are unusual in entering into a summer diapause, and their casts therefore are found almost exclusively between October and May. The worms themselves are sometimes chanced upon coiled up in small, deep chambers if anyone happens to undertake deep digging in the summer. It seems clear that a fertile garden of 'average' size (p. 26) may contain 400,000 earthworms. Cast densities of over 200 per square metre of lawn and weights of 1 kilogramme of cast soil per square metre are not exactly rare.

The importance of earthworms in maintaining garden soil fertility is hard to overvalue. In the course of feeding, they mix and aerate the soil, providing access for air and allowing drainage. They are also hugely important in incorporating organic matter into the soil. Gardeners are advised simply to deposit organic matter on the soil surface in autumn in the certain knowledge that earthworms will drag it downwards far more effectively than they can; and observant gardeners will be familiar with the sight of leaves being hauled down into earthworm burrows.

Charles Darwin's well-known studies of earthworm biology may not have been the most accurate by modern standards, but they were certainly the most extensive, and he was committed to the cause of earthworms in playing a crucial role in soil fertility (Darwin, 1881). He was among the first to determine the quantity of soil moved by the earthworm population and calculated that up to 100 tonnes of soil per hectare are stirred up in the course of a single year. In truth, not much advance has been made since Darwin's time. Agricultural soil studies were made over the years at Rothamsted Experimental Station: the earlier investigations were summarised by Russell (1957) and the later by Davis et al. (1992) in previous New Naturalist volumes, but the garden was a predictably neglected habitat for almost all of them and for modern investigations, it is necessary to refer to American studies.

Other common garden earthworms – beneath lawns and elsewhere – are *Allolobophora chloritica*, which has a characteristic green tinge; *Octolasium lacteum* which is remarkably colourful, bluish overall with a pink or orange clitellum; its relative *O. cyaneum*, blue-grey with a red clitellum and a habit of discharging a milky fluid; *Lumbricus castaneus*, also with a striking orange clitellum; and the red worm *L. rubellus*. The fisherman's brandling *Eisenia foetida* is predominantly a worm of compost bins (p. 53).

In recent years, gardens in parts of Britain have suffered from infestations of introduced southern hemisphere platyhelminths, especially the New Zealand flatworm *Arthurdendyus triangulata* and the Australian flatworm *Australoplana sanguinea* (p. 218), which feed on earthworms and have seriously depleted the worm population in some areas. The New Zealand flatworm was probably first introduced around 1970 and has gradually spread, especially in the south of Scotland and Northern Ireland. In England, it has been found mainly in the north and north-west, but it is also present in the south-east. The Australian flatworm was first found in the Isles of Scilly in 1980 and over the past ten years has been recorded in Lancashire and Cheshire and also the south-west of England, Wales and the Irish Republic. Defra has introduced a Code of Conduct for reporting the discovery of these creatures.

PATHS AND PAVING

Hard landscaping is an expression much beloved of some garden designers. It is a broad term meaning the non-living structural components of a garden – the paths, walls, paving and so on. Whilst at first appearing an uninviting substrate and merely a way to reduce the area of beds and borders, it does have an individual microfauna and microflora; although, rather sadly, too many gardeners seem to equate hard landscaping with sterility and go to extraordinary and costly chemical lengths to ensure that no living thing is allowed to intrude.

Bryophytes readily colonise the crevices between paving. In a study in Paisley, Silverside (2002) singled out silver moss *Bryum argenteum*, a moss of naturally dry, gravelly places, as the commonest urban pavement species, with *B. bicolor* in slightly damper sites. Common liverwort *Marchantia polymorpha* and crescent cup liverwort *Lunularia cruciata* were two common liverworts in Paisley, and certainly *Marchantia polymorpha* is the commonest liverwort of paving cracks in my own garden (Fig. 114). *Marchantia polymorpha* has circular gemma cups, whereas *Lunularia cruciata*'s are lunate.

Concrete and tarmac garden paths become notoriously slippery when wet, a state of affairs brought about by the growth of unicellular green algae and, especially towards the edges, by low-growing mosses such as creeping feather-moss *Amblystegium serpens*. Gravel paths are poor environments for lower plants and fungi because they are intolerant of the instability and movement. The more traditional paving materials of crushed cinders, ash and clinker are now seldom seen because the materials themselves, the waste from coal-fired power stations and blast furnaces, are difficult to obtain. The flora of cinder paths is a special one nonetheless and tends to include bryophytes (and higher plants) that are characteristic or tolerant of fire sites, like the mosses common cord-moss *Funaria hygrometrica* and golden thread-moss *Leptobryum pyriforme*. The fungal flora of this habitat too is characteristic (Fig. 115), and my own first finding of

FIG 114. Common liverwort *Marchantia polymorpha*, familiar on garden paths and plant pots.

FIG 115. *Psathyrella pennata*, a fire-site toadstool growing on a garden cinder path.

that tiny archetypal fire-site toadstool *Omphalina postii* was from just such a garden cinder path. Interestingly, however, other fungi that are so characteristic of fire sites in woodlands and other areas outside gardens, like the ascomycete *Rhizina undulata*, do not seem to grow on cinder paths. Nor are they seen on garden bonfire sites, presumably because these are not left undisturbed for sufficiently long periods.

Plant pots left standing for more than a few weeks will also attract a lush bryophyte growth. My own experience is that *Marchantia polymorpha* is the commonest liverwort in such places and golden thread-moss *Leptobryum pyriforme* and creeping feather-moss *Amblystegium serpens* the commonest mosses. When pots are left undisturbed for more than a season, procumbent pearlwort (p. 116) is also a common higher plant coloniser (Fig. 116).

FIG 116. Procumbent pearlwort *Sagina procumbens* is one of the commonest colonisers of pots left undisturbed for more than a season.

GARDEN WALLS

Garden walls can be rich habitats for small wildlife, although the modern, concrete-based replica brick and stone materials that have understandably replaced the real thing seem to take longer to be colonised. Although new garden walls will in time become colonised by plants, the hard, unyielding quality of modern mortar, brick and artificial stone substitutes mean that it can be a long and rather token process. By contrast, walls built of traditional materials and left for more than two years will generally begin to display a characteristic microflora and microfauna as soil particles accumulate in crevices. Stone walls, especially if unmortared, provide both breeding and hiding places for small animals and habitats for a wide range of flowering plants, ferns and bryophytes.

Bryophytes

Many years ago, Raistrick & Gilbert (1963) conducted a most thorough and fascinating survey of a single building, the field studies centre of Malham Tarn House in West Yorkshire, and recorded in detail the bryophyte, algal and lichen flora of its walls. Bryophytes are usually the first to colonise, and their presence facilitates the more rapid accumulation of soil matter while they in turn begin to provide small amounts of humus. The commonest epilithic, wall-colonising moss is usually wall screw-moss *Tortula muralis*, and it has an ability to establish even on almost featureless brick or stone surfaces. It forms a rich, deep carpet of interconnected cushions on the 45 degree slope of the old handmade tiles on my garage roof. Other mosses commonly found on garden walls include the deep mound-forming capillary thread-moss *Bryum capillare* and the straggly, silky, wall feather-moss *Homalothecium sericeum* together with grey-cushioned grimmia *Grimmia pulvinata* (on the tops rather than the sides), anomalous bristle-moss *Orthotrichum anomalum* and sessile grimmia *Schistidium apocarpum*, the latter two especially frequent on limestone and concrete.

Liverworts, with their greater requirement for moisture, are much less common than mosses on garden walls unless the walls happen to be uncommonly damp. Raistrick & Gilbert (1963) found only two liverworts, common liverwort *Marchantia polymorpha* and greater featherwort *Plagiochila asplenioides*, on the walls of Malham Tarn House (despite an annual rainfall of 1,325 millimetres) compared with 23 mosses. Even then, it is generally only at the base or where there is a constant drip providing almost permanent free water that they will persist. Common liverwort *Marchantia polymorpha* and crescent-cup liverwort *Lunularia cruciata* are those I see most frequently, with forked veilwort *Metzgeria furcata* and wall scalewort *Porella platyphylla* also fairly common. When I was a child in Derbyshire, the base of one of our garden walls, admittedly rather exceptional in being washed by the adjoining little river, supported the most luxuriant growth that I have ever seen of that gloriously robust plant great scented liverwort *Conocephalum conicum.*

Lichens

Old garden walls are classic habitats for lichens. There were 36 species on Malham Tarn House, and it is a shame that in his more comprehensive recent account for the New Naturalist series Gilbert (2000) did not specifically consider the garden environment. He did, however, provide comprehensive lists of the lichens to be expected on 'village' walls of varying geological composition, and stressed how much the lichen flora of residential areas, villages especially, varies enormously as the local building stone varies. Cotswold villages like Burford, for instance, where strict planning regulations restrict house facings to limestone, have no calcifuge species. There is no merit in my repeating Gilbert's detailed lists, but I would simply add my own observations that the commonest of all garden wall lichens must be the more or less crustose *Lecanora muralis* which seems to be everywhere, *Ochrolechia parella* on acidic sandstone walls, *Lecanora*

FIG 117. *Xanthoria* species are among the commonest and most attractive lichens of garden walls.

campestris forming crustose white patches on limestone and the lovely and familiar orange growths of the confusingly similar species of *Xanthoria*. But despite my remarks about the lawn-inhabiting dog lichens *Peltigera* (p. 206f), lichen growth in general is undeniably slow compared with that of plants, and gardeners with new gardens and new walls will inevitably need to be moderately patient for a few years before they see things happening. But the patience will be rewarded. A fairly moist north-facing boundary wall to my garden that I see every day from my study window was built of old bricks 18 years ago. With our Warwickshire rainfall of 620 millimetres, the largest *Xanthoria* colony is now 1,250 millimetres in diameter: not huge, but with perhaps a hundred colonies in total on the wall, they certainly make a fine sight when they are caught in the glow of the morning sun (Fig. 117).

Invertebrates

Garden walls – or similar accumulations of loose stones – can provide important habitats for invertebrates, and the more holes in the wall, the better. Dry-stone walls, especially those in limestone areas, are extremely important for snails, and any gardener with such a wall as a boundary will have traced the numerous slime trails that betray their night-time foraging journeys from there into the vegetable plot. Spiders are attracted to similar sites. When I constructed my wildlife pond, the edges of the liner were initially concealed by masses of pebbles. In the months before these started to be colonised by plant life, they were alive with spiders and on a hot summer's day, many hundreds could be seen sunning themselves, only to dive for cover when someone's shadow approached. The British Isopod Survey (p. 212) revealed that rockeries were, after compost, the most important habitat for woodlice, and I have no doubt that comparable studies with many other invertebrate groups would reveal a similar pattern.

Ferns

Probably the commonest and most widespread garden wall ferns, especially where there is old lime mortar, are species of *Asplenium*, commonly called spleenworts. They make most welcome and beautiful additions to the garden flora. Overall, wall rue *A. ruta-muraria* is probably the commonest and most widespread, with black spleenwort *A. adiantum-nigrum* in more moist and especially coastal gardens and maidenhair spleenwort *A. trichomanes* subsp. *quadrivalens* in slightly drier places. The widespread rusty-back fern *Ceterach officinarum* becomes established in small crevices on well-exposed lime-rich walls that are not subject to excessive drying out, from where it spreads outwards over the wall face. In many old gardens in the Cotswolds, the Pennines and the

FIG 118. Parsley fern *Cryptogramma crispa*, a common wall-inhabiting species on acidic rocks.

far west of Britain, it can form extensive and very beautiful blankets clothing the walls. The calcifuge parsley fern *Cryptogramma crispa* is found extensively on walls of acidic rock in northern and western Britain and is a typical coloniser of slate walls in old Welsh gardens (Fig. 118).

Crevices in old dry-stone walls may be colonised by the two common *Polypodium* species, intermediate polypody *P. interjectum,* typically although not exclusively on limestone walls or among weathered lime mortar on walls of acidic rock, and the less calcicolous common polypody *P. vulgare,* more frequent on sandstone and gritstone walls. Hart's tongue fern *Phyllitis scolopendrium,* with its familiar undivided fronds, is also a common wall coloniser provided it has sufficient year-round humidity. It was the first fern to colonise the inner walls of my garden well when I fitted a glass cover and is still the dominant species there, although it has since been joined by wall rue *Asplenium ruta-muraria* and other species. Larger ferns including species of *Dryopteris* can and do colonise garden walls, especially in wetter western districts, but it is only in really old and generally neglected or wilder gardens that they reach significant size.

OPEN SOIL

By its nature, the open soil of beds and borders is disturbed regularly; in vegetable and annual flowerbeds, at least once a year when it is dug and then again when it is hoed. On longer-term beds, organic mulch will attract its own flora and fauna (p. 258f), but will suppress much soil-inhabiting life. In reality, however, shrubberies and herbaceous borders are often neglected; they are not mulched and the soil is left relatively undisturbed. It is then that unicellular green algae and a characteristic bryophyte flora may develop, including the mosses rough-stalked feather-moss *Brachythecium rutabulum*, common feather-moss *Eurhynchium praelongum*, clustered feather-moss *Rhynchostegium confertum*, common smoothcap *Atrichum undulatum*, bicoloured bryum *Bryum dichotomum* and both common and lesser pocket-mosses *Fissidens taxifolius* and *F. bryoides* together with the leafy liverworts bifid crestwort *Lophocolea bidentata* and creeping finger-wort *Lepidozia reptans*. Few among the larger fungi will tolerate disturbed soil, but there are two common species that seem to thrive in it. The first is the stinkhorn *Phallus impudicus*, generally revealed by its smell rather than its appearance, and which is perhaps the most characteristic large toadstool of disturbed ground generally – it is common on verges during road-widening operations. The second is the parasol *Macrolepiota procera*, one of the largest and most magnificent of all British toadstools.

Ferns are seldom significant colonisers of open beds and borders in gardens, principally because the disturbance gives them insufficient time to become established. Nonetheless, in wilder gardens where bracken *Pteridium aquilinum* already exists, it can be a serious and problematic weed. Among other ferns, *Dryopteris filix-mas* sometimes becomes naturalised, and because it is relatively tolerant of pollution, it can be found in neglected town gardens (Page, 1988).

Many invertebrates seem oblivious of or are actively encouraged by disturbance, and the soil of almost every garden (except it seems, Buckingham Palace – see Langton, 2001) will contain the commonest diplopod, the black millipede *Tachypodoiulus niger*, along with the pest species *Blaniulus guttulatus*. The commonest soil-inhabiting centipedes *Lithobius forficatus* and *Necrophlaeophagus flavus* will be in almost every garden too.

FIG 119. *Lithobius forficatus*, probably the commonest garden centipede.

MULCHED SOIL

Mulching of beds and borders, especially of longer-term plantings, has always been part of a good gardener's stock in trade to maintain soil moisture and keep down annual weed growth, but mulched soil has taken on a special significance as a garden habitat over the past 25 or 30 years since the advent of the widespread availability to gardeners of wood chips. I mentioned in Chapter 5 that a number of species of exotic fungi had appeared on wood chip mulches, but the wider significance has been that several native fungal species previously infrequent in or totally absent from gardens have become relatively common. Thanks to wood chips, even those holy grails of the mushroom collector, the morels *Morchella* spp., are no longer quite as rare in gardens (Overall, 2004). Brian Spooner at the Royal Botanic Gardens, Kew has kindly made available to me his working list of native macro-fungi recorded from wood chips (not necessarily all in gardens). It is a most impressive compilation and is clearly not exhaustive (Table 18).

I am on record as having said that the increasing use of wood chip and other mulches (especially for weed control as herbicide use has declined) has done much for the British woodlouse population. This was largely a conclusion based on my own observations, but my assumption that organic mulches and compost bins are the main garden habitats for these remarkable terrestrial isopods is amply borne out by the British Isopod Survey (p. 212).

TABLE 18. Macro-fungi recorded on wood chip mulches in Britain.

Agaricus lanipes	Agaricus placomyces	Agaricus stramineus (aff.)	Agaricus xanthoderma
Agaricus osecanus	Agaricus porphyrizon	Agrocybe arvalis	Agrocybe cf. pediades
Agrocybe praecox	Agrocybe molesta (dura)	Agrocybe gibberosa	Aleuria aurantia
Anixiopsis sp.	Arrhenia acerosa	Aspicilia contorta	Asterostroma medium
Basidiodendron caesiocinereum	Bolbitius titubans	Bolbitius vitellinus	Botryobasidium conspersum
Bovista nigrescens	Calocybe persicolor	Cercophora lundquistii (cf.)	Cladobotryum sp.
Clitocybe odora	Clitocybe phyllophila	Clitopilus cf. pinsitis	Clitopilus scyphoides
Collybia obscura	Coniochaeta velutina	Conocybe aporos	Conocybe arrhenii
Conocybe cf. kuehneriana	Conocybe lactea	Conocybe rickeniana	Conocybe rugosa
Conocybe siennophylla (cf.)	Conocybe mesospora	Conocybe subpubescens	Coprinus acuminatus
Coprinus auricomus	Coprinus callinus	Coprinus cinereus	Coprinus cortinatus (cf.)
Coprinus cothurnatus (cf.)	Coprinus disseminatus	Coprinus ephemerus	Coprinus erythrocephalus
Coprinus flocculosus	Coprinus galericuliformis	Coprinus hiascens	Coprinus kuehneri
Coprinus lagopus	Coprinus leiocephalus	Coprinus lilatinctus (cf.)	Coprinus marculentus
Coprinus micaceus	Coprinus narcoticus	Coprinus picaceus	Coprinus pseudofriesii
Coprinus sclero-cystidiosus (cf.)	Coprinus scobicola (cf.)	Coprinus subdis-seminatus (cf.)	Coprinus subpurpureus (cf.)
Coprinus pachydermus (cf.)	Coprinus plagioporus	Coprinus xenobius	Coprinus sp. (setulosi)
Crepidotus variabilis	Cristinia rhenana	Crucibulum laeve	Cyathus striatus
Cyathus olla	Encoelia siparia	Entoloma araneosum	Entoloma sordidulum
Geastrum triplex	Grifola frondosa	Gymnopilus penetrans	Hohenbuehelia geogenia
Hohenbuehelia sp.	Hyaloscypha aureliella	Hygrophoropsis ?pallida	Hyphodontia gossypina

TABLE 18. – *cont.*

Hypholoma marginatum	*Hypholoma subericaeum*	*Hypochniciellum coprophilum*	*Lasiosphaeria hispida*
Lepiota cortinarius	*Lepiota pseudolilacea* (cf.)	*Lepiota rubella*	*Lepiota aspera*
Lepiota cristata	*Lepista flaccida* (cf.)	*Leucocoprinus cretatus*	*Leucogyrophana mollusca*
Leucogyrophana pinastri	*Lycoperdon pyriforme*	*Macrocystidia cucumis*	*Macrolepiota rhacodes*
Marasmius rotula	*Marasmius oreades*	*Melanoleuca arcuata* (cf.)	*Melanoleuca cognata*
Melanoleuca oreina (cf.)	*Melanophyllum haematospermum*	*Melanotus horizontalis*	*Micromphale brassicolens*
Micromphale foetidum	*Micromphale impudicum*	*Mollisia cinerea*	*Morchella costata*
Morchella elata	*Mutinus caninus*	*Mycena amicta*	*Panaeolus acuminatus*
Panaeolus cinctulus	*Panaeolus olivaceus*	*Panaeolus semiovatus* var. *phalaenarum*	*Panaeolus subbalteatus*
Peziza arvernensis	*Peziza micropus*	*Peziza petersii*	*Peziza repanda*
Peziza sepiatra	*Peziza varia*	*Peziza vesiculosa*	*Phaeogalera oedipus*
Phaeohelotium geogenum	*Pholiota highlandensis* (cf.)	*Pholiota tuberculosa*	*Physisporinus sanguinolentus*
Pleurocybella porrigens	*Pluteus cinereofuscus*	*Pluteus griseoluridus*	*Pluteus nanus*
Pluteus pellitus	*Pluteus rimulosus*	*Pluteus romellii*	*Pluteus satur*
Pluteus thomsonii	*Preussia funiculata*	*Psathyrella artemisiae*	*Psathyrella candolleana*
Psathyrella conopilus	*Psathyrella corrugis*	*Psathyrella fusca*	*Psathyrella gossypina*
Psathyrella gracilis	*Psathyrella laevissima*	*Psathyrella marcesibilis*	*Psathyrella microrrhiza*
Psathyrella obtusata	*Psathyrella pennata*	*Psathyrella prona* f. *obitarum*	*Psathyrella pseudogracilis*
Psathyrella sacchariolens	*Psathyrella* sp.	*Psathyrella spadiceogrisea*	*Psilocybe crobula*
Psilocybe inquilina	*Psilocybe montana*	*Psilocybe phyllogena*	*Ramaria stricta*
Rhizocarpon obscuratum	*Scutellinia hirta*	*Sphaerobolus stellatus*	*Stachybotrys atra*
Strobilurus esculentus	*Stropharia caerulea*	*Stropharia inuncta*	*Stropharia squamosa*

TABLE 18. – *cont.*

Tubaria conspersa	*Tubaria furfuracea*	*Tubaria hiemalis*	*Tubaria* sp.
Tulasnella saveloides	*Verticillium biguttatum*	*Volvariella caesiotincta*	*Volvariella hypopithys*
Xylaria hypoxylon			

Although there is now official encouragement through the British Mycological Society for toadstools to be referred to where possible by an English name as well as their conventional scientific name (Holden, 2003), most of those in the table are not common enough to have been included in the new list and so I have referred to them all by scientific names only.

ROCK GARDENS

The rock garden, alpine trough or alpine house is arguably one of the least favourable garden environments for wildlife. The use of stone or gravel mulches to keep the soil cool and moist and to limit soil splash and soil-borne pathogens from reaching the flowers, creates an alien habitat for most British wildlife, although the trough itself, whether of real or artificial stone, can be an important substrate for lichens.

CLOCHES AND GREENHOUSES

Cloches provide temporary shelter and warmth for many small creatures, while greenhouses are especially important for many aliens from warmer climates (p. 15f), as well as offering year-round shelter and the possibility of year-round breeding for native species. Among bryophytes especially common in greenhouses are creeping feather-moss *Amblystegium serpens*, Kneiff's feather-moss *Leptodictyum riparium*, common cord-moss *Funaria hygrometrica*, golden thread-moss *Leptobryum pyriforme*, crescent-cup liverwort *Lunularia cruciata* and common liverwort *Marchantia polymorpha*. Many indigenous pests, although important outdoors, achieve even greater significance in the warmth of the greenhouse. Among them are numerous aphids, the root mealybug *Rhizoecus falcifer* which is particularly serious on plants growing in dry potting composts, and several species of woodlouse, especially *Armadillidium nasutum*, *Porcellio laevis* and *Androniscus dentiger*. But whilst the greenhouse may be sheltered, it is also one of the most controllable of garden environments, and one in which unwanted intruders, even small organisms, are soon spotted and eradicated.

By contrast, moreover, the protection afforded by the greenhouse structure itself, especially from fairly host-specific spore-dispersed diseases, does in some instances mean that problems which are common and important outdoors are seldom found, even when susceptible plants are grown. Tomato blight *Phytophthora infestans* and peach leaf curl *Taphrina deformans*, for instance, are especially infrequent in greenhouses.

ORCHARDS

The orchard, even a solitary fruit tree, is largely an undisturbed environment. If a tree is large enough, it will provide a nesting site for some garden birds, almost the only garden habitat for mistletoe *Viscum album* (Fig. 120) and, in the old bark, one of the best habitats for algae, some bryophytes and lichens, as well as many invertebrates. Gilbert (2000) gave a fascinating account of a tree-trunk

FIG 120. Mistletoe *Viscum album* is often found on old garden apple trees.

FIG 121. *Cladonia* species occur on old tree stumps.

ecosystem, albeit on ash trees and not in a garden, but the general pattern and variety of life is similar. Gilbert identified seven categories of tree-trunk dweller: green plants such as algae together with lichens (there were no bryophytes on his trees) which formed the base of the food chain; herbivores which browsed on them; omnivores and decomposers; carnivores preying on the herbivores, omnivores and decomposers; travellers going up and down the trunk to feed in the canopy; resting animals basking in the shade, and accidental species such as aphids and capsids that had fallen out of the canopy.

Even less appreciated than trees are tree stumps, although in drawing attention to them, I feel a pang of guilt. I have spent many years telling gardeners to be rid of stumps for the simple reason that they provide the commonest means of entry into gardens for honey fungus *Armillaria mellea*. That said, if they are allowed to remain, they will form a habitat for numerous other species of saprobic fungi, many lichens (*Hypogymnia physodes* and several beautiful species of *Cladonia* such as *C. pyxidata* are highly characteristic (Fig. 121)), some bryophytes like the foliose liverwort creeping finger-wort *Lepidozia reptans*, and of course huge numbers of wood-destroying insects and other invertebrates.

GARDEN PONDS

Water gardens are extremely rich habitats for smaller organisms, not all of which are horticulturally desirable. There are many authoritative texts on pond life which are as applicable to garden ponds as to natural ones, so I will simply confine myself here to those microscopic forms that in some way make their presence rather obvious to gardeners. Algae are present in large quantities in every pond, but they can create problems when excessive nutrients in the water encourage unicellular forms such as *Chlamydomonas*, *Volvox* and *Chlorella* to cause the familiar pea-soup effect, or filamentous types such as *Spirogyra*, *Rhizoclonium*, *Enteromorpha* and *Cladophora* to be manifest as blanket weed. Although blanket weed itself provides a habitat for other microscopic organisms, pond algae overall are considered unsightly, they obscure other forms of aquatic life and they can lead to a diminution of the oxygen supply. Gardeners' options include physically pulling out blanket weed as well as biological, mechanical or ultraviolet filtration, chemical algicides such as photosynthesis inhibitors, or submerging bags or rafts of barley straw or lavender clippings to act as natural algicides. In 2003, the RHS was advocating 'roughly 25–50 grams of straw per square metre of water surface', although there seems some doubt about how the algicidal effect is produced, and even whether the use of straw is now legal. The most widely accepted explanation for the algicidal effect is that the straw decomposes by bacterial action and releases lignins which, after intermediate reactions, ultimately liberate hydrogen peroxide. The hydrogen peroxide in turn inhibits the growth of algae. The EU, however, seems to have deemed this an unapproved method of chemical control and has banned it.

The invertebrate life of ponds, both above and below the water surface and also at the air–water interface, is legion. It is extremely well documented, and I do not intend to dwell on it here save to draw attention to one small aspect of its value in aiding garden biodiversity. In the ten years before I constructed my own wildlife garden and specific wildlife pond, I recorded five species of dragonfly in the garden. In the five years since, I have recorded fifteen.

Before leaving microscopic aquatic organisms, and to emphasise that there will be life wherever you look, I wonder how many wildlife gardeners think of adding *Saprolegnia* species (Oomycetes) to their list of recorded organisms. They will be present in a large number of ponds as the causes of one of the commonest fish diseases.

GARDEN PESTS

Now from microscopic fungi in ponds to microscopic fungi elsewhere. Every garden plant is host to at least some micro-fungi and invertebrate pests, and chapter if not verse on the commoner and more important species can be found in Buczacki & Harris (2005). But because pest species have a special resonance for gardeners, rather more attention has been paid to their relative frequencies. I have mentioned elsewhere the increase in occurrence of the vine weevil that followed the widespread use of peat in potting composts (p. 254). The RHS, on the basis of the number of enquiries received by its Advisory Service, was describing the weevil as the top garden pest in 2003. It was usually the top insect pest, although woodlice and slugs generally outranked it, but it had not won the overall prize since 1999. The complete 2003 top ten was:

1. vine weevil *Otiorhynchus sulcatus*
2. lily beetle *Lilioceris lilii*
3. slugs and snails
4. chafer grubs in lawns
5. rabbits
6. cushion scale *Chloropulvinula floccifera*
7. soft scale *Coccus hesperidum*
8. glasshouse red spider mite *Tetranychus urticae*
9. deer
10. ants

Nonetheless, these RHS lists change appreciably year by year and in 2005, the vine weevil had dropped to number three. The list then was:

1. slugs and snails
2. lily beetle
3. vine weevil
4. rosemary beetle *Crysolina americana*
5. grey squirrel
6. leatherjackets *Tipula* spp.
7. chafer grubs
8. soft scale
=9. cushion scale
=9. glasshouse mealybugs

These are interesting lists, but I suspect they say almost as much about the
geographical distribution of the membership of the RHS (and to some extent
about the plants they grow) and the number of gardeners keen enough to send
samples for identification as it does about pests. Lily beetle, for instance,
although now widespread, was for a long time essentially a pest of south-eastern
England. I surmise that a top ten pest list for the north-west would be rather
different.

Valuable information on the relative occurrences of different micro-
organisms can also be found in several databases (see, for example, the British
Mycological Society database (http://194.203.77.76/fieldmycology/)). However,
it is perhaps worth drawing attention to some objective data on the relative
frequencies of different types of major pest and disease organism in gardens
as revealed by two London surveys – that by Honey *et al.* (1998) of the recently
created wildlife garden at the Natural History Museum and the two volumes
edited by Plant (1999; 2001) of the highly comprehensive survey of the garden
at Buckingham Palace to which numerous experts contributed.

Admittedly, neither was a typical garden, much less an average domestic
garden, but the data are better than most available and the Buckingham Palace
survey certainly set a high standard. Among the fungi, Honey *et al.* found
'an overwhelming preponderance of powdery mildews (Erysiphales)', most of
which were dismissed as '*Oidium* sp.' together with some common and widely
distributed rusts (Uredinales), no smuts (Ustilaginales) and a few ascomycetes.
At Buckingham Palace, 24 species of rust and 45 powdery mildews as well as a
considerable number of plant pathogenic species were recorded among 630 fungi
(Henrici, 2001). I should add in passing that the publications describing the
results of these two surveys, especially that of Buckingham Palace, also contain
much information on the presence of other groups of garden-inhabiting
organisms, large and small, with some analysis of their significance.

BUTTERFLIES AND MOTHS

*Don't ever let anyone tell you that beauty doesn't matter. By most people's reckoning,
butterflies and to some degree moths … are the most beautiful and obvious of insects.
They have therefore attracted attention and interest far out of proportion to their
numerical or zoological importance. There are four butterflies (out of around 60) and
five moths (out of around 2,500) on the list of species protected under the Wildlife and
Countryside Act 1981; there are only four other insects (out of around 21,000). There are
societies for the conservation of butterflies but they give rather little attention to the*

larger moths and even less to the minor ones; and no-one seems in the least interested
in conserving even the rarest of aphids, lice or fleas. (Buczacki, 2002)

Yes, it is a sad truth that while ladybirds are welcome in gardens, along with
dragonflies, perhaps the larger moths and above all the butterflies, no-one is
really interested in inviting much else – although gardeners are now being
encouraged to put out boxes for bumblebees and nests for *Osmia* bees. 'Plants
to attract butterflies' have indeed become a *sine qua non* for any wildlife garden,
although the contribution such plants may or may not make to butterfly
conservation is generally ignored and even the value of growing larval food
plants in gardens is now being questioned (p. 246). Given this general interest
in butterflies, however, it comes as a surprise to realise that even here gardens
have been neglected areas of study (Vickery, 1995). I can only endorse Vickery's
comments, which of course could apply equally to almost every other animal
group:

> *Many individuals have kept records of the butterflies in their own gardens and a few*
> *have published these ... Although such records are interesting and can be helpful to the*
> *management of that particular garden, extrapolation to the garden habitat in general is*
> *fraught with inaccuracy. Only surveys involving many gardens can give an accurate*
> *picture ...*

Limited surveys have been performed by a number of individuals such as
Owen (1991) and bodies including WATCH, the junior branch of the Royal Society
for Nature Conservation, which organised a summer count in 1981; the Essex
Wildlife Trust, which surveyed 460 gardens during 1991; and the RSPB's Young
Ornithologists Club, which oversaw a summer (school holidays) survey of 288
gardens in 1992. The most serious study was probably that reported by Warren &
Stephens (1989) and Stephens & Warren (1992) who surveyed 24 Dorset gardens
during 1985. One of the most original features of the Dorset survey lay in its
attempt to relate butterfly incidence to garden design, although the findings
were fairly obvious. It was found that gardens broken up by internal hedges or
borders attracted more butterflies than those with large areas of hard surface.

The British Butterfly Conservation Society (now known as Butterfly
Conservation) launched a national garden butterfly survey in 1990. This ran for
three years and involved over 1,000 gardens; in practice, during 1991 and 1992,
two parallel surveys were run, one for Butterfly Conservation members and the
other for members of the Women's Institute. Recorders compiled such data as
the frequency of butterflies visiting gardens, the dates of first sightings and the

presence of particular nectar plants. Full details of the survey were published by
Vickery (1995) from which a number of clear conclusions can be drawn. The five
commonest butterflies were the large white *Pieris brassicae*, small white *P. rapae*,
red admiral *Vanessa atalanta*, small tortoiseshell *Aglais urticae* (Fig. 122) and
peacock *Inachis io*, although their exact placings on the list varied slightly
(Table 19).

There were understandable regional variations too. Fewer than 10 per cent
of gardens in the north of England compared with a third of southern gardens
could expect more than 18 species. No Scottish gardens recorded more than
12 species. There were trends concerning the type and size of garden, although
these largely confirmed what could reasonably have been guessed. More butterfly
species were recorded in large than in small gardens, more in rural than urban
gardens, more in gardens that completely surrounded a house (which presumably were generally larger), and more in sunny than shaded gardens. A particular
value of these surveys for gardeners, however, lay in their attempts to relate
butterfly incidence to the types of plant present (Table 20).

Vickery pointed out that 'It is generally agreed that butterflies visit gardens
primarily in order to feed on nectar plants' but that in the past 'Extrapolation
from observations in a single garden to the garden habitat as a whole has led to
many inaccuracies in published lists of supposed good butterfly nectar plants'.

FIG 122. Small tortoiseshell *Aglais urticae* caterpillar on stinging nettle *Urtica dioica*.
The extent to which butterflies use nettles in gardens is disputed.

TABLE 19. The 22 species of butterfly recorded most commonly in British gardens in surveys conducted by Butterfly Conservation, as a percentage of the total number of gardens recorded (after Vickery, 1995).

BUTTERFLY SPECIES		YEAR				
		1990 Butterfly Conservation Survey	1991 Butterfly Conservation Survey	1991 Women's Institute Survey	1992 Butterfly Conservation Survey	1992 Women's Institute Survey
small tortoiseshell	Aglais urticae	97	98	94	99	99
small white	Pieris rapae	93	93	84	93	88
large white	Pieris brassicae	92	94	92	97	92
red admiral	Vanessa atalanta	91	92	87	98	97
peacock	Inachis io	83	88	96	96	95
orange tip	Anthocaris cardamines	79	80	77	86	85
meadow brown	Maniola jurtina	76	78	68	80	68
holly blue	Celastrina argiolus	75	73	56	74	62
green-veined white	Pieris napi	71	69	39	60	40
comma	Polygonia c-album	71	81	64	75	62
speckled wood	Pararge aegeria	61	68	44	59	55
gatekeeper	Pyronia tithonus	61	65	56	70	68
small copper	Lycaena phlaeas	60	47	32	42	28
brimstone	Gonepteryx rhamni	56	60	53	64	56
painted lady	Cynthia cardui	56	64	50	72	49
common blue	Polyommatus icarus	46	45	46	54	39
wall	Lasiommata megera	39	30	34	37	41
small skipper	Thymelicus sylvestris	36	38	19	32	19
large skipper	Ochlodes venata	33	25	5	24	10
ringlet	Aphantopus hyperantus	17	17	9	21	6
small heath	Coenonympha pamphilus	15	9	6	11	12
marbled white	Melanargia galathea	9	8	–	6	6

TABLE 20. Nectar plants used as food sources by butterflies in gardens throughout the British Isles, in surveys conducted by Butterfly Conservation 1991–2; ranked by two-year mean (based on Vickery, 1995).

PLANT	NUMBER OF BUTTERFLY SPECIES REPORTING FEEDING	
	1991	1992
Buddleja spp.	27	29
Lavandula × *intermedia*	21	26
Aubrieta deltoidea	15	20
Hebe spp.	13	22
Scabiosa spp.	20	23
Centranthus ruber	18	23
Origanum vulgare	19	21
Rubus spp.	16	24
Eupatorium cannabinum	16	22
Thymus vulgaris	13	24
Lobelia erinus	18	18
Mentha spp.	17	19
Sedum spectabile	17	19
Ligustrum spp.	17	18
Erigeron spp.	14	19
Aster spp. [summer]	14	18
Aster spp. [autumn]	14	18
Iberis spp.	12	20
Tagetes patula	15	17
Tagetes erecta	15	16
Solidago canadensis	16	14
Alyssum spp	12	17
Erica spp.	13	16
Myosotis alpestris	13	16
Phlox spp.	9	20
Coreopsis spp.	13	15
Nepeta × *faasenii*	13	15
Dianthus barbatus	11	16
Hesperis matronalis	9	17
Erysimum cheiri	12	13
Phaseolus coccineus	9	13
Lunaria annua	8	10
Primula spp.	6	8

In these surveys, there was a positive relationship between the presence and frequency of a butterfly species in a garden and the number of favourite nectar plants – four of the top five butterflies fed on the largest number of nectar plants while the least common fed on the least number. Common migrants such as red admiral and painted lady *Cynthia cardui* used fewer nectar plants than common residents of similar percentage presence. The greater the variety of nectar plants in a garden, the greater the number of species of butterfly. In the 1992 survey, it was found that gardens with fewer than 20 different nectar plants had only a 31 per cent chance of recording more than 14 butterfly species, while those with more than 20 plants had a 65 per cent chance of doing so.

Little information was obtained about butterfly breeding in gardens, although there seemed to be a trend for it to be commoner in rural than urban gardens. The species recorded breeding were the same as those noted by Stephens & Warren (1992) – small white, large white, orange tip *Anthocaris cardamines*, holly blue *Celastrina argiolus*, small tortoiseshell, peacock, comma *Polygonia c-album*, speckled wood *Pararge aegeria*, gatekeeper *Pyronia tithonus* and meadow brown *Maniola jurtina*. In a separate survey of nettle patches in gardens, Vickery found that only about half were used by nettle-feeding nymphalids for egg laying (Vickery, 1995). Stephens & Warren (1992) also found that nettle patches were not generally used and the jury still seems to be out on whether these so often recommended components of a wildlife garden really are of any merit (see also p. 273).

A further survey, called predictably enough Garden Butterflies Count, was held during 2002. It was billed as the biggest survey of garden butterflies and moths ever undertaken in the United Kingdom, and more than 30,000 survey packs were distributed to members of the public. Over 11,000 responded and the survey was repeated in 2003, although with slightly lower overall support. It was then discontinued through lack of sponsorship. The top five species were the same as those reported in the earlier surveys and no startlingly obvious new information was uncovered (Table 21).

The conclusion from these surveys and the many hours of work put in by numerous well-intentioned persons is equivocal. Just what does yet another butterfly survey really tell us? And how much has butterfly conservation in the wide sense benefited from them? Where are the surveys of the countless other species of garden insect, and where is the research and practice that should be drawing on the raw data of the surveys? As is evident throughout the whole area of garden natural history, a little has been done with the best of motives, but a vast amount remains.

TABLE 21. Butterfly Conservation Garden Butterfly Counts, 2002 and 2003.

2003 RANKING	SPECIES	PERCENTAGE OF GARDENS WITH EACH SPECIES IN 2003	PERCENTAGE OF GARDENS WITH EACH SPECIES IN 2002 (RANKING IN BRACKETS)
1	red admiral *Vanessa atalanta*	95	81 (3)
2	large white *Pieris brassicae*	92	87 (1)
3	small white *Pieris rapae*	91	83 (2)
4	small tortoiseshell *Aglais urticae*	89	73 (5)
5	peacock *Nymphalis io*	86	75 (4)
6	painted lady *Vanessa cardui*	83	53 (6)
7	comma *Polygonia c-album*	66	50 (9)
8	meadow brown *Maniola jurtina*	64	54 (8)
9	gatekeeper *Pyronia tithonus*	60	49 (10)
10	orange-tip *Anthocaris cardamines*	57	41 (12)
11	speckled wood *Pararge aegeria*	56	50 (11)
12	brimstone *Gonepteryx rhamni*	50	36 (13)
13	holly blue *Celastrina argiolus*	49	52 (7)
14	[hummingbird hawk moth *Macroglossum stellatarum*]	39	16 (18)
15	green-veined white *Pieris napi*	33	30 (14)

CHAPTER 9

The Role of the Gardener as Conservator

I T IS IMPOSSIBLE TO open a gardening magazine or to see a television gardening programme today without coming face to face with a conservation message. Gardeners are constantly being asked to conserve, preserve, protect, save, do and don't to the extent that if we undertook it all there would surely be little time left to mow the lawn. To what extent is this an attempt to salve our consciences, and to what extent can gardeners really do anything meaningful? I have touched in earlier chapters on the ways that gardens can be used to attract passing creatures and in Chapter 6 I referred to studies showing that a material contribution can be made to bird nesting sites. Here I want to explore the theme more widely.

ENCOURAGING WILDLIFE

Michael Majerus, author of the New Naturalist volume on ladybirds, gave guidelines for attracting ladybirds to the garden (and mentioned in passing that he recorded over half the British species in his own garden in 1995) (Majerus, 1996). Among Majerus's important suggestions were: do not use general (wide-spectrum) pesticides in the garden; maintain a diversity of plant species; plant species that will encourage aphids (not a suggestion that most gardeners would instantly entertain, although Majerus advises plants such as lime, oak, birch and hawthorn which will not be detrimental to 'flowers and vegetables'); plant native plant species; have a garden pond; leave at least a small area of weeds; have some late-summer-flowering nectar plants; do not remove all mildewed foliage until mid-October as some ladybirds including the 22-spot ladybird *Thea 22-punctata* feed on mildew; plant a few species such as pampas grass *Cortaderia selloana* and gorse *Ulex europaeus* which are effective at providing overwintering sites; plant mixed rather than single species hedges; and provide shelter for those species like the 2-spot ladybird *Adalia 2-punctata* that prefer to overwinter inside buildings. Although Majerus did not mention them, perhaps because they were not available in 1996, specially designed ladybird 'houses' (along with bee houses and other types of invertebrate lodging place) are now sold for this purpose by some environmental supply companies (Fig. 123).

All Majerus's advice is sound and reasoned, not much of it contentious, and most of his suggestions generally not too hard to carry out. But ladybirds – like

FIG 123. Purpose-made boxes are sold to encourage hibernating ladybirds although they are just as likely to be used by other insects.

birds – are fairly obvious creatures and therefore fairly obvious targets for our efforts. Some of the organisms that I considered in Chapter 8 are at least as deserving of our assistance but much less obvious, and one of the most unexpected and unappreciated contributions that gardeners can make towards aiding biodiversity lies with encouraging the lower plants and fungi. Much can be done relatively easily to encourage the growth of macro-fungi, but the potential is greater still. Leaving piles of logs, especially hardwood logs, should be a *sine qua non* for any wildlife garden as they provide shelter for a large number of invertebrates (although gardeners should, of course, resist the temptation too regularly to peep underneath and should always replace the logs carefully in the same position). They are also most important substrates for bryophytes and wood-rotting fungi. The fact that a combination of wood-destroying insects and fungi will gradually cause the logs to disappear should be taken as a positive rather than a negative result. Much less appreciated is the potential that wildlife gardens offer for the conservation and encouragement of grassland fungi, including members of the Clavariaceae, Hygrophoraceae, Entolomaceae and Geoglossaceae; and, most especially, the waxcaps *Hygrocybe* spp.

Waxcaps

Paradoxically, closely mown turf, the very type of grassland that is less satisfactory for the encouragement of flowering plant diversity, can be ideal for waxcaps (Fig. 124). Overall, it is encouraging to note that the United Kingdom is particularly important for grassland fungi; in many parts of Europe, intensive agriculture on the one hand and lack of grassland management leading to a reversion to scrub on the other have led to a serious decline in these species (Fungus Conservation Forum, n.d). Of the 11,000 or so records of *Hygrocybe* in the British Mycological Society Fungal Records Database (http://194.203.77.76/fieldmycology/), there are approximately 550 from lawn or garden habitats. Moreover, since 2000, fungi have been included among the criteria for designation of a site as an SSSI, and all those sites considered in the first two years were waxcap grassland habitats – at least three of them lawns – at Roecliffe Manor in Cheshire, Milham Ford School in Oxfordshire and Llanerchaeron in Ceredigion (a National Trust property). The lawns at Roecliffe Manor, which is now an SSSI on the basis of its 24 taxa of waxcap grassland fungi, support five Red Data List fungal species: beige coral *Clavulinopsis umbrinella*, dotted fanvault *Camarophyllopsis atropuncta*, *C. foetens*, pink waxcap *Hygrocybe calyptriformis* and big blue pinkgill *Entoloma bloxamii*, making it a quite outstanding mycological example of unimproved grassland habitat in England.

FIG 124. Scarlet waxcap *Hygrocybe coccinea*. A waxcap lawn is one of the most rare and beautiful of fungal habitats and can be recreated in gardens.

With relatively little effort, gardeners can assist in the conservation of waxcaps, and the Fungus Conservation Forum publication cited gives useful guidance. It is entirely realistic to believe that 'waxcap lawns' could be made fashionable in the same way that careful publicity and reeducation a decade ago encouraged the growing of wild flower meadows, although some species are more likely to appear than others, and the finest waxcap grasslands will take decades if not hundreds of years to develop. I am grateful to Shelley Evans, my colleague in the British Mycological Society, for much of the following guidance. Realistically, from a re-seeded lawn it may be feasible to encourage possibly one or two species in a decade, but it would be a slow process to obtain a full colour range of the more attractive and rare types. From an 'abused' lawn, things should happen rather more quickly. It is known that the addition of inorganic fertilisers, moss killers and lime has an immediate effect on fruit-body production – the fruit-bodies disappear, although it is not known how well the underlying mycelium can cope or recover. Nonetheless, in most cases, when applications of moss killer and fertiliser cease, some recovery will take place with time. One study found that the more common species such as snowy waxcap *Hygrocybe virginea* and blackening waxcap *H. conica* can reappear after 10 years, but that more sensitive (and high value indicator) species like splendid waxcap *H. splendidissima* could take over 30 years to recover.

The waxcap lawn requires regular mowing and the clippings removed. This should continue until early autumn when the fungi begin to fruit and the grass may be allowed to grow. Absence of mowing has been shown to have a detrimental effect on fruit-body production and of course there will be changes in the associated plant communities (Keizer, 1993). A feature of a typically good waxcap lawn is the presence of moss cover. In Wales, spring turf-moss *Rhytidiadelphus squarrosus* has proved an important species, and in an extensive ecological study in Holland, Arnolds (1981, 1982) described several fungi including parrot waxcap *Hygrocybe psittacina*, glutinous waxcap *H. glutinipes* and vermilion waxcap *H. miniata* as saprotrophic species associated with the moss. It is quite acceptable to walk on a waxcap lawn and use it recreationally in the same way as usual; and, oddly enough, some trampling is even thought to be beneficial to certain groups like the earth tongues *Geoglossum* spp. Overall, the conclusion seems to be that looking after and encouraging a waxcap lawn is a good deal less work than trying to destroy it!

Mammals, invertebrates and birds

A Mammal Society survey (p. 151) showed that the average gardener is likely to see just seven different mammals in their garden (hedgehog, pipistrelle, grey squirrel, field vole, wood mouse, house mouse and fox) and, according to Gaston & Thompson (2002): '... if you live in a city ... it doesn't matter what you do or how hard you try to attract [them] you will never see any more'. That seems to me a gross and oversimplified generalisation which depends in considerable measure on what you mean by 'in a city'. I know city gardens where I could easily almost double the list by adding mole, Daubenton's bat, brown rat, bank vole, rabbit and common shrew. Nonetheless, Gaston & Thompson used this paucity of mammals to justify concentrating their Sheffield University project on invertebrates 'because that's where the real biodiversity of gardens is to be found'.

This careful and detailed study merits closer examination to see what evidence it produced that gardens do have conservation value. The 61 gardens studied were carefully selected to offer a range of garden types, ages and sizes, right across the city of Sheffield from the urban heart to the edge of open countryside. In each garden, Gaston & Thompson's group sampled terrestrial invertebrates with pitfall traps and flying insects with Malaise traps. They also analysed leaf litter and identified all plants present. Over 37,000 individual invertebrates in over 786 species were identified, but even this survey was limited by the timescale and the lack of expertise in some taxonomic groups. Clearly, Gaston & Thompson did not overestimate when they said there were probably tens of thousands of invertebrate species in gardens; some very common, some rare, some new to science. They reached a number of significant conclusions, most notably that it is a myth that only large gardens are 'good for wildlife'. Whilst these contain more biodiversity, there is no qualitative difference between a large and a small garden. Second, they believed their results showed that suburban gardens are as valuable for wildlife as those in rural areas. But third, and most controversially, they believed their results showed:

> ... no evidence at all that the number of native plants in your garden has any effect on the invertebrate wildlife which your garden supports ... gardens that had many different plants were better than gardens that had few different plants. But it absolutely didn't matter whether those plants were alien or native, it was simply the total biodiversity which was important. There is nothing wrong with native plants and if you want to plant lots of native plants in your garden, it won't do any harm, but it won't necessarily do any specific good in attracting wildlife.

That conclusion is highly controversial; the supporting data were not published, there is much information to the contrary from elsewhere, cited in other parts of this book, and it certainly flies in the face of my own experience: I can walk from my own 'normal garden' to my own native plant garden and be almost literally overwhelmed by the difference. It is also counter to the view offered by bodies and organisations with much longer experience in these matters, such as the British Trust for Ornithology:

> It is well known that native species of plant generally support a more diverse community of animals than non-native species, simply because the two groups have existed alongside one another for many generations and have developed complex relationships. (Toms, 2003)

None of this, however, is to say that Gaston & Thompson were totally wrong – or even totally flying a kite, which may have been closer to the truth. It was of considerable interest and surprise, for instance, that Owen (1991) found the alien *Buddleja davidii* the most widely used food plant for moth larvae in her Leicester garden. Eighteen species fed on it. And Comba, Corbet, Barron *et al.* (1999), in a detailed study of nectar production and insect visits to nasturtium *Tropaeolum majus* (Fig. 125), larkspur *Consolida* sp., snapdragon *Antirrhinum majus*, winter-flowering pansy *Viola* × *wittrockiana*, tagetes *Tagetes patula* and hollyhock *Alcea rosea*, concluded that: 'Garden flowers can be valuable to wildlife if they produce nectar, pollen and/or seeds'. However, many garden flowers originating in Europe are bee-pollinated and are often yellow, blue or purple with a corolla

FIG 125. *Tropaeolum majus*, an exotic species extensively visited by insects.

tube no longer than a bee's tongue. In a later, more complex study, Corbet *et al.* (2001) found a number of exotic plants of little value for British insects – *Salvia splendens*, for example, which, like many tropical flowers, probably co-evolved with humming birds, has such deep flowers that British bees could only reach the nectar by crawling down the corolla. Some double-flowered garden forms of *Petunia*, *Saponaria* and *Lotus* secrete little or no nectar, and except in *Calendula* where doubling involved a change in the proportion of disc and ray florets rather than modification of individual flower structure, exotic or double flowers in general were little exploited by insect visitors. In a related study (Comba, Corbet, Hunt & Warren, 1999), it was shown that even in native plants, production of nectar must be taken in conjunction with other factors such as flower structure. Some deep flowers, for instance, may be preferentially valuable to long-tongued bumblebees as their nectar cannot be reached by honey bees.

Speaking at the same RHS conference at which Gaston & Thompson's views were expounded, Baines (2002), himself a tireless campaigner for wildlife gardens, commented that he felt the remarks were only true 'as long as there is a broader landscape from which to draw the wildlife in the gardens'. He believed that gardens are successful for much wildlife, especially many bird species, because they represent an equivalent habitat to the woodland glade. And he has long believed in the principle of the garden being a 'service station' in the wider landscape (Baines, 1985). For example, he considers that grape hyacinths *Muscari* spp., although not native plants, are valuable because they provide a supply of nectar for insects early in the year when there is little otherwise available.

I have cited ample evidence for the importance of gardens in assisting the conservation of some bird species, the report by Bland *et al.* (2004) being especially revealing (p. 142). Evans (2002) has also pointed out that the data from BTO surveys (p. 142) suggested that 'as we turn our environment into an agricultural desert ... gardens actually provide a refuge' for declining bird species. More than 50 per cent of the entire United Kingdom population of house sparrows and starlings is associated with gardens, along with 25 per cent of song thrushes and 10 per cent of bullfinches. Gardens have become particularly important for many species because of changes in farming practices – clearing of ditches and similar invertebrate habitats, the switch from spring to autumn sowing of cereals with the consequent loss of overwinter stubble, and the removal of hedgerows and dead wood. By way of compensation for what is therefore lacking, says Evans, gardens can provide three important features – nesting sites, adult food and chick food. Nesting sites are most obviously provided by nest boxes (p. 145), but the presence of trees, shrubs, hedges and buildings all play an important part. My own experience with gardeners has shown that management is at least as important. Provision of a hedgerow is all very well, but if you clip it at precisely the time the local blackbirds are incubating, its conservation value will instantly be reduced to nought. Provision of buildings is not difficult – after all, every garden has a house attached to it – but ensuring that the decorator or window cleaner does not disturb (or remove) house martin nests is the rather important rider. Whilst most people know that to disturb roosting bats transgresses the law, rather fewer would admit to knowing that house martins are also blessed with protection.

Bird food is most obviously provided by bird tables and bird feeders (p. 136ff), but appropriate planting is also essential: fruiting shrubs, herbaceous perennials with persisting seed heads and so forth. However, it is important also to bear in mind the significance of something I wrote some years ago – that the modern garden is largely a garden of hybrids. An important consequence of this for wildlife is that a smaller proportion of the plants sets seeds than was the case in gardens of an earlier generation. So the fewer the sterile hybrids, the fewer double flowers, the better for birds, rodents and other creatures. Gardeners should also bear in mind that it is impossible to satisfy the needs of every bird and every creature all of the time. Evans (2002) commented that the RSBP Big Garden Birdwatch (p. 147) demonstrated, for example, that reed buntings *Emberiza schoeniculus* only tend to enter gardens in February or March and use artificial seed sources when the natural seed supply is at lowest. Bullfinches, by contrast, are commonly found in gardens in June, feeding on young fruit and buds, and sometimes nesting. And as with nesting sites, in many instances it is as important for gardeners to desist as to do. Growing of seeding perennials is only of value if the seed heads are not cut back in the cause of autumnal tidiness. Removal of ivy from trees and structures can also be a mixed blessing. Filling the crowns of trees, ivy can render them unstable, and on the crumbly bricks and lime mortar of old houses, it can be highly destructive, so here needs must and the ivy should go. But on modern bricks and mortar it should do no harm, and its provision of food and shelter for many creatures can justify its retention. And on many an old wall, as in my own garden, it is the ivy that holds the whole thing together.

Biological pest controls

The range of biological pest controls available to gardeners has increased significantly in recent years and has given greater impetus to a move away from the use of wide-spectrum chemical control measures. The most important currently available are summarised in Table 22 and, in theory at least, their use should have long-term benefits for garden wildlife. However, I am all too aware that many gardeners still view their effectiveness with circumspection. I suspect this has as much to do with perception and gardener mentality than actual efficacy. You can see a chemical spray kill aphids and caterpillars before your eyes. Miracles and biological control take longer. I am reminded of the fate in the garden market some years ago of a chemical called propachlor. This was a pre-emergence weedkiller in granular form which was effective for six to eight weeks and safe to use among most garden plants. As it did not affect weeds once they had emerged from the seed, it was applied to weed-free soil – after planting

TABLE 22. Biological pest controls available for garden use.

PEST	BIOLOGICAL CONTROL ORGANISM	NOTES ON USE AND LIMITATIONS
aphids	*Aphidoletes aphidimyza* (a predatory midge)	greenhouse use at a minimum air temperature of 10°C
aphids	*Aphidius matricariae* (a parasitic wasp)	greenhouse use at a minimum air temperature of 10°C
aphids and other pests	*Chrysoperla carnea* (a lacewing)	greenhouse/outdoor use at a minimum air temperature of 10°C
caterpillars	*Bacillus thuringiensis* (a bacterium)	greenhouse/outdoor use; applied as a spray. Will kill all caterpillars, not only pest species
fungus gnats	*Hypoaspis miles* (a predatory mite)	greenhouse use at a minimum air temperature of 12°C
glasshouse whitefly	*Encarsia formosa* (a parasitic wasp)	greenhouse use at a minimum air temperature of 18°C
glasshouse whitefly	*Delphastus pusillus* (a predatory ladybird beetle)	greenhouse use at a minimum air temperature of 15°C
mealybug	*Cryptolaemus montrouzieri* (a predatory ladybird beetle)	greenhouse use at a minimum air temperature of 20°C
red spider mites	*Phytoseiulus persimilis* (a predatory mite)	best in a greenhouse at a minimum air temperature of 10°C
scale insects (soft scale only)	*Metaphycus helvolus* (a parasitic wasp)	greenhouse use at a minimum air temperature of 22°C
slugs	*Phasmarhabditis hermaphroditica* (a bacteria-carrying nematode)	outdoor use at a minimum soil temperature of 5°C
soil pests (some)	*Steinernema carpocapsae* (a bacteria-carrying nematode)	outdoor use at a minimum soil temperature of 14°C
thrips	*Amblyseius cucumeris* (a predatory mite)	greenhouse/outdoor use at a minimum air temperature of 10°C and high humidity
vine weevil (larvae)	*Heterorhabditis megadis* (a bacteria-carrying nematode)	outdoor use at a minimum soil temperature of 12°C
vine weevil (larvae)	*Steinernema carpocapsae* (a bacteria-carrying nematode)	outdoor use at a minimum soil temperature of 14°C

FIG 126. Whitefly scales parasitised by the small South American wasp *Encarsia formosa*.

or among young seedling plants. It was, however, soon withdrawn from sale, not for reasons of toxicity, but because the manufacturers were unable to persuade people to use a weedkiller before they could see any weeds.

Garden ponds

Trevor Beebee has shown most convincingly that a garden pond can aid the conservation of amphibians (p. 158), although of course ponds provide succour for many other creatures too, and I have no doubt that groups devoted to conserving water fleas, water boatmen and rat-tailed maggots issue comparable advice to their members (Fig. 127). But because water gardening has become horticulture's new rock and roll, and a 'water feature' is something every garden must have, it is easy to fall into the trap of thinking that any pond will do. Beebee & Griffiths (2000) gave advice specifically intended to encourage amphibians, but the guidelines have overall relevance too. The major considerations were that the pond should be at least 50 centimetres deep in the centre with shelves of varying depth; should be in as sunny a position as possible; should have a range of marginal and submerged plants ('preferably native British species' (p. 163ff)); should have no fish; should be colonised naturally by the animals; should be cleared out once a year; and the surface should be kept ice-free. Beebee & Griffith also pointed out that the materials from which the pond is constructed are not important. In practice, the advice given by the British Dragonfly Society on its website (www.dragonflysoc.org.uk) is essentially the same, except that its

FIG 127. A garden pond is one of the most valuable of wildlife habitats.

recommendation is to build as large a pond as possible. Beebee & Griffiths were concerned only with amphibians and reptiles, but their advice regarding the remainder of the garden is equally valuable for the conservation of other creatures too – have some unkempt areas and rocks to provide shelter; have some uncultivated patches in full sun; limit the use of pesticides; be careful with lawnmowers and strimmers; and, most tellingly, use an electronic cat deterrent.

Compost

The value of compost-making in the garden has been touched on several times in this book, and a well-functioning compost bin undoubtedly provides a valuable and obvious source of organic matter for soil amendment and mulching. In my own 0.5 hectare garden, I have eight substantial compost bins and a powerful shredder to prepare the ingredients. Almost nothing is wasted, and the combined output means we make just enough for our needs and never have to buy organic matter. Ironically, however, as far as wildlife conservation is concerned, a compost bin is at its best when it is not functioning optimally. Because the chemical reactions taking place in compost making are exothermic (give out heat), the temperature rises are considerable and even a normal garden compost bin (at least in the centre) should reach 75°C, which is clearly too high for most creatures to survive. Whilst many invertebrates will occupy the cooler periphery, the space available there may be inadequate for hibernating mammals and reptiles, and I think there is much to be said for maintaining a compost *heap*, exposed to the elements, for wildlife conservation, in addition to the bins used for 'proper' compost production.

THE *SPHAGNUM* CONTROVERSY

So much for things that gardeners *can* do; now for some things they should not. I earlier described the hanging basket as the garden equivalent of the Sitka spruce plantation; a pretty depressing and barren habitat, scoring less than one on a biodiversity value scale of nought to ten. Ironically however, it has until recently played a disproportionately significant role in the depletion of at least one important wild species. The use of *Sphagnum* moss as a hanging basket liner led to widespread collection of moss from a number of British wetland sites over a period of many years. I know of one wet birchwood locality in Hampshire (part of a designated sssi since 1990) that as recently as the late 1970s was being raided on a regular basis by a leading tree and shrub nursery for its extensive *Sphagnum* beds. Unapproved collection of *Sphagnum* from the wild in Britain was rendered illegal in 1981 by the Wildlife and Countryside Act (which also created sssis). Nonetheless, large quantities of live *Sphagnum* are presently imported into the United Kingdom for horticultural purposes from a number of countries including Canada, the Falkland Islands and especially New Zealand, although data on precise quantities are impossible to obtain as, bizarrely, *Sphagnum* moss falls under the New Zealand government's category of 'confidential exports'.

The United Kingdom, along with Japan and other Asian countries, is the major market for New Zealand *Sphagnum* moss. However, in marked contrast with the extremely powerful lobby opposed to the use of *Sphagnum* peat in gardens (see below), the implications of its use for both British and New Zealand biodiversity seem to have escaped the attention of horticulturists and naturalists. Although moss for hanging baskets is sometimes described by retailers in Britain as originating in 'moss farms', an expression that presumably helps to salve people's consciences, the Australasian species *S. cristatum* is in reality collected in an almost unregulated manner from an area of around 1,300,000 hectares of privately owned land in New Zealand. The moss pickers say that they try to leave approximately 10–20 per cent of the shorter strands in the swamp and it is claimed that after three to five years, the moss will have regenerated. It is said with apparently naïve optimism by a major producer (www.moutere.com) that 'by the simple process of market forces, supply and demand, the swamp areas are being maintained, as near as can be determined, in their original state'. This is hardly what I would call farming. But irrespective of the environmental impact in New Zealand, the possible significance of the importing into British gardens of large volumes of a non-native bryophyte and its associated flora and fauna appears to have escaped almost everyone's attention. This seems strange in view of the major impact that the arrival in gardens here of Australian and New Zealand flatworms has had on our native fauna (p. 217f). On horticultural grounds, the trade is in any event fairly indefensible. There are perfectly satisfactory hanging basket liners made from alternative absorbent materials, and the use of simple and inexpensive automated watering systems means that hanging baskets need never dry out.

PEAT

Sphagnum moss, plant containers and the British horticultural trade lead me inevitably to considerations of the use of peat in gardens. I shall not dwell in detail on peat production and the destruction of lowland raised bogs which has become a highly emotive subject, because many of the considerations do not have an impact within the garden itself – although let it never be forgotten that the domestic garden market was part of the driving force (see below). Nonetheless, what have become known as 'growing media' are an intrinsic and unavoidable part of the modern garden environment and a little background is relevant.

The fact that soil behaves differently when confined in a pot or other container was recognised centuries ago. Structure is lost, drainage impeded and the whole alternates between being dry and hard and being waterlogged. By the nineteenth century every serious gardener had devised their own means of surmounting the problem by adding varying amounts of organic and/or other matter to produce what became known as a 'potting compost'. The multiplicity of individual formulae and the difficulty of replicating them, however, led to serious scientific attempts to produce uniform standards. The greatest and most enduring success came at the John Innes Horticultural Institute, then based at Merton in Surrey. (The eponymous John Innes whose name has passed into the currency of gardening language had nothing to do with the compost. He was a London property speculator who on his death in 1904 bequeathed his fortune to horticultural research and endowed the institute.) Over a period of around six years in the 1930s, two of the John Innes staff, William Lawrence and John Newell, set out to overcome the problems and formulate composts that would give consistently predictable and reliable results. They used heat to sterilise a standard 'medium clay' loam, added *Sphagnum* peat to improve porosity, grit to aid drainage and a standard fertiliser mixture (called John Innes Base), and so developed a range of composts for different needs – John Innes Seed for seeds and cuttings, John Innes Potting Compost No. 1 for short-term growth, No. 2 for intermediate growth and No. 3 for long-term growth.

The John Innes composts became the norm for gardeners, although most continued to mix their own from standard ingredients using the John Innes formulae. Following the Second World War, proprietary bagged John Innes composts became more widely available, but a shortage of good quality loam gradually began to present difficulties. Originally, the finest loam had come from stacked and partly rotted turves which ensured the soil had sufficient organic matter to supply nitrogen to the plant over a long period. The unregulated stripping of turf and sale of agricultural soil was outlawed, however, and the available soils from building sites and other areas were unsuitable. It was also recognised that heat sterilising of the loam results in some disadvantageous changes to its chemistry.

Alternatives were sought and, following extensive research, a wide range of proprietary bagged 'soil-less' composts became available from the 1960s onwards. Almost all were based substantially on peat; either *Sphagnum* peat or the darker, stickier sedge peats derived mainly from sedges *Carex* spp. and common reed *Phragmites australis*. Their properties were significantly different from those of the soil-based composts, especially in respect of their ion-exchange capacity, which had a bearing on the availability of nutrients, and the fact that because peat itself contained almost no plant nutrients, these had to be added as artificial fertiliser. Some fertiliser was added at the time of manufacture, but its efficacy was finite, and so supplementary liquid feeding became an increasingly important part of a gardener's work (Bunt, 1976). Only in the past few years has the advent of artificial resin-based slow-release fertiliser granules eased the burden of container-plant feeding.

Peat-based plant composts had a golden period of around 30 years before they fell victim to the ever-increasing public awareness of the fragility of the natural environment. Pressure groups began to exert their influence on public, industry and politicians and drew attention to the largely irreparable damage being caused to lowland raised bogs which were called 'among the most fragile of natural habitats'. 'Banning peat' became something of an environmental bandwagon, and media gardening experts weighed in with the best of intentions, although not always equipped with much more than emotion to counter the arguments put forward by such vested interests as the Peat Producers Association. The biggest problem lay in finding a peat substitute, and as one of the first people in Britain to begin experimenting with Sri Lankan coir residue as a growing medium in the early 1980s, I became all too aware that peat is uniquely different from everything else in many respects of its chemistry and physical properties. The options were set out in detail in 1991 by the pressure group Friends of the Earth (Pryce, 1991). *Inter alia*, the report's conclusions were that 'the excavation of peat from designated wildlife sites, such as Sites of Special Scientific Interest, should be banned forthwith' and that 'if open ground landscape and horticultural media ... and the amateur/retail sector were to go "peat-free", some 60 per cent of peat usage could be accounted for'.

Peat alternatives

Over a period of around 20 years, coir, composted paper, sewage sludge, straw residues, hops and grain, sawdust, seaweed and many other materials were assessed and either rejected or adapted. The term 'peat-free composts' became a catchword for any retailer wanting to present a 'green' image. The John Innes Composts too saw something of a resurgence with new sources of loam becoming available, although almost no-one seems to have noticed that the John Innes soil-based composts themselves contain a significant peat component. One by one, gardening 'experts', publications, radio and television programmes and organisations fell into line in turning away from peat and advocating the alternatives, although, not for the first time in its existence, the RHS was not exactly leading from the front. By 2002, it was saying 'There are situations in the garden where the substitution of peat is now possible. In other situations a cautious approach is necessary' (Anon, 2002c). By 2004, the Society could still only say 'The RHS aims to transfer 90 per cent of its own growing media requirements to peat alternatives by 2010' (Anon, 2004). By contrast, the National Trust, the largest landowner in the country, was as early as 1999 setting itself a two-year timetable to phase out the use of peat as a constituent of composts and was:

> ... actively working towards the elimination of peat use in all its gardens apart from exceptional circumstances, such as raised peat beds and ericaceous plantings that are integral to the history of the site. (Calman, 1999)

Following the release of this statement, the Peat Producers Association wrote to the National Trust 'expressing its concerns', and an undated publication, apparently from the late 1990s (Anon, n.d.b) set out its own agenda, claiming that without peat '... horticulture would not exist as we know it today, and our gardens, parks and window boxes would be drab shadows of their present glory'. It stated:

The entire horticultural peat industry in Great Britain utilises a mere 5,000 hectares
in total and will require a further 1,000 hectares over the next quarter of a century.
An area of just 6,000 hectares out of 1.64 million would seem to be fairly insignificant.

Sites such as Flanders Moss (Carse of Stirling), Ballnahone (County Antrim) and Thorne (Yorkshire) 'have been returned to nature conservation'.

Nonetheless, despite the enormous media coverage and propaganda, nearly 3.5 million cubic metres of peat was still being used in British horticulture in 2000; 96 per cent as growing media and 66 per cent by amateur gardeners (Anon, 2000a). Around two-thirds of the total was imported, mainly from Ireland and the Baltic States. A glance at any high street garden centre will reveal the reality that home gardeners are still buying peat-based products in large quantities and seem destined to continue to do so for some while.

There seems little doubt that the use of peat in gardens, most importantly as the bulk of the medium in which countless thousands of container plants have been raised, sold and bought, has had a number of obvious consequences for garden wildlife. Two species that were once important but relatively minor garden inhabitants, the vine weevil (p. 233) and the annual weed, hairy bitter-cress (p. 114), have been catapulted to the forefront of gardeners' concerns. I believe there is also some evidence for club root disease of brassicas caused by

FIG 128. Brassicaceous weed species at the edge of a commercial peat bog – a possible source of club root disease.

Plasmodiophora brassicae, originating in peat bogs, which might thus serve as a source for the contamination of previously disease-free gardens (Fig. 128).

BARK

The modern garden also absorbs other organic materials, most notably as soil amendments and mulches, and among them one of the most important is bark: chipped, shredded or composted. It is a by-product of the softwood timber industry and approximately half a million tonnes are produced annually in Britain alone. In its various forms, bark is a valuable mulching material and although it has virtually no nutrient content, it has the merit of an attractive appearance and smell (Fig. 129). But largely because of the cost of transporting

FIG 129. Wood chip mulches have introduced a fascinating new habitat to many gardens.

and packaging such a bulky substance of fairly low density, branded bark is and is always likely to be fairly expensive and so, understandably, gardeners with access to raw bark have been tempted to use it in their own gardens. This must be done with caution, however, for two main reasons. Some barks, particularly those of spruces and Douglas fir, contain chemicals, especially various terpenes, that are toxic to plant growth. Pine and larch barks generally have little toxic effect. By stacking the bark for several weeks, the monoterpene content is reduced by about 75 per cent because the temperature quickly elevates to over 50°C and the stack is invaded by thermophilic bacteria. The stacking also results in a raising of the pH from about 4.5 to a more acceptable 5.5 and the elevated temperature has the incidental effect of eradicating the second potential problem – honey fungus *Armillaria mellea*, which may be present in untreated bark.

There is a widespread belief that the use of bark mulches (and perhaps increasing use of leaf mould) has given succour to the British woodlouse population (p. 226), and it seems almost inevitable that a considerable increase has taken place in gardens in numbers of both individuals and species of many natural inhabitants of woodland litter. A characteristic and distinctive range of macro-fungi too has come to be associated with bark and wood mulches (p. 226 & 227ff). Real woodlands are absent from all except the largest gardens, and individual trees yield little permanent litter cover and create quite different microclimatic relationships between shade, temperature, light and moisture – it is important to realise that a solitary garden tree is not a very small wood. The use of bark and wood chip mulches may play a rather important and perhaps generally unappreciated role therefore in the conservation of what are, for the most part, small and little-observed creatures. The relative significance for them of such indigenous materials vis-à-vis exotic products such as crushed cocoa shell seems, predictably, not to have been investigated.

NATURAL STONE

As I explained in Chapter 2, the British have long had an interest in and commitment to rock or alpine plant gardening, and following the initial, often bizarre attempts at it in the nineteenth century, a more natural approach to rock garden construction evolved. Unfortunately, the better and more natural the rock garden appeared, the more damage its creation did to the wider landscape, and by the late twentieth century the unauthorised collection of stone from the countryside was causing severe damage in some areas. Expanses of limestone pavement in Yorkshire and the Lake District were especially vulnerable. Ward & Evans (1976) surveyed 537 limestone pavement areas and reported only 3 per cent with no detectable damage; by implication, much of it had been caused by gardeners. Although protection was available for such places under several pieces of legislation, including the sssI and specific Limestone Pavement Order provisions of the Wildlife and Countryside Act 1981, it was clear that a public awareness campaign was needed, and somewhat belatedly the gardening media, RHS and others played an important part in this (Anon, 1997).

The biggest fillip, however, both for gardeners and for the natural environment, has come from on the one hand the development of inexpensive concrete paving slabs in a wide range of styles that are highly passable replicas of the genuine article, and on the other from the increasing availability at garden centres of real stone in cut or massive form that has been legally obtained from 'approved sites'. Gardeners may find it a curious commentary, however, on the commercial appeal of modern home gardening that real stone for their gardens can be transported economically halfway round the world – presumably, one hopes, from comparably 'approved sites' elsewhere. A sample of Haworth Moor Natural Stone, its name redolent of Wuthering Heights, Fred Trueman and Yorkshire pudding, was recently delivered to me still in the original shipping crate that betrayed its real origin as India.

CHAPTER 10

The Garden as an Inspiration for the Naturalist

E ARLY IN THE morning of Friday 24 November 1854 the Revd Miles Berkeley sat down at his desk at the family home in the village of King's Cliffe, Northamptonshire, and quickly wrote a short note by candlelight before commencing his parish duties. His correspondent was Christopher Broome, lawyer and fellow amateur mycologist, an old friend who lived at Batheaston, near Bath. It was the height of the Crimean War, and after some customary comments on specimens that had been sent to him for identification, Berkeley continued: 'I have no faith in Prussia and less in Lord Aberdeen. My melons and cucumbers have died off this year very unpleasantly ...' (Natural History Museum, London: Broome Correspondence).

Miles Berkeley (1803–89) (Fig. 130) was the outstanding British nineteenth-century authority on fungi, consulted by naturalists the world over and looked to with respect as a fount of knowledge on many other matters too – he was, for instance, approached in 1865 to advise on: 'the most appropriate genus of South American orchids to be represented on Prince Albert's monument' (Natural History Museum, London: Berkeley Correspondence). Among tens of thousands of other identifications, he named the fungi that Charles Darwin collected on the *Beagle* voyage. He was the intimate friend of both Sir William Hooker (1785–1865) and Sir William's son Sir Joseph Hooker (1817–1911), successive directors of the Royal Botanic Gardens, Kew.

Berkeley's note to Broome echoed the character of countless letters to other colleagues. Natural history, especially mycology, was the principal thrust, with current affairs and gardening taking an important if smaller secondary role. Self-evidently he maintained a garden with some pride and interest. He was not alone among his nineteenth-century contemporaries in this respect, sprinkling

FIG 130. The Revd Miles Berkeley (1803–89), one of many early British naturalists who also cultivated a garden.

horticultural comment and observation (and especially an obsession with melons) through his correspondence. Stretching back through the preceding centuries, other naturalists too had enlivened their writings with comparable notes. What sets these observations apart from the journals, diaries and books of full-time gardeners lies in their seeing the garden through naturalists' eyes.

In Chapter 1, I gave a number of reasons for the importance and popularity of gardens and gardening in Britain. But I have also long thought and often said that at least as important today is our national connection with other living things. We are not only a nation of gardeners, we are also a nation of naturalists. Is there any other country where approaching two per cent of the entire population belongs to a wildlife conservation organisation (membership of the Royal Society for the Protection of Birds recently passed one million)? But while many of the great naturalists of the past, like Berkeley, clearly owned and maintained gardens, how general a trend was this? And more importantly, what part did gardens and gardening play in their lives and scientific endeavours? Do their experiences parallel mine and show the two to be inextricably linked and interrelated, or were natural history and horticulture perceived and treated as two separate but parallel pursuits? What can we discover from their writings or from the gardens they have left behind?

EARLY NATURALIST-GARDENERS

Ray Desmond's monumental *Dictionary of British & Irish Botanists and Horticulturists* (1994) contains around 10,000 biographical entries. Desmond spent 'the best part of eight years' scanning books and long runs of periodicals to obtain his information. A considerable proportion of the subjects of the entries left behind correspondence, and Desmond tells us where to find it. To scour those letters for references to gardening in the lives of naturalists (or even natural history in the activities of horticulturists) would be a wonderful thing to do; fascinating and probably rewarding. Sadly it would take several lifetimes (and even then would exclude people who were principally zoologists) and therefore is an option not open to me. A search of more limited biographical compilations might help. I looked at the 101 short biographies in Michael Salmon's fascinating account of British butterfly collecting (Salmon, 2000), and I found:

> Robert Adkin (1849–1935) – 'Later in life, when failing health restricted his mobility, Adkin studied insect pests in his garden ...'
> Frederick Bond (1811–89) – '... he fished; he shot and stuffed birds and made a collection of their eggs; and he cultivated ferns and other plants in his garden and greenhouse ...'
> Percy May Bright (1863–1911) – '... his large garden was full of scented flowers, especially those attractive to butterflies and moths ...'
> Henry Harpur Crewe (1828–83) – a good botanist ... a keen horticulturist ... expert on wallflowers ... entomologist ...'
> Peter William Crib (1920–93) – 'remarkably skilled at breeding butterflies ... Possibly part of his secret was that he was a good gardener ...'
> William Henry Harwood (1840–1917) – 'He perfected the method [sleeving] in his modest back garden on North Station Road in Colchester, and used it to rear many British species of moths and butterflies ...'
> Abel Ingpen (1796–1854) – '... a keen gardener and contributed articles to the *Horticultural Magazine* ...'

Hmm; not especially promising. Other compilations such as Michael Darby's *Biographical Dictionary of British Coleopterists* (www.coleopterist.org.uk/biogdict) are comparably unrevealing. It is evident that anything approaching a comprehensive survey would be impossible, and I have chosen instead therefore to look at a handful of individuals who were pivotal in the development of British natural history and about whom I already knew something.

JOHN RAY

John Ray (1627–1705) has a greater right than most of his rivals to be accorded the epithet 'the father of English natural history'. He was born in a cottage adjoining a smithy at the village of Black Notley just south of Braintree in Essex. After an academic career at Cambridge, and much travelling, he died in the same village and left as part of his legacy to the nation several outstanding and outstandingly important books, most notably his epochal *Historia Plantarum* of 1686–8. He also left a considerable correspondence from which Charles Raven pieced together arguably the finest biography ever written of a British naturalist (Raven, 1942). Raven deduced that:

> *Even if he did no scientific work until after his election to a fellowship in 1649* [a Minor Fellowship at Trinity, the year after graduating BA] *he must have been profoundly interested in nature; for his breadth of range, his power of acute and accurate observation, his flair for discriminating the vital from the superficial, bespeak not only natural gifts but early habit.*

Gratifyingly, at an early age Ray was also interested in gardens and the cultivation of plants. One of his contemporaries at Cambridge was John Worthington (1618–71), Master of Jesus from 1650 to 1660 and Vice-Chancellor in 1657–8. From him we first learn that at Trinity, Ray had a garden. In a letter to Samuel Hartlib (c.1600–62), ex-patriot East Prussian, philosopher, pamphleteer, 'the Great Intelligencer of Europe', and friend of Milton, Worthington wrote 'He hath a little garden by his chamber which is as full of choice things as it can hold: that it were twenty times as big I could wish for his sake' and later 'it hath at least 700 plants in it' (Crossley & Christie, 1847–86). Raven reasoned that Ray's 'chamber' and garden may have been the same as those occupied a few years later by Isaac Newton, although this was based on the false premise that only two sets of rooms could have had gardens; there were others, although it is now impossible to say with certainty where Ray's garden lay (Jonathan Smith, Trinity College Library, pers. comm.: Fig. 131).

One of Ray's earliest writings was a 'Catalogus Plantarum non domesticarum quae aluntur Cantabrigiae in Hortis Academicorum et Oppidanorum' which he adumbrated in 1660 in a letter to Willughby (Lankester, 1848). It seems never to have been printed, and the manuscript is now lost. However, he had plans, so he told Willughby, to produce another catalogue, 'a Horti Angliae', based on lists obtained from all the noted gardens of the time. He already possessed the list

FIG 131. Trinity College Cambridge in 1689 showing gardens alongside the college buildings although it is not possible to identify the location of John Ray's garden specifically.

prepared by Philip Stephens and William Browne in 1658 of the Oxford Botanic Garden (the senior British botanic garden, endowed by Sir Henry Danvers in 1621), and that of the Tradescants' remarkable Lambeth garden, prepared by John Tradescant junior in 1656. From these and others, including that of his own garden, he intended to produce a catalogue including only 'such plants as do not grow wild anywhere in England'. Thus far, Ray was setting the pattern to be followed by countless others – the garden was for the cultivation of the exotic. It does not appear to have been a place to study natural history, but it is nonetheless hugely gratifying to find that, although the 'Horti Angliae' would be a list only of non-native species, some British plants did find their way, deliberately, into the garden itself. At the beginning of Ray's botanical studies in the early 1650s, he wrote of growing wild plants in his 'little garden' and it was only later, when his projected 'Horti Angliae' had been expanded to become the *Historia Plantarum*, that most of the numerous references to the garden relate to alien species and cultivated forms.

Ray's natural history career only began properly when he rode out of Cambridge on Monday 9 August 1658. Following his ejection from the university four years later (for refusing to condemn a Covenant for reform of the Church), he was to spend much of the next 20 years travelling the country, botanising, being introduced by his friend Francis Willughby (1635–72) to zoology, recording wild plants and animals, and also visiting gardens to make notes of cultivated species – although the latter was still a separate if parallel activity. In 1679, Ray and his wife moved back to Essex and to 'Dewlands', the cottage in his native village of Black Notley that he had bought for his mother and where she had lived until her death in March of that year. There was a 'good strip of garden in front' but 'not much room for growing plants' – it was 'a cold soil and an ill-situated place', exposed to north and east winds (Raven, 1942). An undated drawing shows a typical cottage garden with trees. It is hard to believe that Ray's twin interests of natural history and gardening remained completely separate during the remaining 25 or so years of his life that he spent there, although on this matter his writings are frustratingly vague. The garden was essentially absent from *Ornithologia*, the result of his remarkable collaboration with Willughby and 'The foundation of scientific ornithology' (Newton, 1893–6). The 'garden bird' had not been invented in the seventeenth century, and *Sylvia borin* was still the pettychaps. The garden was also largely unmentioned in his works on mammals and, less surprisingly, fishes, although it is evident that it did provide the material for many of his later observations on 'insects' – 'in those days, everything from an amoeba to an earthworm' (Raven, 1942) – that were to appear in *Historia Insectorum*. He found the red underwing moth *Catocala nupta* 'sitting on the outside of the bedroom window' and 'it was in his own home and by the efforts of his family and a working man, Thomas Simson or Simpson, who may probably have been in his employ, that the bulk of the material was procured' (Raven, 1942). Simson seems to have lived next door and worked in the garden, implying at least that the plot was large enough to require labouring assistance, although these were the later years of Ray's life by which time he was becoming seriously infirm. Ray wrote that 'my little daughters caught many of this species [probably the burnished brass *Diachrysia chrysatis*] flying at dusk in our garden' (*Historia Insectorum*). It appears, therefore, to have been necessity occasioned by infirmity rather than choice that prompted Ray to see his own garden as a site for natural historical study and collection.

JAMES PETIVER

To be a naturalist at a time when the discipline of your choosing was in its infancy gave you a good chance of becoming its father. But as John Ray had been dubbed the father of natural history in its entirety, it was left to others to garner the subsidiary roles. So it fell to James Petiver (c. 1665–1718) to become 'the father of British butterflies'. His lepidopterous claim to fame was principally that he pioneered butterfly naming. The brimstone was the first (Petiver, 1695) and many others followed. But was his interest in butterflies triggered by his horticulture? It seems probable, as he was by profession an apothecary, and had a physic garden which he evidently put to uses other than those initially intended. He was visited in 1710 by the German scholar Zacharias Conrad von Uffenbach (1683–1734), who was in England to study manuscripts in university libraries and who later commented, amidst a general damnation of English museum curation, that herbs grown in Petiver's garden were at least as likely to be used in botanical exchanges or placed in his museum as to be used for their 'proper purpose' (Quarrell & Mare, 1934). Petiver seems to have travelled little outside the immediate area of London, but was a prodigious acquirer and cataloguer of natural history specimens gathered by people who did travel and his own immense collections were purchased after his death by Sir Hans Sloane (1660–1753). Despite his interests being more in the exotic than the home grown (Stearns, 1952), it seems likely that in a modest way he was among the first of British naturalists to appreciate his own, albeit professional, garden as a habitat and collecting ground.

SIR JOSEPH BANKS

Sir Joseph Banks (1743–1820) was arguably the wealthiest of all British naturalists, inheriting the substantial if relatively new money of three preceding generations of well-connected lawyers and landowners (Fig. 132). He also inherited the family seat of Revesby Abbey in Lincolnshire, although the house Banks knew is not the Revesby Abbey undergoing a long-term restoration today. This dates only from 1844; the preceding property and home in which Banks grew up was built around 1670, some distance from the eponymous ruined twelfth-century Cistercian abbey. By the time his great-grandfather bought it in 1714, the house was attached to around 2,000 acres (800 hectares) and gradually, increasingly large amounts of Lincolnshire came under the Banks family's ownership. At the time of Joseph Banks' inheritance, the immediate gardens and deer park alone extended to some 340 acres (140 hectares) with 'vast woods behind' and 'vast fens in front' (O'Brian, 1987). O'Brian says that 'Young Joseph Banks was very fond of fishing, as he was of most country pursuits ...' and whilst it is famously recorded that his conversion to botany took place at the age of 14 one evening during a stroll down a country lane when he was at Eton, it seems inescapable that the basis of

FIG 132. Sir Joseph Banks (1743–1820) was probably inspired to take up natural history by the gardens of his Lincolnshire home.

his passion for natural history was laid in the Revesby Abbey gardens and adjoining family land.

There is no question that Banks was seriously influenced by gardens after 1761 when his father died and his mother took a new house at 22 Paradise Row, Chelsea (later to become Royal Hospital Road), close by the Apothecaries Physic garden, then under the charge of Philip Miller and within reach of the many other nurseries and market gardens for which the then still rural Chelsea was well known. Horace Walpole (1717–97), son of Sir Robert Walpole, was also nearby at Orford House, his father's favourite residence. Its wonderful gardens, extended by Horace and including a huge orangery, were all achieved at the expense of Chelsea Hospital, of which he had been paymaster general.

The most celebrated and in some ways the most formative years of Banks' life as a naturalist came, just as Darwin's some 63 years later, when he travelled as naturalist on a Royal Navy ship around the world. Between 1768 and 1771, he accompanied James Cook in the *Endeavour* and was lifted 'from the ranks of gentlemen naturalists to become a figure of international scientific significance' (Gascoigne, 2004). In 1773, Banks became official botanical adviser to King George III, and in effect the first director of the Royal Botanic Gardens, Kew. But Kew, then as now, was considered no place to study natural history; and matchless though its collections are, nor in truth has it ever been much of a garden. Although the King's Gardens at Kew were 'in their first conception pleasure grounds' (O'Brian, 1987), the Royal Botanic Gardens are and always have been principally magnificent living catalogues where the floras of the world can be studied.

By this time, Banks was living for much of the year in London, and in 1776 he took a large house, No. 32 Soho Square. The house was big enough to accommodate his expanding herbarium and became 'a virtual research institute' (Gascoigne, 2004), but it had no garden and this appears to have been a continuing frustration. By 1779:

> ... he was much taken up with finding a country house or villa within dining distance of London, for he and his ladies cruelly missed a garden of their own. Soho Square was all very well; it looked out into trees, and it was to remain their principal dwelling; but a real garden was essential to complete happiness. (O'Brian, 1987)

They found what they were seeking in a house called Spring Grove, 'a little off the Hounslow Road in Isleworth'. The locality was also called Heston and sometimes Smallberry Green. The house is now a conference facility of West Thames College. There is no evidence that Banks used the garden for much more than relaxation, pleasure and for a certain amount of horticultural diversion and experimentation; it was not a work place, and certainly not a place to study natural history. The three houses and their gardens, Revesby, Soho Square and Spring Grove, were to remain Banks' homes until his death at Spring Grove in 1820. So this most influential, well connected and wealthy of all British botanists, traveller and explorer of far-flung places, apparently never saw that his own garden could offer him at least some of the natural history that he travelled round the world to find.

GILBERT WHITE AND HIS CONTEMPORARIES

Towering above all others in his gardening comments, as he towers above the foundation of British local natural history, was the Reverend Gilbert White of Selborne (1720–93). Whilst White is most familiar to the general public through his book *The Natural History and Antiquities of Selborne*, first published in 1789, it is perhaps not widely enough appreciated that this work did not arise *de novo*, but was based on the individual diary entries he had been accumulating in his journals. Arguably, there has never been a more comprehensive set of observations of British natural history made by one person than those recorded by White almost daily from the age of 30 for a period of over 40 years until his death in 1793. It is perhaps appreciated even less that three separate sets of observations were produced. The more celebrated, known as the 'Naturalist's Journal', was not commenced until 1768, when it took over from a predecessor diary called the 'Garden Kalendar' which he had started 17 years earlier, on Monday 7 January 1751, when he recorded that he had sown two rows of Spanish-beans (broad beans *Vicia faba*). Greenoak (1986) suggested these may have been 'Seville long-pod'; they were self-evidently a winter-hardy variety comparable with the modern 'Aquadulce'. White's records throughout the 17 years of the 'Garden Kalendar' are largely horticultural, chronicling the dates of sowing and harvesting his crops and ornamentals and the performance of his various plants.

The year 1751 was perhaps an unfortunate one in which to start, as in Britain the weather pattern was evidently one of the strangest and, for a gardener, the most frustrating. There are several references to the difficult conditions in that first year. On 22 March, he wrote: 'There had been a glut of wet for five weeks, & the Ground was rather too moist; but worked pretty well'. He also remarked that it was wet on 2–3 April when he established an asparagus bed, and even though his gardening knowledge and experience were then limited, he already had a perceptive eye for a catch crop as, after having planted the asparagus, he '... sowed a thin Crop of Onions upon them'. As the seasons pass, the records fluctuate between one aspect of gardening and another. Taking as an example the year 1759, the mid-year of the 'Garden Kalendar', there are 141 separate entries, 78 of which include at least one reference to cucumbers and melons (and sometimes several). Like most serious gardeners of the seventeenth, eighteenth and nineteenth centuries, and just like Miles Berkeley during the Crimean War, White was much obsessed with cucurbits and other semi-tropical plants which were grown on hot beds of fresh animal manures and straw. Yet nowhere did he mention or discuss the fact that the technique is simply an attempt to mimic the conditions in which such cucurbits grow naturally in their native habitats.

Inevitably, for a gardener, weather observation and comment soon began to make their appearance – there are numerous references to rainfall and especially to frost, and these gradually assume greater significance. The winter of 1755–6 beggars belief: 'A terrible winter for Earthquakes [sic], Inundations, Tempests, & continual Rains ...' And the final 'Garden Kalendar' entry, for 31 December 1787, was unashamedly meteorological: 'It froze under people's beds. Great rimes, & beautiful sunny days'.

There is little comment on animal life or even on the local flora in the earlier years of the 'Garden Kalendar', although from the late 1750s a few natural history observations do begin to appear. On 12 February 1759 'the air full of gnats and ... & the surface of the Ground full of spiders' webs ...'. There came the first

FIG 133. The gate leading from the garden of Gilbert White (1720–93) at The Wakes, Selborne, into the open countryside.

reference to birds (to a species that long fascinated White): on 13 April 1759 'Saw seven swallows, the first this Year ...'; then on 16 April 1759 'Heard the first nightingale in my fields'; 4 May 1759 'saw the first Redstart, & Cherrysucker' (spotted flycatcher *Muscicapa striata*); 8 June 1761 'The Rooks are perchers: there are but two; & one of the old ones was some how destroyed as soon as they were hatched' and two weeks later some botany: 'Discovered a curious *Orchis* in the hollow shady part of Newton-lane, just beyond the Cross. It is the *Orchis alba bifolia minor, Calcari oblongo ...*' (lesser butterfly orchid *Platanthera bifolia*). On 20 May 1761 came the first proper analysis of a natural history observation when White made detailed comment on the behaviour of the field cricket *Gryllus campestris*, a then largely unstudied creature and one that is still local in its distribution. But despite the entry being in 'Garden Kalendar', the crickets that White and his brother Thomas examined were caught not in the garden of The Wakes, but in 'a steep, rocky pasture-field'.

Coincident with the latter period of the 'Garden Kalendar' came the second set of records and the start of a complete transformation in White's notes and, seemingly, his interest. The second set is 'Flora Selborniensis', a 'Calendar of Flora', in which White noted the flowering times of local native plants together with 'some co-incidences of the coming, & departures of birds of passage, & insects; & the appearing of Reptiles: for the Year 1766'. Weather notes persisted, but there was little horticultural comment, although on some days the entries for 'Garden Kalendar' and the 'Flora' do complement or even duplicate each other. The 'Kalendar', for instance, recorded that on 10 November 1766 he 'Trimmed the vines against the House', but it was in the 'Flora' three days later that he reported he had 'Finished dressing the vines'.

Then came the biggest change. The third of White's sets of records is the 'Naturalist's Journal', a work still littered with gardening tasks and comments, where meteorology also has a significant presence, but where natural history predominates. What prompted White to abandon his gardening records and embark on a work essentially of natural history? Had gardening simply become too repetitive? Perhaps he had fallen into the trap of which I heard a parallel a few years ago. The features editor of a national newspaper, with almost no knowledge of or interest in horticulture himself, told his gardening correspondent that he thought his regular 'Jobs for the Week' section ought to end and that he should write something more inspirational instead. 'We've been telling people to sow their beans in February and prune their roses in March for years; we don't need to go on doing it' was the explanation. The fact that gardening is inevitably cyclic but that even the most accomplished gardeners need reminders clearly escapes the uninitiated. It seems unlikely, however, that White was becoming bored or less interested in horticulture, simply that he was becoming more interested in natural history.

The 'Naturalist's Journal' has one particularly outstanding omission. A gardener's diary of today with no mention of butterflies would be unthinkable: the emergence of hibernating nymphalids and the first sightings of the orange tip or the brimstone are primal events in the gardening year. Indeed, the encouragement of butterflies is consistently one of the major reasons that gardeners are now encouraged to plant and develop 'wildlife gardens' with their obligatory (but arguably valueless) patch of stinging nettles (p. 239). Yet the 'Naturalist's Journal' is almost silent on the subject. It mentions the brimstone once, when it appeared on 18 February 1779; and even that unavoidable garden insect, the large white, has but a single reference, albeit an unusual one: on 23 August 1781: 'Tho' white butterflies abound, & lay many eggs on the cabbages; yet thro' over-heat & want of moisture they do not hatch, & turn to palmers [caterpillars]; but dry & shrivel to nothing'. At the time White was writing these lines, serious interest in butterflies was barely a century old. Although the likes of John Ray, James Petiver and Sir Hans Sloane formed butterfly collections at an early date, they were inveterate collectors of almost everything, and the first Aurelian Society was not founded until around 1730. For Gilbert White, butterflies were clearly of relatively little remark, either as things of beauty or impact.

It is tempting to interpret White's three diaries as recording the birth of a great interest in natural history, and of a great naturalist himself, from the inspirations and observations of gardening. Unfortunately, however, this was not a simple evolution, and it seems to have happened under the influence of others. The earliest explanation for this can be found in the second edition of a popular work, and one White would have known – Stillingfleet's *Tracts* (1762).

Benjamin Stillingfleet (1702–71), botanist, poet, operatic librettist and, thanks to the eccentricities of his wardrobe, the origin of the name bluestocking, is credited with popularising the Linnean system in England. When he revised his *Miscellaneous Tracts relating to Natural History, Husbandry, and Physic. To which is added the Calendar of Flora*, first published in 1759, he added translations of a number of dissertations that had been written in Sweden under Linnaeus' supervision and including a 'Calendar of Flora' for the year 1755. Foster (2000) has elaborated on this:

> The idea of the calendars ... was linked to a high, humanitarian purpose: the
> improvement of rural economy ... Sympathy with this high purpose led White to
> contribute. The first stage was to record natural phenomena other than that of the

garden – this is what he began in July 1765 [when within 'Garden Kalendar' is found 'A Calender of Flora, & the Garden']; *but he soon realised he knew less about wild plants than was necessary for the task and rapidly acquired a copy of Hudson's Flora Anglica (1765), the first English flora to be organized on Linnean principles.*

But it was the year 1767 that was to be an *annus mirabilis* in White's life as a naturalist and an *annus horribilis* for his gardening. In the spring of that year, he visited London for several weeks to see his brothers Benjamin and Thomas, and it is thought to have been in Benjamin's bookshop at the Horace's Head, 63 Fleet Street, that he first met a man who was to become an abiding influence on his future life and work. Thomas Pennant (1726–98), Welsh traveller and academic, was arguably the leading zoologist of his day, and certainly the leading zoological author. Benjamin White had published his major opus *British Zoology* around 1776 and he and Gilbert White soon began to correspond with Pennant on a regular basis. Probably at Pennant's suggestion, his friend the Welsh lawyer and antiquary Daines Barrington (1727/8–1800) sent White a copy of his own diary 'The Naturalist's Journal', and White was hooked. Gardening now took a lesser place in his affections and the writing of his own natural history journal began. It was later, in the form of letters to Pennant and Barrington, that *The Natural History and Antiquities of Selborne* came into being.

There is little evidence from their own writings that Pennant and Barrington were gardeners, although Pennant especially may have been a horticultural dark horse. He lived at the family home, Downing Hall at Whitford, near Holywell in Flintshire (Fig. 134), and although it is recorded that he placed in the garden an ancient Celtic inscribed stone he had found in the nearby parish of Caerwys (Westwood, 1876–9), his abiding interests were generally believed to be natural history and topography. Downing Hall was improved by Pennant's son David and others, but was purchased by commercial interests for its land in 1920, burned down two years later and was finally blown up by the army in the 1950s (James Wragg, pers. comm.). On a visit in 2003, I found some stone rubble, underground vaults and evidence of what could well have once been a magnificent garden with watercourses, but which is today completely overgrown and a tranquil woodland. Barrington clearly had some gardening interest – among the subject matter of his earlier publications was the somewhat bizarre blend of 'the history of archery, gardening, and card-playing in England' (Miller, 2004), and towards the end of his life, he was one of the superintendents of the King's Bench Temple gardens to which he devoted much energy.

It is often difficult and sometimes impossible to ascertain from White's natural history writings which observations were made in his garden and which

FIG 134. Remains of the garden at Downing Hall, the former home of Thomas Pennant (1726–98).

in the surrounding countryside. He certainly never made any comment on the differences between his garden and the outside environment. It does appear, nonetheless, that while the garden was clearly the basis for the horticulture, rather little natural history was observed there. Such observations as: 'Glow-worms appear'd again pretty frequent; but more in the Hedges, & bushes than in June, when they were out on ye turf' ('Garden Kalendar', 8 August 1765) or: 'The brambling, fringilla montifringilla, appears. The cock is a fine gay bird' ('Garden Kalendar', 16 April 1767) could have been made anywhere in the neighbourhood. White's most celebrated discovery of a native creature was his recognition of the harvest mouse *Micromys minutus* which he described as 'very common in these parts'. It has always struck me as remarkable that neither he nor anyone else had previously realised that they were distinct from 'field-mice' (the wood mouse *Apodemus sylvaticus*), as they are so markedly different in both size and habit. Nonetheless, the celebrated entry (almost the last) in the 'Garden Kalendar' on 4 December 1767 read:

> *Sent two field-mice, a species very common in these parts (tho' unknown to the zoologists) to Thomas Pennant Esq of Downing in Flintshire. They resemble much in colour ye* Mus domesticus medius *of Ray; but are smaller than the* Mus domesticus vula: seu minor *of the same great Naturalist. They never enter houses; are carried into ricks, & barns with ye sheaves, abound in harvest; & build three nests,*

composed of blades of corn, up from the ground among the standing wheat: &
sometimes in thistles. They breed as many as eight Young at one time.

There is no evidence that White found the harvest mouse in his garden, and
it seems likely it was in fields nearby, as it was in 1998 when Laurie Woods, a
volunteer gardener at The Wakes, found a nest while making a late crop of hay
in an orchard near the house (Anon, 1998*b*).

White's famous first British observation of the noctule *Nyctalus noctula* was
also described with no reference to locality: 'The large species of bat appears'
('Naturalist's Journal', 22 April 1769) and it too was probably not in his garden.
Nonetheless, perhaps the most intriguing of White's observations of new species,
and one that *was* certainly made in his garden, is that reported in 'Naturalist's
Journal' for 11 May 1782:

> *An uncommon, & I think a new little bird frequents my garden, which I have great*
> *reason to think is the Pettichaps. It is common in some parts of the kingdom, & I have*
> *received formerly several dead specimens from Gibraltar. It much resembles the white*
> *throat, but has a more white, or rather silvery breast & belly ...*

Officially, the lesser whitethroat was first described as a British bird by
Latham in 1787 (Supplement to *A General Synopsis of Birds*) but, as James Fisher
(1947) pointed out:

> *It is significant that only the first volume of Latham's Synopsis was published (in 1781)*
> *by Gilbert's brother Benjamin, and that the other volumes were published by another*
> *firm (Leigh & Sotheby). Probably there was some quarrel between Latham and the*
> *White family; certainly Gilbert never refers to Latham's work, which leads us to believe*
> *that he may have discovered the lesser whitethroat independently of Latham.*

CHARLES DARWIN

If there is an inexorable progress through British natural history down the
centuries, then all its roads lead eventually to Charles Darwin. It is with Darwin
that we at last find a naturalist who not only understood his garden, but also
used it as a source for his thinking and as a testing ground for some of his ideas.
Darwin's life is too well known and his work too well chronicled to justify any
repetition here, but the importance of the garden at Down House, his Kent
home for the last 40 years of his life, is perhaps less widely appreciated. The land

belonging to Down House – around 18 acres (7 hectares) of the silty alkaline soils of the area – spilled almost imperceptibly into the surrounding countryside of the North Downs, and after the family moved there in September 1842, Darwin:

> … undertook his major works at home, fitting out his estate as a place for natural history researches of a gentlemanly kind. He had the house renovated and extended, the lawns landscaped, gardens dug, and the road outside his study window lowered to keep passers-by from peering inside. A grove of trees was planted where he laid out his thinking path, the 'Sandwalk', and he began (but abandoned) a country diary, following in the footsteps of the Revd Gilbert White. (Desmond et al., 2004)

The sandwalk was central to Darwin's life. It was a circular path around the perimeter of a small wood, part of an area that Darwin purchased from his neighbour Sir John Lubbock (1834–1913, banker, politician, naturalist and archaeologist and author of a popular nature book Ants, Bees, and Wasps (1882)). There Darwin took his daily constitutional, lost in thought but no doubt inspired by what he saw in the garden around him.

The garden was initially very much the province of his wife Emma who oversaw the herbaceous borders and the lawn with its fine established trees – mulberry, Scots pine, yew and sweet chestnut. But as Darwin took on more of the role of the country gentleman, and purchased additional adjoining land, he began to model it to suit both the family's needs and his own scientific requirements. The long, narrow enclosed kitchen garden was not only productive in yielding fruit, vegetables and cut flowers for the house, but also provided an ideal trial area for experiments in plant breeding. And it was after the publication of The Origin of Species in 1859 that the garden began to assume a special significance. After 1860, Darwin was devoting his energies to two principal areas, one related to selection, variation and emotion, especially in man and mammals, and the second encompassing a broad area of botany. The initial inspiration for the botanical researches seems to have come almost equally from his own garden (and Darwin was fortunate in that his garden embraced an adjoining meadow of around 15 acres (6 hectares) so he had 'countryside' almost on his doorstep) and from wider afield, although it was generally back in the garden (and, after 1863, in his greenhouses) that the ideas were tested experimentally.

It was on holiday in south Devon in 1861 that the extraordinary subject of orchid fertilisation first gripped Darwin's imagination. It was this that led to the publication of On the Various Contrivances by which British and Foreign Orchids are Fertilised by Insects (1862), and then to him erecting the first hothouse so that he could continue his studies through the winter of 1862–3. He had first taken an interest in insectivorous plants in Sussex in 1860, initially in the native British sundews, but then in exotic species, and these too found a home in the greenhouses where the studies continued for many years to culminate in the publication of *Insectivorous Plants* in 1875.

But it was the kitchen garden trial ground that, in a very literal sense, proved the most fertile area (Fig. 135). Studies and experiments with potatoes, radishes, onions, sweet peas, marrows, beans, asters and many other plants provided the raw material for numerous papers, and for the books *The Movements and Habits of Climbing Plants* (1875), *The Effects of Cross and Self-Fertilisation in the Vegetable Kingdom* (1876), *The Different Forms of Flowers on Plants of the same Species* (1877), *The Power of Movement in Plants* (1880) and, above all, for *The Variation of Animals and Plants under Domestication* (1868):

> *Many annuals come true: thus I purchased German seeds of 34 named sub varieties of one race of ten-week stock* (Matthiola annua), *and raised a hundred and forty plants, all of which, with the exception of a single plant, came true. In saying this, however, it must be understood that I could distinguish only twenty kinds out of the thirty four named sub-varieties; nor did the colour of the flower always correspond with the name affixed to the packet; but I say that they came true, because in each of the 36 short rows every plant was absolutely alike, with the one single exception. Again, I procured*

FIG 135. Reconstructed greenhouse and experimental kitchen garden plots at the home of Charles Darwin (1809–82), Down House in Kent.

packets of German seed of twenty-five named varieties of common and quilled asters,
and raise a hundred and twenty-four plants; of these, all except ten were true in the
above limited sense; and I considered even a wrong shade of colour as false …
(Darwin, 1868)

That is genuine horticulture and so, with such studies, Darwin's garden came
to share his immortality.

And where better than in one's own garden to examine and investigate those
archetypal garden animals, worms. Darwin, like many a gardener before and
since, was utterly fascinated by them. He measured their endeavours and
calculated the results of their labours by many ingenious experiments (p. 217),
the intrigue of almost a lifetime finally bearing fruit in *The Formation of Vegetable*
Mould through the Action of Worms (1881), published shortly before his death.

Darwin, it seems to me, was the ultimate, almost the unique, embodiment of
the naturalist-gardener, a man who was inspired equally by plants in the wild and
plants in cultivation, and who realised that the one could teach much about the
other. For the first time, the garden and the world beyond it were not disparate
and separate entities, but variations of the greater environment in which all
livings things exist. It is both a tribute to Darwin and a telling commentary on
natural history since that in large measure his studies were unique. We have
slipped back. The unavoidable conclusion is that whilst the great naturalists of
the past observed some natural history in their own gardens, their writings, when
they reveal anything of locality, suggest that most of their study was in open
countryside nearby. The garden in some measure may have provided them with
the inspiration to look beyond its boundaries but, above all, then *as now*, the
garden was simply not perceived as a habitat or environment on a par with
anything outside it. It is telling that:

Apart from Philip Miller, who was in charge of the Chelsea Physic Garden and thus
straddled the worlds of both medicine and horticulture, [Thomas] *Martyn's Botanical*
Society [1721–6] *shared no members with another small contemporary body, the Society*
of Gardeners … (Allen, 1994)

CONCLUSION

So what judgement is to be made of them: of Francis Willughby, who travelled
the length and breadth of Britain and much of Europe collecting natural history
specimens, but forgot to look in his own garden; and the Tradescants, *pater et*

filius, whose collection of natural curiosities was 'far and away the largest and most comprehensive of its day' (Leith-Ross, 1984), but who clearly preferred to stock the gardens they created with plants from almost anywhere except their native England whose vegetation took second place? It is all too easy with hindsight to apportion blame. As Leith-Ross pointed out:

> *The first half of the seventeenth century was a period of intense horticultural activity ... Old World plants, for long cultivated with great skill in Persia, were gradually working their way westward via Vienna and Antwerp, and plants from America, even more exciting because they were entirely new, were also arriving.*

It was small wonder then that the contemporary garden was little more than a living museum of exotic curiosities. In explaining 'the suitableness of the study of Natural History for a clergyman residing in the country ...', J. C. Loudon (cited by Allen, 1994) wrote: '... the horticulturist exercises his gentler pursuit within his garden ... but the naturalist is abroad in the fields, investigating the habits and searching out the habitats of birds, insects, or plants ...' What a pity.

Sadly it is today impossible to see the gardens of almost any of our great naturalists; at least not in anything approaching the condition in which they knew them. Where, for instance, is the garden of the man with whom I began, Miles Berkeley, the Northamptonshire naturalist cleric who grew melons and cucumbers and admired the crocuses beneath his window? The extent of the garden is not clear from his own accounts and today sadly is unrecognisable. The house has become the village school, and the garden lies beneath the tarmac of its car park. Pennant's garden is gone, so has Banks', while Ray's cannot be identified. Two exceptions, however, are the most important. Both Gilbert White's garden at The Wakes, Selborne in Hampshire and Charles Darwin's at Down House in Kent are unusual in remaining in a form their creators would have recognised; and both are undergoing a programme of restoration – Down House by English Heritage who acquired it in 1996, although it had been open to the public as a museum since 1929, and The Wakes by Gilbert White's House & The Oates Museum Trust. The Wakes was opened to the public by the Trust in 1955, although serious restoration of the garden began later, and the work there has been described by Fisher (2000).

And what of the great naturalists of our own time, as evidenced, perfectly legitimately, by the authors of previous New Naturalist volumes? In Peter Marren's thumbnail biographies of 96 authors of Volumes 1 to 81, gardening is mentioned as an interest or occupation, but rarely, even among the professional botanists like the late Max Walters (*Wild Flowers; Mountain Flowers; Wild and*

Garden Plants) or horticulturists like Christopher Page (*Ferns*), although W. B. Turrill (*British Plant Life*) was a keen gardener and listed gardening among his recreations in *Who's Who*. Winifred Pennington (*The Lake District*) and John Raven (*Mountain Flowers*) were also described by Marren as gardeners. William Stearn, who co-authored *The Art of Botanical Illustration* and wrote the standard work on botanical Latin, reassuringly described himself as having gardening as a recreation, although John Ramsbottom (*Mushrooms and Toadstools*), who also wrote *A Book of Roses* and certainly belonged to horticultural societies, was silent on his recreational pursuits. The only New Naturalist author to give gardening as his sole recreation in *Who's Who* was the virologist Kenneth Smith (*Measles, Mumps and Mosaics*). Marren's comment on Wilfrid Blunt (1901–87), Stearn's co-author of *The Art of Botanical Illustration*, was perhaps the most telling: 'Lifelong fascination with flowers, but not one to dirty his hands weeding: once posed by waist-high ornamental urn commenting: "This is the sort of gardening I like".' It is nonetheless revealing and reassuring that Billy Collins himself, founder of the New Naturalist series, was reputedly a keen gardener, although he did not list it among his recreations in *Who's Who*.

CHAPTER 11

The Garden as a Natural History Educator

L IKE MOST GARDENERS today, the foundations of my knowledge were laid in the garden where I grew up. My father and uncle were enthusiastic amateur gardeners and it was by joining them in their gardening tasks and following their example that I grasped the basics (Fig. 136). But I was equally blessed by the regular afternoon's gardening at primary school. Our headmaster too was a keen gardener and set us weekly tasks to undertake. The pride in our plot – and in our meticulously kept tools – lives with me still, even though the school garden itself is now under tarmac as an extension to the car park, and the fine 'Conference' pear tree outside the staff room has long gone. Once I reached secondary school, the constraints of GCE syllabuses meant that gardening was a luxury the timetable could ill-afford. There was, nonetheless, some scope for using the school garden – such as it was – for parts of the then new and reformist Nuffield Foundation Biology courses for O-level and A-level, that at least encouraged some practical studies and the use of live plants and animals – and incidentally, were also responsible for the demise of large numbers of common frogs. Forty years on, concerns, at least with A-level biology, arose again. There had been no new curriculum initiative since Nuffield, and there was 'evidence that much teaching in the subject results in little student involvement, lacks variety and is dull' (Lock, 1998). A new scheme, Salters-Nuffield Advanced Biology, was piloted in 2002 in England and Wales (Hall *et al.*, 2005). It is structured on nine topics, five for the AS grades and four for the final A2. From the perspective of gardening and natural history, it too looks like a missed opportunity. The only glimmer of hope seems to be in the A2 topic called 'On the wild side' and the sentence 'Students will see that successful conservation

FIG 136. The author learned to garden by following his father's example.

requires an understanding of the interactions between wildlife and human populations ...'.

There seem to me to be two problems with biological education and in each, biology is divorced from gardening – and both subjects from natural history. The subject of biology is taught in schools, and the courses contain little or no compulsory gardening, although where scope does exist for including it – especially at some primary schools and at independent schools with freedom outside the National Curriculum – individual and interested teachers can help. There are certainly some enterprising biological projects that involve gardening in such journals as *Biological Education* and *Field Studies*, available for those who have time to pursue them. For younger children, a new book attempts a proper integration of gardening with natural history (Buczacki & Buczacki, 2006).

By contrast, horticulture/gardening is principally taught to aspiring professional horticulturists at horticultural and similar colleges, and in some measure to enthusiastic amateurs at part-time and evening courses. But hardly anywhere it appears is gardening instruction properly integrated with natural history. I did a sample trawl through one college's offerings of the syllabuses of the Higher National Certificate/Diplomas in Horticulture, Garden Design, Turf Management, Organic Gardening, Landscape and Garden Design, Nursery Production and even Environmental Management; and for anyone with any sort of interest in natural history, they looked pretty bleak. The widely used RHS General Certificate in Horticulture was slightly more promising and did embrace some taxonomy, and even a tiny bit of ecology. But there appeared no real indication that there was a genuine integration of these with horticulture.

So where is this integration of natural history and horticulture to come from? Its absence seems to be a manifestation of a wider anxiety that I and at least some of my fellow biologists share. Whole organism studies, at all levels of biology, have largely been abandoned in the pursuit of ever smaller subjects that are examined in ever greater depth. Molecular biology reigns, and as far as classification and taxonomy is concerned, a whole generation (at least) has been missed out and future biologists will have to start afresh to learn scientific names and the natural orders of things. As I said in my presidential address to the British Mycological Society a few years ago, on the specific topic of mycology, but it could apply equally to entomology and many other disciplines:

> I do fear that a time will come, not so many years hence, when a generation will have grown up that can recite by heart the genome of organisms without ever knowing what the organisms are, what they look like, what they do or where they live. And some of these people will call themselves mycologists ... (Buczacki, 2002)

We require a complete rethink of the way we teach people about living things – and a good start would come from the reintroduction into everyday use of the term natural history, which has for far too long been out of fashion (except in the New Naturalist series) in favour of 'conservation', 'biology', 'environmental studies' and 'ecology', which really mean something quite different. We simply cannot go on ignoring whole organism studies and whole organism/habitat interactions.

SOURCES OF INFORMATION

The public today obtains its gardening information from a variety of sources. Books, magazines, television, radio, the internet, lectures and gardening societies are the most important. I am not concerned here with their overall role in influencing gardeners' actions, ideas and purchasing proclivities, but I do want to examine what, if any, part they do and should play in showing gardens as habitats and in demonstrating their significance for wildlife.

Television

Television is the all-powerful medium so it is the appropriate place to start (Fig. 137). In Britain, on a typical day in 2005, there were around 26 hours of gardening television, spread across five or six channels and encompassing about 15 different programme titles. That adds up to 9,500 hours of television gardening every year, although, of course, only a small proportion is original programming because all programmes are repeated – ad nauseam, some might say. In the cause of my research, I sat through the equivalent of a sample week and even endured watching myself. I saw nothing that had much to do with wildlife; and in truth, not a huge amount that had anything to do with horticulture. It is no coincidence that the programmes fell into the category of Entertainment rather than Documentary. In the same sample week that

FIG 137. Television production in the author's garden.

I surveyed the gardening output, there were 33 programmes occupying 120 hours on 15 channels that were loosely described as 'nature'. Almost none touched on the natural history of the British Isles, let alone the garden, but most concentrated on such topics as sharks, snakes, big game and 'insects from hell'.

And never, it seems, the twain shall meet. I cannot believe I am alone in having offered programme proposals that married gardening and natural history and that would have shown the role and importance of the garden as a habitat, but no commissioning editor has been interested. In some measure, the problem lies with the great difficulty television seems to have in creating hybrids. The people and departments who commission gardening programmes are not usually the same as those who commission natural history. Television likes pigeonholing; programme ideas that do not fit a predetermined stereotype seldom get off the ground. It also likes 'focus groups': assemblages of viewers and others who are supposed to represent public opinion and give their own opinions on what programmes should be made. But just as in catch-22, if they have never seen or been exposed to anything different, they cannot possibly know what is possible. By and large, television also likes to be safe. Time and again, one sees well-tried presenters who can perform reasonably reliably in front of the camera, irrespective of whether they have the knowledge or background to understand and interpret what they are being asked to say. Someone, at some time, needs to grasp that gardens are extremely important and interesting habitats, and to use knowledgeable people to demonstrate this to the viewing public. It is all very well to pay lip service to a gardening conservation message (p. 241), but it is high time television used its undoubted power to turn it to real effect.

Books

Despite many portents of gloom over the past 30 years and numerous predictions that the printed word has had its day, book and magazine sales are still reasonably healthy. The halcyon days when gardening and cookery were the reliable stand-bys of every non-fiction publisher may have passed, and the number of gardening titles released each year may have declined, but there are still plenty of them. Sadly, here, yet again, an opportunity is being missed. The bulk of modern gardening books fall into one of three categories. There are so-called garden design books, sometimes but not always written by accomplished garden designers. They are usually pleasing to the eye, but contain advice and plans that not one person in a thousand ever does, wants to or could turn into reality. Second, there are basic practical books describing the principal gardening tasks, generally dependent for their sales on a well-known media author, but seldom containing anything novel, original or individual and merely representing the recycling of well-worn facts, a few of which might even lie within the compass of the author's own experience. And third, there are semi-monographic reference books on different types of plant or plants for different purposes – grasses, conifers, plants for dry soils and so on. These are usually authoritative, written by people who know their subjects and tend to be the most read and used (as opposed to merely bought) among all gardening titles, depending on their level and approach, by both experienced and novice gardeners.

On another shelf in the bookshop, sometimes but not invariably close by, there are the natural history titles, almost always written with authority by knowledgeable authors, and divided on the one hand into sumptuously illustrated volumes with glorious photographs, often linked to a television series, and on the other, authoritative and often definitive works of reference, most falling into the category of field guides. But again, and as with television, there are few hybrids, few books that blend gardening and natural history; largely because at many publishing houses, just as at many television production companies, the commissioning editors are different and there is perceived to be a different audience for each.

Magazines

The first gardening magazine in anything remotely like the modern sense, as opposed to learned journals that embraced some horticulture, was the appropriately titled *Gardener's Magazine*, launched by John Loudon in 1826. It was quarterly at first, then bimonthly, then monthly, and continued until Loudon's death in 1843. It too was pretty learned; but then it was aimed principally at professional gardeners employed by big houses who knew their craft, and it contained a good deal of what in today's terminology would be called biology or even ecology. It is particularly telling that between 1826 and 1838, Loudon was also editing his *Magazine of Natural History*, a duality of scope few editors would attempt today. Loudon's efforts spawned imitators – and some plagiarists – *The Horticultural Register* by Joseph Paxton in 1831, Paxton's *Magazine of Botany* in 1841, William Robinson's *The Garden* in 1871 and others. All embraced at least some botany and zoology, and it was in the most celebrated of all, *The Gardener's Chronicle*, which began publication in 1841, that the Revd M. J. Berkeley published his seminal studies of the cause of potato blight. The publication set out its mission to be 'A weekly record of everything that bears upon horticulture and garden botany' and it blended the best gardening and the best science of the day in a manner that has never been equalled. *The Gardeners' Chronicle* still exists in name, but there the similarity with its august forebear ends, as it is now a weekly magazine for the horticultural trade.

The ultimate in Victorian breadth in encompassing gardening and natural history, and a publication to which Darwin himself contributed, must have been George Johnson and Robert Hogg's *Journal of Horticulture and Cottage Gardener and Country Gentleman, a Magazine of Gardening, Rural and Domestic Economy, Botany and Natural History*, which by the 1870s had become *The Journal of Horticulture, Cottage Gardener, Country Gentleman, Bee-Keeper and Poultry Chronicle – A Journal of The Homestead, Poultry-Yard, Apiary and Dovecote*. I can just imagine a publisher attempting to get that on to a railway-station bookstall today.

Like *The Gardener's Chronicle*, another important early publication also survives, but this time still in august form. Serial publications of the RHS began with its *Transactions* in 1805, which metamorphosed through the *Proceedings, Journal First Series, Proceedings* (again), *Proceedings New Series* and *Journal New Series* to its current manifestation as *The Garden*. It is the leading popular, large circulation magazine for serious gardeners (almost by definition, as those receiving it are all members of the RHS), but its wildlife and even its wildlife gardening content is woefully small.

One of the biggest disappointments, however, is *Amateur Gardening*, the oldest surviving truly popular publication for the home gardener, which also appeals to the professional. From its launch in 1884 until the 1990s, it led the field in practical gardening information, but sadly, its direction then changed just as the importance of wildlife gardening and the garden as a habitat began to be appreciated. It is now a distinctly tabloid title. As a publication for the more serious modern amateur gardener, it has been eclipsed by its weekly rival *Garden News*.

It may be that some of the older titles carry too much traditional baggage and find it difficult to embrace natural history; the newer magazines seem much more ready to be flexible. A good representative example is *Gardens Monthly* which, in a typical issue in 2005, contained a liberal sprinkling of wildlife matter across its contents. The biggest selling modern gardening magazine is the monthly BBC *Gardeners' World*, but it is in an unusual position because the same publisher also produces another leading title, BBC *Wildlife*. This has not, however, prevented it from having a strong wildlife gardening content since its launch in 1991. Much more significantly, it also has frequent features on strictly wildlife matters such as profiles of birds and other garden visitors.

Perhaps more encouraging than the relatively poor overall representation in gardening magazines of natural history (as opposed to a lip service recognition of wildlife gardening) is the fact that wildlife magazines are beginning to include gardening contributions. The RSPB magazine *Birds*, with a quarterly readership of around two million, is among those leading the way, with several pages devoted to gardening matters.

The internet

The internet is now vast and apparently all-embracing. But in truth, it seems to do little to help my cause. There is a plethora of gardening websites, far too many to count or appraise, but the overall impression is that they are either mimicking gardening magazines, mimicking garden centres or both. I am sure there are websites that blend wildlife and gardening information, but I have not found many.

ENCOURAGING THE YOUNG GENERATION

Time and again, horticulturists pay lip service to a desire to 'attract younger people into gardening'. But you need to own or have access to a garden and/ or have some responsibility for its upkeep to be likely to have an interest in gardening. Attracting young people into natural history is never presented as a problem; which indeed it is not. You need no responsibilities and need to own nothing to have an interest in wildlife. An opportunity is being missed throughout most of the media and certainly throughout much of education to promote gardening and natural history simultaneously to the benefit of both subjects and of everyone who participates. So if the formal information and education channels are not helping, we should take matters into our own hands.

In large measure, and at an amateur level, gardening is about doing; natural history about observing. I have indicated elsewhere that watching their feeding behaviour is a primary reason for the interest gardeners have in attracting birds. But there are examples among insect behaviour that are at least if not more compelling, and if people could be persuaded that garden butterfly, bee, spider or even hoverfly watching is a worthwhile pursuit, I am sure they would not take too long to be hooked on natural history. I will digress for a moment to say that is precisely how my own dual interests began – they came through emulating my boyhood hero, the pioneer African wildlife film-maker Armand Denis, in our home garden, where I tracked down whatever creatures I could find with my box Brownie camera. Admittedly, many garden creatures are elusive and live in dark and inaccessible places, but flower-visiting insects are remarkable compelling exceptions. It is relatively easy to obtain interesting and valuable data on flower selection by butterflies, to observe their varied basking behaviour (Heinrich, 1993) and to see how their territorial activity depends on the microclimatic landscape of the garden (Dennis, 1992). Hoverflies are easy to watch, even if not always easy to identify, and their flower-visiting and territorial behaviour can prove fascinating for child and adult alike (Gilbert, 1983). I have already touched on the fact that bees have recently become one of the few groups of garden insects to have joined butterflies and dragonflies as subjects for gardeners' attention, and they do make fascinating creatures for observation and study. Boxes to attract bumblebees and mason bees (*Osmia* species) are now widely available (Fig. 138), and the sort of studies that Corbet and her co-workers have made on flower selection by different bees (p. 247) can be richly rewarding. The New Naturalist volume *Bumblebees* (Benton, 2005) has provided a huge stimulus to bee study and conservation in gardens.

I have complained throughout this book about the paucity of data on animal behaviour and activity – as opposed to mere presence – in gardens. It is gardeners themselves, young and old, who have it in their scope to put this right.

FIG 138. Proprietary nest boxes may be bought for mason bees. They betray their presence by sealing tubes in which their eggs have been laid.

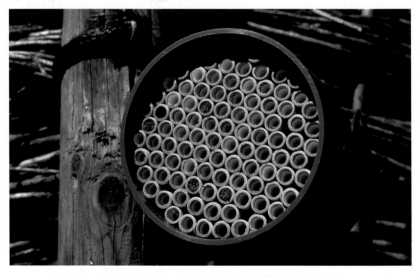

CHAPTER 12

The Future of the Garden and its
Likely Role in our Natural History

I N EARLY 2005, the RHS in association with the wildlife trusts launched
'a major new project to bring the worlds of gardening and nature
conservation closer together'. Thanks presumably to someone
employed by a public relations consultancy, it was called the 'Wild about
Gardens Project'. Its aims were to 'celebrate' what gardeners are doing to
support wildlife, to 'increase understanding' of the significance of local wildlife
characteristics, and to 'build on existing research' into the wildlife potential
of domestic gardens.

Ultimately, all the important pursestrings in twenty-first century Britain are
held by the Treasury and the Government. So what can gardeners expect from
their political leaders? It is little surprise that neither the word 'garden' nor the
word 'wildlife' appeared in any meaningful way in the 2005 general election
manifestos of the main political parties. The Labour Party promised to cut down
on fly-tipping and to build 60 per cent of new homes on brownfield sites (but
see p. 29). The Liberal Democrats did mention wildlife and even biodiversity,
but only insofar as a commitment to protect them in developing countries. The
Conservatives said nothing. Perhaps it is naïve to expect anything more from
the big parties when there are much bigger political fish to be fried. But what
of the 'Greens'? The Green Party, the first ecology party in Europe, was founded
in 1973. Originally called People, it changed its name first to the Ecology Party
and then in 1985 to The Green Party. Its manifesto spoke of ecotaxes and zero
waste strategies, but made no specific appeal to or promises for gardeners.
There was not much help, it seems, from politicians of any persuasion.

THE IMPACT OF GARDENS ON WILDLIFE

Gardening and the impact of gardens on wildlife are inseparable from the overall viability of gardening as a pursuit and gardening as an industry. One might hope that the more gardens and gardeners there are, the greater the likelihood that wildlife will be affected beneficially. Disappointingly, the Government review document *Opportunity Age – Meeting the Challenges of Ageing in the 21st Century* (Anon, 2005*b*) had nothing to say about gardens and gardening, but it may be that after many years of conventional wisdom suggesting to us that retirement brings with it the opportunity and desire to do more gardening, the move to raise the retirement age might just reverse that trend. Shorter working weeks and increased leisure time do not necessarily mean more gardening and gardeners, and even if they do, they do not necessarily mean more worthwhile plants or a better environment for wildlife. It all too often seems to be the increased obsession with 'easy gardening', 'labour-free gardening' and 'instant gardening' that is being catered for by our national population of around 2,000 garden centres, many of which are now, in any event, little more than venues for a family day out rather than anything to do with serious horticulture. Where I do see some grounds for optimism is in the comparable population of smaller nurseries which collectively sell a splendid range of species and cultivars; in the fairly small but generally high-quality suppliers of native plants and seeds; and in the ever-increasing membership of bodies like the RSPB, the RHS, the wildlife trusts and the National Trust, all of which, to some degree and in different ways, encourage people to look at and appreciate the wider environment and/or to see just what can be achieved in gardens. If nothing else, at least they have the potential to inspire.

I become slightly irritated when having visited the Chelsea Flower Show I am asked almost every year by a broadcast or newspaper interviewer to give my views on the 'current trend' or 'this year's theme'. The Chelsea Flower Show does not have a theme, and there is no annual caucus of gardeners, garden designers and other pundits to set the style for gardens in the coming 12 months. If several of the show gardens at Chelsea or any of the other horticultural shows do appear similar, it is usually mere coincidence. And so it is with trying to forecast 'trends' in gardening generally – and to extrapolate from them to see any impact on wildlife. If nurserymen and garden product retailers really could foretell the future, they would be wealthy folk indeed. And little can be learned with the benefit of hindsight. People's gardens do not change wholesale every few years. As I walk around my local town of Stratford-upon-Avon today, I cannot

FIG 139. Native wild flower mixture grown in pots and used in a flower-show display garden.

honestly say the gardens I see are appreciably different from when I first knew them 30 years ago. Some are more tidy, some less so; some have fewer roses, some more. Individual gardeners may well change a garden they have newly bought and they may like certain plants their predecessor did not; but to look for an overall trend so significant that it is likely to cause shifts in wildlife species populations seems to me to look in vain; with two possible exceptions, one beneficial, one not.

Decking

From time to time, and almost always through the influence of television, a particular plant will suddenly become popular or a particular feature will suddenly assume significance – or even some innovation will become apparent.

But most are transient and certainly none anything like universal. Among plants, I recall the excitement about Rose 'Super Star' in the 1960s, a multitude of hostas in the 1970s, and Potentilla 'Red Ace' in the 1980s. All survived and all are still available, but most of the new introductions launched with such fanfares by the horticultural trade each season sink without trace in a few years. Over the past few decades, I suppose the only planting style that might be a candidate was the conifer and heather garden that now seems as redolent of the sixties as The Beatles and the prawn cocktail. There were certainly a considerable number of these biodiversity depauperate creations in urban housing estates, but good sense has prevailed and most have gone. No, it is something more recent – decking – that is almost the exception that proves the rule.

Although wooden platforms and boards have always had a place in gardens of certain traditions, most especially those of China and Japan, decking was more or less invented for the modern garden by the clutch of television makeover programmes that sprouted in the 1990s, to wither not long after the millennium turned. It is easy to see how and why. Given the ludicrous notion of creating a garden in a weekend as an entertainment, wooden boards and gravel offered the cheapest and quickest way of covering significant areas of ground without

FIG 140. The rose has declined in popularity in modern gardens.

FIG 141. Decking is appropriate in oriental gardens which are born of a different tradition, but sadly has been used to cover many hectares of otherwise productive home garden in Britain.

actually embarking on anything horticultural. Manufacturers sprang to the opportunity, marketing not only the boards themselves but 'decking paint', 'decking screws', 'decking brushes' and the other DIY paraphernalia that went with them. There is no way of knowing how many of the 20 odd million British gardens now contain some decking, but in those ten or so years of television influence, many hectares of valuable home garden were covered in the stuff, leaving a legacy of discolouring and eventually disintegrating timber, lost planting space and, as I indicated on p. 39, almost no benefit to wildlife other than as a growing medium for green algae and wood-rotting fungi. I cannot, thank goodness, foresee anything else as counterproductive to wildlife encouragement imposing itself on our collective national garden in the foreseeable future. But there has been and continues to be one, probably positive, trend in the deliberate growing in gardens of native plants, especially attractive native flowers.

Wild flower seeds

I can remember the headlines on the gardening page of a national tabloid newspaper as recently as the mid-1980s when John Chambers, owner of one of the first of the serious native plant nurseries, issued his seed catalogue. 'Weeds for Sale' was the banner. And that was essentially most gardeners' reaction. It was a reaction that was tempered when in the late 1980s he first displayed wild flowers at the Chelsea Flower Show, and then from 1990, when designer Julie Toll began to stage gardens there in which native plants took the dominant role. It was tempered even more when she won gold medals with them. However, the attitude has not completely gone away, especially among gardeners of the older generation, but overall the atmosphere has undoubtedly changed. Every major seed catalogue today has at least some wild flower seeds on offer – and the more reputable now guarantee that they are of British provenance to avoid any contamination of the native gene pool. And there are several specialist nurseries and seed companies selling nothing but native plants. I have been unable to obtain data indicating how many people buy them and how many gardens contain them, but clearly there must be sufficient numbers to ensure commercial viability. The encouragement is there to see for anyone who drives a car and uses a motorway, as the use of native plants on motorway-side planting now seems almost *de rigueur* (Fig. 142). I have said that wild flower planting is 'probably positive' because the relative merits of native and alien plants as wildlife benefits are still being argued. I am convinced, but not everyone else is.

GM PLANTS

Even if there is still disagreement about the merit of planting native species, at least no-one seems to think it is harmful. The same cannot be said of genetically modified (GM) plants, over which highly charged and emotive arguments still rage. Will the home garden of the future contain GM plants, and if so, what will be their impact?

Aside from the well-known anxieties held by the general public about the edibility of GM plants, the main wildlife issues are concerned with the leakage into the environment of alien genes and the threat that is posed by, for example, the use of insect-resistant crops that could pass their resistance genes on to wild relatives. The wild relatives, so the reasoning goes, would also be less attractive to insects. Insect populations would suffer in consequence, and so in turn would insect-eating birds and thence other creatures up the food chain. I can see much merit in these concerns, but it is not appropriate to enter into the debate here.

FIG 142. Oxeye daisy *Leucanthemum vulgare* is now *de rigueur* for motorway verges.

No GM plants are presently grown in commercial agriculture in the UK, let alone in gardens, and none can be grown without Government and EU approval. The home garden has therefore had no role to play in the GM debate and moreover, each request for approval must receive a comprehensive prior assessment of any potential risk to human health or the environment. These assessments involve considerable cost and no applications for growing non-food crops or uses of any sort in the UK have yet been made. So the time when the option exists for growing GM plants on the allotment may be a very long way off, but one day gardeners just might be faced with extremely awkward decisions, and it is worth musing briefly on the information that may be put before them.

There have been two relevant pronouncements from highly significant quarters. In his presidential address to the 2000 RHS Chelsea Flower Show, Sir Simon Hornby played down the environmental threat from GM crops by equating them with the results of conventional plant breeding and said that over 90 per cent of the plant material in the show marquee was already the result of genetic modification over hundreds of years. He said the whole show was about hybrids and cultivars. And in 2002, Lord May, distinguished former Chief Scientific Adviser to the Government, and then President of the Royal Society, was quoted as saying that invasive alien plants escaping from gardens posed a greater threat to the environment than GM crops.

THREATENED SPECIES

In 2005, the long-awaited new *Vascular Plant Red Data List for Britain* was published (Joint Nature Conservation Committee, 2005). It included 1,756 plants, of which around 20 per cent were considered to be threatened with extinction – generally not, as some sections of the media seemed to imagine, from the planet, but certainly from Britain. The authors restricted their coverage to true natives – although there were differences of opinion about the status of some neophytes – and as such, a large number of the species I have considered in this book had no relevance. It was, however, pointed out that plants of arable land had suffered the greatest decline – generally through loss of habitat – although some upland species had been seriously affected by overgrazing. Some consideration was given to ways to reverse the trend and it was hoped that new environmental farming initiatives which pay for farmers to restore habitats might help. Less intensive grazing and reflooding of drained wetlands were mentioned too. What was of interest is that nowhere in the list itself, nor in the publicity matter accompanying it, was any mention made of a role that gardens might play in helping to reverse the decline. This is not meant as a criticism; rather it is a confirmation of a fact that many partially informed observers fail to realise. Although gardens may well provide suitable conditions for a large number of threatened species, growing native plants in gardens, even rare and vulnerable native plants, is of little or no value in helping to retain them as viable British species; and that will not change in the years to come. It may well give pleasure, pride and satisfaction to gardeners and, with the huge proviso that the seed is obtained from an approved British source, it will certainly do no harm. In a purely arithmetical sense, it might increase their numbers slightly if the garden population is allowed to set seed and the seedlings allowed to grow, although it will do nothing to redress the loss of habitats and other factors that have reduced the wild populations. But I return again to my belief that it will continue to be valuable in providing food and shelter for possibly threatened animals and therefore is to be warmly encouraged on that count.

THE FUTURE

Ultimately, any prediction of the appearance and content of the garden of say 50 or 100 years hence is fraught with uncertainty. I referred earlier to the document *Gardening in the Global Greenhouse* (p. 60) and its attempts to predict the future character of Britain's gardens by reference to what used to be called global warming but now tends to be known as climate change in deference to the fact that not everywhere is becoming, or will be, warmer all of the time. In terms of garden wildlife, its forecasts were pretty limited, but even if we look at wildlife indirectly through the types of plants gardeners grow, I find it hard to see any sort of dramatic, climatically induced shift, at least in the next 50 or so years. There may be a few more 'Mediterranean-style' plants (p. 59); 'Golden Delicious' (Fig. 143) may become a more widely grown apple (and given warm summers, will taste wonderful too); and 'International Kidney' (a.k.a. 'Jersey Royal') may become a more popular early potato. But as long as we continue to have a winter minimum temperature below freezing – as long as we still have frosts – there will be no seismic change in the nature of our garden flora, and cold-blooded creatures will still need to pass into some dormant state, and some of the warm-blooded ones to hibernate or migrate. Apart from in a few odd sheltered maritime spots, there have been no consistently frost-free winters in Britain for many thousands of years, and the type of climate change now being countenanced will certainly not alter that record.

FIG 143. Apple 'Golden Delicious', a variety that may become more popular in British gardens as summers turn warmer.

What seems more likely is that garden wildlife and the importance of gardens for wildlife in general will alter not because gardens themselves change, but because the environment beyond them does. It will be the loss of traditional feeding and breeding sites that will bring hitherto less familiar birds and other creatures into gardens; it will be the plants – whatever they are – and the supplementary artificial feeding and breeding encouragements they find there that will help to retain them.

References

Aarstad, J. S. & Miller, D. E. (1978). Corn residue management to reduce erosion in irrigation furrows. *Journal of Soil & Water Conservation* **33**: 289–91.

Addison, J. (1712). *Spectator* **414**, 25 June.

Allan, M. (1982). *William Robinson, 1838–1935: Father of the English Flower Garden.* London: Faber & Faber.

Allen, A. A. (1964). The Coleoptera of a suburban garden. *The Entomologist's Record and Journal of Variation* **76**: 261–4.

Allen, D. A. (1994). *The Naturalist in Britain – a Social History.* Second Edition. Princeton: Princeton University Press.

Amherst, A. (1896). *A History of Gardening in England.* London: Bernard Quaritch.

Anon (1997). *The Use of Limestone in Horticulture.* London: Royal Horticultural Society.

Anon (1998a). United Kingdom Parliament. Minutes of Evidence taken before the Environmental Audit Committee, Tuesday 7 July 1998. London: Stationery Office.

Anon (1998b). Harvest mice return to home of 'father of English natural history'. *Daily Telegraph*, 24 August.

Anon (2000a). *Monitoring and Assessment of Peat and Alternative Products for Growing Media and Soil Improvers in the UK (1996–1999).* London: Department of the Environment, Transport and the Regions.

Anon (2000b). *Pesticides Safety Directive Newsletter 25.* York: Pesticides Safety Directive.

Anon (2002a). *All About Bird Tables.* Wildlife Information Leaflet. Sandy: RSPB.

Anon (2002b). *Conserving Water in Buildings.* Worthing: Environment Agency National Water Demand Management Centre.

Anon (2002c). *Conservation and Environment Guidelines. Peat and the Gardener.* Wisley: Royal Horticultural Society.

Anon (2003a). Badger problems: advice to householders. *Rural Development Service Technical Advisory Note WM07.* Westbury on Trym: Defra.

Anon (2003b). *Housing Statistics Summary No. 13, Survey of English Housing Provisional Results 2001–2002.* London: Office of the Deputy Prime Minister.

Anon (2004). *Conservation and Environment Guideline Leaflet – Peat and the Gardener.* Wisley: Royal Horticultural Society.

Anon (2005a). *The Yellow Book.* Guildford: The National Gardens Scheme Charitable Trust.

Anon (2005*b*). *Opportunity Age – Meeting the Challenges of Ageing in the 21st Century.* London: dti.

Anon (n.d.*a*). *Gardens and Biodiversity.* Wisley: Royal Horticultural Society.

Anon (n.d.*b*). *Peat – How Production Today Benefits Our Environment Tomorrow.* Glastonbury: Peat Producers Association.

Arnolds, E. (1981). *Ecology and Coenology of Macro Fungi in Grasslands in Drenthe, The Netherlands. Vol. 1. Part 1. Introduction and Synecology.* Vaduz: Bibliotheca Mycologica.

Arnolds, E. (1982). *Ecology and Coenology of Macro Fungi in Grasslands in Drenthe, The Netherlands. Vol. 2. Parts 2 & 3. Autecology and Taxonomy.* Vaduz: Bibliotheca Mycologica.

Asher, J., Warren, M., Fox, R., Harding, P., Jeffcoate, G. & Jeffcoate, S. (2001). *The Millennium Atlas of Butterflies in Britain and Ireland.* Oxford: Oxford University Press.

Bailey, J. P. & Conolly, A. P. (2000). Prize-winners to pariahs – A history of Japanese knotweed s.l. (Polygonaceae) in the British Isles. *Watsonia* **23**: 93–110.

Baines, C. (1985). *How to Make a Wildlife Garden.* London: Elm Tree Books.

Baines, C. (2002). Biodiversity in practice. *In: Gardens: Heaven or Hell for Wildlife?* London: Royal Horticultural Society.

Baker, P. J., Ansell, R. J., Dodds, P. A. A., Webber, C. E. & Harris, S. (2003). Factors affecting the distribution of small mammals in an urban area. *Mammal Review* **33**: 95–100.

Barnett, E. A., Fletcher, M. R., Hunter, K. & Sharp, E. A. (2002). *Pesticide Poisoning of Animals 2000: Investigations of Suspected Incidents in the United Kingdom.* York: Central Science Laboratory, Defra.

Beales, P. (1977). *Classic Roses.* Second Edition. London: Harvill.

Bean, W. J. (1973). *Trees and Shrubs Hardy in the British Isles.* Eighth Edition. London: John Murray.

Beebee, T. J. C. (1979). Habitats of the British amphibians (2): suburban parks and gardens. *Biological Conservation* **15**: 242–57.

Beebee, T. (1996). Twenty years of garden ponds. *British Herpetological Society Bulletin* **56**: 2–6.

Beebee, T. & Griffiths, R. (2000). *Amphibians and Reptiles.* London: HarperCollins.

Benton, T. (2006). *Bumblebees.* London: HarperCollins.

Bhatti, M. & Church, A. (2000). 'I never promised you a rose garden': gender, leisure and home-making. *Leisure Studies* **19**: 183–97.

Bisgrove, R. & Hadley, P. (2002). The impacts of climate change on gardens in the UK. *In: Gardening in the Global Greenhouse.* Oxford: UK Climate Impacts Programme, Royal Horticultural Society and National Trust.

Bland, R. L., Tully, J. & Greenwood, J. D. (2004). Birds breeding in British gardens: an underestimated population? *Bird Study* **51**: 97–106.

Bosanquet, F. S. T. (Trans.) (1907). *The Letters of Caius Plinius Caesilius Secundus: The Translation of Melmoth.* London: George Bell & Sons Ltd.

Branigan, K. (1973). *Town and Country. The Archaeology of Verulamium and the Roman Chilterns.* Bourne End: Spur Books.

Braun-Blanquet, J. (1936). Social life among plants. *Plant Sociology: the study of plant communities.* New York: McGraw-Hill.

Buczacki, S. T. (1986). *Ground Rules for Gardeners.* London: Collins.

Buczacki, S. (1988). *Creating a Victorian Flower Garden.* London: Collins.

Buczacki, S. T. (2001). Berkeley's legacy –

who cares? *Mycological Research*
105: 1283–94.

Buczacki, S. (2002). *Fauna Britannica.*
London: Hamlyn.

Buczacki, S. & Buczacki, B. (2006). *Young Gardener.* London: Frances Lincoln.

Buczacki, S. T., Cadd, S. E., Ockendon, J. G. & White, J. G. (1976). Field evaluations of systemic fungicides and derivatives of dithiocarbamic acid for the control of clubroot. *Annals of Applied Biology* **84:** 51–6.

Buczacki, S. & Harris, K. (2005). *Pests, Diseases & Disorders of Garden Plants.* Third Edition. London: Collins.

Bunt, A. C. (1976). *Modern Potting Composts.* London: George Allen & Unwin.

Cahill, K. (2001). *Who Owns Britain?* Edinburgh: Canongate.

Calman, M. (1999). *Statement on the Use of Peat in National Trust Gardens.* London: National Trust.

Cannon, A. (1999). The significance of private gardens for bird conservation. *Bird Conservation International* **9:** 287–97.

Carson, R. (1962). *Silent Spring.* Boston: Houghton Mifflin.

Centre for Aquatic Plant Management (2000). *Australian Swamp Stonecrop. Information Sheet 14.* Bristol: Long Ashton Research Station.

Chamberlain, D. E., Vickery, J. A., Glue, D. E. & Conway, G. (2003). Gardens as winter feeding refuge for declining farmland birds. BTO *Research Report No. 342.* Thetford: British Trust for Ornithology.

Cheffings, C. M. & Farrell, L. (Eds) (2005). *Species Status No. 7. The Vascular Plant Red Data List for Great Britain.* Joint Nature Conservation Committee.

Clapham, A. R., Tutin, C. G. & Warburg, E. F. (1962). *Flora of the British Isles.* Second Edition. Cambridge: Cambridge University Press.

Clegg, J. (1965). *The Freshwater Life of the British Isles.* Third Edition. London: Warne.

Clement, E. J. & Foster, M. C. (1994). *Alien Plants of the British Isles.* London: Botanical Society of the British Isles.

Clover, C. (2005). Has Prescott got his sums right on housing crisis? *Daily Telegraph,* 16 May.

Comba, L., Corbet, S. A., Barron, A., Bird, A., Collinge, S., Miyazaki, N. & Powell, M. (1999). Garden flowers: insect visits and the floral reward of horticulturally-modified variants. *Annals of Botany* **83:** 73–86.

Comba, L., Corbet, S. A., Hunt, L. & Warren, B. (1999). Flowers, nectar and insect visits: evaluating British plant species for pollinator-friendly gardens. *Annals of Botany* **83:** 369–83.

Corbet, S. A., Bee, J., Dasmahapatra, K., Gale, S., Gorringe, E., La Ferla, B., Moorhouse, T., Trevail, A., Van Bergen, Y. & Vorontsova, M. (2001). Native or Exotic? Double or single? Evaluating plants for pollinator-friendly gardens. *Annals of Botany* **87:** 219–32.

Crossley, J. & Christie, R. C. (Eds) (1847–86). *The Diary and Correspondence of Dr John Worthington.* 2 vols in 3. London: Chetham Society.

Cunliffe, B. (1971). *Excavations at Fishbourne. Vol. I. The Site.* London: Society of Antiquaries.

Darwin, C. (1868). *The Variation of Animals and Plants under Domestication.* London: John Murray.

Darwin, C. (1881). *The Formation of Vegetable Mould, through the Action of Worms with Observation of their Habits.* London: John Murray.

Davis, B. N. K. (1979). The ground arthropods of London gardens. *London Naturalist* **58:** 15–24.

Davis, B., Walker, N., Ball, D. & Fitter, A.
(1992). *The Soil.* London: HarperCollins.

Defra (2002). *Countryside Survey 2000.
Accounting for Nature: Assessing Habitats in
the UK Countryside.* London: Department
of the Environment, Transport &
Regions.

Dennis, R. L. H. (1992). *The Ecology of
Butterflies in Britain.* Oxford: Oxford
University Press.

Desmond, A., Browne, J. & Moore, J. (2004).
Charles Robert Darwin. *In: Oxford
Dictionary of National Biography.* Oxford:
Oxford University Press.

Desmond, R. (1994). *Dictionary of British &
Irish Botanists and Horticulturists.* London:
Taylor & Francis and The Natural History
Museum.

Elliott, B. (1985). Some sceptical thoughts
about William Robinson. *The Garden*
110: 14–17.

English Nature (2003). *Sustainable housing
with biodiversity at its heart.* Press Release,
10 September. Peterborough: English
Nature.

Evans, A. (2002). Gardens: heaven or hell
for birds? *In: Gardens: Heaven or Hell for
Wildlife?* London: Royal Horticultural
Society.

Evans, K. & Trudgill, D. L. (1992). Pest
aspects of potato production. Part 1: the
nematode pests of potatoes. *In:* Harris,
P. M. (Ed.) *The Potato Crop: Scientific Basis
for Improvement.* London: Chapman &
Hall.

Evelyn, J. (1664). *Sylva, or a Discourse of
Forest-Trees and the Propagation of Timber.*
London: Thomas Martyn.

Falk, J. H. (1976). Energetics of a suburban
lawn ecosystem. *Ecology* **57**: 141–50.

Farrer, R. J. (1907). *My Rock Garden.* London:
Edward Arnold.

Feeny, P. (1976). Plant apparency and
chemical defense. *In:* Wallace, J. W. &
Mansell, R. J. (Eds) *Biochemical Interactions
Between Plants and Insects.* New York:
Plenum Press.

Fisher, C. (2000). The restoration of Gilbert
White's garden at Selborne. *Hortus*
56: 1–20.

Fisher, J. (Ed.) (1947). *The Natural History of
Selborne, by Gilbert White.* London: Cresset
Press.

Flegg, J. (2002). *Time to Fly – Exploring Bird
Migration.* Thetford: British Trust for
Ornithology.

Fleming, N. (2004). Countryside Survey
2000. *Daily Telegraph,* 16 October.

Foster, P. (2000). Gilbert White, naturalist,
poet, priest and scholar (1720–93). *Selborne
Paper No. 1.* Selborne: Gilbert White's
House & The Oates Museum.

Foster, P. & Standing, D. (2003).
Landscape and labour – Gilbert White's
garden. *Selborne Paper No. 2.* Selborne:
Gilbert White's House & The Oates
Museum.

Fungus Conservation Forum (n.d.).
*Grassland Gems: Managing Lawns and
Pastures for Fungi.* Salisbury: Plantlife
International.

Gahan, A. B. (1924). Some new parasitic
Hymenoptera with notes on several
described forms. *Proceedings of the U.S.
National Museum* **65**: 1–23.

Gascoigne, J. (2004). Sir Joseph Banks.
In: Oxford Dictionary of National Biography.
Oxford: Oxford University Press.

Gaston, K. & Thompson, K. (2002).
Evidence for Significance. *In: Gardens:
Heaven or Hell for Wildlife?* London: Royal
Horticultural Society.

Gerarde J. (1597). *The Herball or Generall
Historie of Plantes.* London: John Norton.

**Gibbons, D. W., Reid, J. B. & Chapman, R.
S.** (1993). *The New Atlas of Breeding Birds in
Britain and Ireland: 1988–1991.* London:
T. & A. D. Poyser.

Gilbert, F. S. (1983). The foraging ecology of hoverflies (Diptera, Syrphidae): circular movements on composite flowers. *Behavioral Ecology and Sociobiology* **13**: 253–7.

Gilbert, O. (2000). *Lichens*. London: HarperCollins.

Godwin, H. (1975). *The History of the British Flora*. Second Edition. Cambridge: Cambridge University Press.

Greenoak, F. (Ed.) (1986). *The Journals of Gilbert White Volume 1*. London: Century.

Groenman-van-Waateringe, W. (1978). The impact of Neolithic man on the landscape in the Netherlands. *In*: Limbrey, S. & Evans, J. G. (Eds) *The Effect of Man on the Landscape: the Lowland Zone*. CBA Research Report **21**: 135–46.

Hall, A., Reiss, M. J., Rowell, C. & Scott, A. (2005). Designing and implementing a new advanced level biology course. *Journal of Biological Education* **37**: 162–7.

Harding, P. T. & Sutton, S. L. (1985). *Woodlice in Britain and Ireland: Distribution and Habitat*. Huntingdon: Natural Environment Research Council.

Harlan, J. & de Wet, J. (1965). Some thoughts about weeds. *Economic Botany* **19**: 16–24.

Harvey, J. (1979). The medieval garden before 1500. *In*: Harris, J. (Ed.) *The Garden. A Celebration of One Thousand Years of British Gardening*. London: Mitchell Beazley.

Harvey, J. H. (1981). *Mediaeval Gardens*. London: Batsford.

Heimbach, F. (1997). Field tests on the side effects of pesticides on earthworms: influence of plot size and cultivation practices. *Soil Biology and Biochemistry* **29**: 671–6.

Heinrich, B. (1993). *The Hot-blooded Insects*. Berlin: Springer-Verlag.

Henderson, J. L. (1945). The beetles of a suburban London garden in Surrey. *Entomologist's Monthly Magazine* **81**: 63–6.

Henderson, J. L. (1946). More beetles of a suburban London garden in Surrey. *Entomologist's Monthly Magazine* **82**: 38–9.

Henrici, A. (2001). Non-lichenised fungi in Buckingham Palace Garden. *In*: Plant, C. W. (Ed.) The natural history of Buckingham Palace Garden, London. Part 1. *London Naturalist* **79** (Supplement).

Hessayon, D. (1983). *The Armchair Book of the Garden*. London: Century Publishing.

Hessayon, D. G. & Hessayon, J. P. (1973). *The Garden Book of Europe*. London: Elm Tree Books.

Hide, G. A. & Lapwood, D. H. (1992). Disease aspects of potato production. *In*: Harris, P. M. (Ed.) *The Potato Crop: Scientific Basis for Improvement*. London: Chapman & Hall.

Highfield, R. & Clover, C. (2003). Building more new homes could benefit wildlife. *Daily Telegraph*, 10 September.

Hingley, M. (1979). *Fieldwork Projects in Biology*. Poole: Blandford.

Holden, E. (2003). *Recommended English Names for Fungi in the UK*. Salisbury: Plantlife International.

Honey, M. R., Leigh, C. & Brooks, S. J. (1998). The fauna and flora of the newly created wildlife garden in the grounds of The Natural History Museum, London. *The London Naturalist* **77**: 17–47.

Hooker, W. J. (1986). *Compendium of Potato Diseases*. St Paul: American Phytopathological Society.

Jekyll, G. (1932). (Ed. Jekyll, F. & Taylor, G. C.) *A Gardener's Testament. A Selection Of Articles And Notes*. London: Country Life.

Jellicoe, G., Jellicoe, S., Goode, P. & Lancaster, M. (1986). *The Oxford Companion to Gardens*. Oxford: Oxford University Press.

Joint Nature Conservation Committee (2005). *Vascular Plant Red Data List for Britain.* London: JNCC.

Keizer, P. J. (1993). The influence of nature management on the macromycete fungi. *In*: Pegler, D. N., Boddy, L., Ing, B. & Kirk, P.M. (Eds) *Fungi in Europe: Investigations, Recording and Conservation.* Kew: Royal Botanic Gardens.

Koryszko, J. (2001). Cut-worm observations. *Bulletin of the Amateur Entomologists' Society* **60**: 205.

Landsberg, S. (1995). *The Medieval Garden.* New York: Thames & Hudson.

Langley, B. (1728). *New Principles of Gardening, or the Laying-out and Planting Parterres.* London.

Langton, P. H. (2001). Centipedes and millipedes (Myriapoda) in Buckingham Palace Garden. *In*: Plant, C. W. (Ed.) The natural history of Buckingham Palace Garden, London. Part 2. *London Naturalist* **80** (Supplement).

Langton, S. D., Cowan, D. P. & Meyer, A. N. (2001). The occurrence of commensal rodents in dwellings as revealed by the 1996 English House Condition Survey. *Journal of Applied Ecology* **38**: 699–709.

Lankester, E. (Ed.) (1848). *The Correspondence of John Ray: Consisting of Selections from the Philosophical Letters Published by Dr. Derham, and Original Letters of John Ray, in the Collection of the British Museum.* London: The Ray Society.

Lawson, W. (1618). *A New Orchard and Garden. Or the Best Way for Planting ... With the Country House-wife's Garden ...* London: B. Alsop for R. Jackson.

Lean, G. (2003). Prescott plans new homes on green sites. *Independent*, 2 February.

Leather, S. R. (1986). Insect species richness of the British Rosaceae – the importance of host range, plant architecture, age of establishment, taxonomic isolation and

species area relationship. *Journal of Animal Ecology* **55**: 841–60.

Leith-Ross, P. (1984). *The John Tradescants – Gardeners to the Rose and Lily Queen.* London: Peter Owen.

Linklater, A. (2002). *Measuring America.* New York: Walker & Co.

Lock, R. (1998). Advanced-level biology – is there a problem? *School Science Review* **80**: 25–8.

Majerus, M. (1996). Ladybird, ladybird, fly to my home! (or how to attract ladybirds to your garden). *Bulletin of the Amateur Entomologists' Society* **55**: 83–90.

Majerus, M. (1994). *Ladybirds.* London: HarperCollins.

Manley, G. (1952). *Climate and the British Scene.* London: Collins.

Miller, D. P. (2004). Daines Barrington. *In*: *Oxford Dictionary of National Biography.* Oxford: Oxford University Press.

Miller, P. (1731). *The Gardener's Dictionary.* London: The Author.

Milne, R. I. & Abbott, R. J. (2000). Origin and evolution of invasive naturalized material of *Rhododendron ponticum* L. in the British Isles. *Molecular Ecology* **9**: 41–6.

Mitchell, A. (1985). *The Complete Guide to Trees of Britain and Northern Europe.* Limpsfield: Dragons World.

Moore, M. T., Hillman, G. C. & Legge, A. J. (2000). *Village on the Euphrates.* Oxford University Press, Oxford.

Morris, C. (Ed.) (1947). *The Journeys of Celia Fiennes.* London: Cresset Press.

Mound, L. A. (1962). *Aleurotrachelus jelinekii* (Frauen.) (Homoptera: Aleyrodidae) in southern England. *Entomologist's Monthly Magazine* **97**: 196–7.

Murphy, P. & Scaife, R. (1991). The environmental archaeology of gardens. *In*: Brown, A. E. (Ed.) Garden archaeology. *Research Report* **78**. York: Council for British Archaeology.

Murray, J. A. H., Bradley, H., Craigie, W. A. & Onions, C. T. (Eds) (1961). *Oxford English Dictionary*. Oxford: Oxford University Press.

Newton, A. (1893–96). *A Dictionary of Birds*. London: Adam and Charles Black.

O'Brian, P. (1987). *Joseph Banks; a Life*. London: Collins Harvill.

Overall, A. (2004). Morels abound. *Field Mycology* **5**: 83–4.

Owen, J. (1991). *The Ecology of a Garden*. Cambridge: Cambridge University Press.

Page, C. N. (1988). *Ferns*. London: Collins.

Parkinson, J. (1629). *Paradisus in Sole, Paradisus Terrestris*. London: Humfrey Lownes and Robert Young.

Petiver, J. (1695). *Musei Petiverianai centuria prima rariora naturae*. [Later published in Anon (1764) *Jacobi Petiveri Opera, historiam naturalem spectantia*. London: John Milan.]

Plant, C. W. (Ed.) (1999). The natural history of Buckingham Palace Garden, London. Part 1. *London Naturalist* **78** (Supplement).

Plant, C. W. (Ed.) (2001). The natural history of Buckingham Palace Garden, London. Part 2. *London Naturalist* **80** (Supplement).

Polaszek A., Evans G. A. & Bennett F. D. (1992). Encarsia parasitoids of *Bemisia tabaci* (Hymenoptera: Aphelinidae; Homoptera: Aleyrodidae): a preliminary guide to identification. *Bulletin of Entomological Research* **82**: 375–92.

Pollard, E., Hooper, M. D. & Moore, N. W. (1974). *Hedges*. London: Collins.

Preston, C. D. & Croft, J. M. (1997). *Aquatic Plants in Britain and Ireland*. Colchester: Harley Books.

Preston, C. D., Pearman, D. A. & Innes, T. D. (2002). *New Atlas of the British & Irish Flora*. Oxford: Oxford University Press.

Pretty, J. (2001). *Some Benefits and Drawbacks of Local Food Systems*. Sustain AgriFood Network, 2 November 2001. (www.villagekey.com/localfood.html)

Pryce, S. (1991). *The Peat Alternatives Manual*. London: Friends of the Earth.

Quarrell, W. H. & Mare, M. (Ed. and Trans.) (1934). *The Travels of Zacharias Conrad von Uffenbach*, London: Faber & Faber.

Rackham, O. (1986). *The History of the Countryside*. London: J. M. Dent.

Raistrick, A. R. & Gilbert, O. L. (1963). Malham Tarn House: its building materials, their weathering and colonization by plants. *Field Studies* **1**: 89–115.

Raman, K. V. & Radcliffe, E. B. (1992). Pest aspects of potato production. Part 2: the insect pests. In: Harris. P. M. (Ed.) *The Potato Crop: Scientific Basis for Improvement*. London: Chapman & Hall.

Raven, C. (1942). *John Ray: Naturalist*. Cambridge: Cambridge University Press.

Ray, J. (1686–88). *Historia Plantarum*. London: M. Clark for H. Faithorne.

Repton, H. (1803). *Observations on the Theory and Practice of Landscape Gardening, &c.* London: T. Bensley for J. Taylor.

Robinson, F. N. (Ed.) & Benson, L. (General Ed.) (1992). *The Riverside Chaucer*. Third Edition. Oxford: Oxford University Press.

Robinson, W. (1883). *The English Flower Garden*. London: John Murray.

Roxburgh, S. H. & Wilson, J. B. (2000). Stability and coexistence in a lawn community: experimental assessment of the stability of the actual community. *Oikos* **88**: 409–23.

Rubinstein, J. C. (2004). Eadmer of Canterbury. In: *Oxford Dictionary of National Biography*. Oxford: Oxford University Press.

Russel, L. M. (1949). The North-American species of the genus *Trialeurodes*. U.S.D.A. *Miscellaneous Publications* No. **635**.

Russell, E. J. (1957). *The World of the Soil*. London: Collins.

Russell, E. W. (1973). *Soil Conditions and Plant Growth*. Tenth Edition. London: Longman.

Salisbury, E. (1961). *Weeds and Aliens*. London: Collins.

Salmon, M. A. (2000). *The Aurelian Legacy*. Colchester: Harley Books.

Scattergood, J. (Ed.) (1983). *John Skelton: The Complete English Poems*. New Haven: Yale University Press.

Sharrock, R. (1694). *An Improvement in the Art of Gardening*. Third Edition. London.

Silverside, A. J. (2002) www-biol.paisley.ac.uk/courses/silverside/PCE/PCEUrbanB.html

Simmons, I. G. (1998). *An Environmental History of Great Britain, From 10,000 Years Ago to the Present*. Edinburgh: Edinburgh University Press.

Soper, T. & Lovegrove, R. (1989). *Birds in your Garden*. Exeter: Webb & Bower.

Sorour, J. & Larink, O. (2001). Toxic effects of benomyl on the ultrastructure during spermatogenesis of the earthworm *Eisenia fetida*. *Ecotoxicology and Environmental Safety* 50: 180–8.

Southern, R. W. (1963). *Saint Anselm and his Biographer: A Study of Monastic Life and Thought 1059–c.1130*. Cambridge and London: Cambridge University Press.

Stace, C. (1997). *New Flora of the British Isles*. Second Edition. Cambridge: Cambridge University Press.

Stamp, L. D. (1946). *Britain's Structure and Scenery*. London: Collins.

Stearns, R. P. (1952). James Petiver – promoter of natural science, c.1663–1718. *Proceedings of the American Antiquarian Society* 62: 243–65.

Step, E. (1921). *Animal Life of the British Isles*. London: Warne.

Stephens, D. E. A. & Warren, M. S. (1992). *The Importance of Garden Habitats to Butterfly Populations*. Wareham: Joint Committee for the Conservation of British Insects.

Stewart, V. I. & Salih, R. O. (1981). Priorities for soil use in temperate climates. *In*: Stonehouse, B. (Ed.) *Biological Husbandry*. London: Butterworths.

Stillingfleet, B. (1762). *Miscellaneous Tracts relating to Natural History, Husbandry, and Physic. To which is added the Calendar of Flora*. Second Edition. London: R. and J. Dodsley, S. Baker and T. Payne.

Switzer, S. (1718). *Ichnographia Rustica*. London.

Thompson, K., Hodgson, J. G., Smith, R. M., Warren, P. H. & Gaston, K. J. (2004). Urban domestic gardens (III): composition and diversity of lawn floras. *Journal of Vegetation Science* 15: 371–6.

Toms, M. (2003). BTO/CJ *Garden BirdWatch Book*. Thetford: British Trust for Ornithology.

Turner, C. (1968). A note on the occurrence of *Vitis* and other new plant records from the Pleistocene deposits at Hoxne, Suffolk. *New Phytologist* 67: 333–4.

US Environmental Protection Agency (1988). *Pesticide Fact Sheet Number 191: Metaldehyde*. Washington, DC: Office of Pesticides and Toxic Substances, Office of Pesticide Programs, US EPA.

Valkonen, J. P. (1994). Natural genes and mechanisms for resistance to viruses in cultivated and wild potato species. *Plant Breeding* 112: 1–16.

Vickery, M. (1995). Gardens; the neglected habitat. *In*: Pullin, A. S. (Ed.) *Ecology and Conservation of Butterflies*. London: Chapman & Hall.

Walters, M. (1993). *Wild and Garden Plants*. London: HarperCollins.

Ward, S. D. & Evans, D. F. (1976). Conservation assessment of British limestone pavements based on floristic criteria. *Biological Conservation* 9: 217–33.

Warren, M. S. & Stephens, D. E. A. (1989). Habitat design and management for butterflies. *The Entomologist* **108**: 123–34.

Westwood, J. O. (1876–1879) *Lapidarium Walliae: the Early Inscribed and Sculptured Stones of Wales*. Oxford: Oxford University Press.

White, G. (1789). *Natural History and Antiquities of Selborne*. London: T. Bensley.

Wilkinson, D. & Smith, G. C. (2001). A preliminary survey for changes in urban Fox (*Vulpes vulpes*) densities in England and Wales, and implications for rabies control. *Mammal Review* **31**: 107–10.

Willmott, D. M., Hart, A. J., Long, S. J., Edmondson, R. N. & Richardson, P. N. (2002). Use of a cold-active entomopathogenic nematode *Steinernema kraussei* to control overwintering larvae of the black vine weevil *Otiorhynchus sulcatus* (Coleoptera: Curculionidae) in outdoor strawberry plants. *Nematology* **4**: 925–32.

Wilson, E. O. (Ed.) (1988). *Biodiversity*. Washington: National Academy Press.

Woods, M., MacDonald, R. A. & Harris, S. (2003). Predation of wildlife by domestic cats *Felis catus* in Great Britain. *Mammal Review* **33**: 174–88.

Worsley, G. (2002). *England's Lost Houses*. London: Aurum Press.

Yalden, D. (1999). *The History of British Mammals*. London: T. & A. D. Poyser.

Zeepvat, R. J. (1991). Roman gardens in Britain. *In*: Brown, A. E. (Ed.) Garden archaeology. *Research Report* **78**. York: Council for British Archaeology.

Index

The New Naturalist Library